MAKING IT CRAZY

MAKING IT CRAZY

AN ETHNOGRAPHY OF PSYCHIATRIC CLIENTS IN AN AMERICAN COMMUNITY

Sue E. Estroff

Foreword by H. Richard Lamb, M.D.

UNIVERSITY OF CALIFORNIA PRESS
Berkeley Los Angeles London

University of California Press
Berkeley and Los Angeles, California

University of California Press, Ltd.
London, England

First Paperback Printing 1985
ISBN 0-520-05451-2
Library of Congress Cataloging in Publication Data

Estroff, Sue E.
Making it crazy.

Bibliography: p. 289
Includes index.
1. Mentally ill—Rehabilitation—United States. 2. Community mental health services—United States. 3. Sheltered workshops—United States. 4. Supplemental security income program—United States. 5. Psychiatric research—Field work. I. Title
RC439.5.E84 362.2'2'0973 79-64660

Printed in the United States of America

2 3 4 5 6 7 8 9

This book is for D. H.—
who would have wanted us
to learn from his agony and
our incalculable loss.

A good part of the struggles of mankind centre round the single task of finding an expedient accommodation—one, that is, that will bring happiness—between this claim of the individual and the cultural claims of the group; and one of the problems that touches the fate of humanity is whether such an accommodation can be reached by means of some particular form of civilization or whether this conflict is irreconcilable.

—Freud (1961:43)

CONTENTS

FOREWORD

In an era of rhetoric about deinstitutionalization, it is refreshing to have solid clinical data from a perceptive observer who does not have a vested interest in this matter, that is, one who is neither mental health professional, nor patient, nor union official, nor legislator. Amid the heated discussions about the advantages and benefits or the problems and scandals of the mentally ill living in the community, the kind of objective information provided by this book is essential.

What is the everyday world of the psychiatric patient really like? If we try to understand it within the context of our own experiences and our own frame of reference, we can easily misconstrue and misinterpret most of what we see. But living with the clients in their world, as Estroff did, gives us a whole new perspective. Further, she tried to approach her task without preconceived theories, letting the patients determine what was and is important to learn and understand. This has, undoubtedly, contributed to her new and fresh insights.

Equally important is the author's recognition that taking a patient's perspective of the treatment process does not necessitate casting staff in the role of villains, even though the perspective and point of view of the patients and the staff may differ markedly. Thus, she avoids the error made by so many of "taking sides" and still graphically describes the patients' world and how that world is perceived by them.

What are the effects when mental health professionals, even enlightened, dedicated ones, try to help? In looking at this, the author questions many of our cherished beliefs. And that is good.

The author's observation about "meds," the use of psychoactive drugs, should be read by everyone working in this field. There is no doubt in my mind that the phenothiazines, lithium, and the other major tranquilizers are among the great advances of modern psychiatry. But at what price? We need to know so we can minimize adverse effects and weigh the costs against the benefits. Estroff observes that being given "meds" is interpreted by the mentally ill as a message that they are crazy people who will never get well. She observes that side effects contribute to clients' looking different, and therein lies the paradox of "meds"—they keep you from being crazy, but they reveal your crazy identity and defects to others. This does not mean that we should stop dispensing psychoactive medications. Far from it. But we do need a balanced view of the results of our ministrations.

This book makes a contribution in taking a searching look at both the beneficial aspects and the unintended adverse effects of income maintenance programs, in particular, Supplemental Security Income (SSI). On the positive side, SSI provides a dependable source of income that makes it possible for the mentally ill, who are unable to support themselves through work or private funds, to live outside of state hospitals and to be maintained in the community. But SSI may also perpetuate and encourage the crazy life by making it attractive (i.e., a source of income) and also by rewarding the demonstration and continuation of inadequacy (i.e., not working). And, the author points out, all the while society is rewarding disability, it is also placing a negative value on disability and the disabled. On this issue, our society would have to be diagnosed as chronically schizophrenic.

Perhaps it should not come as a surprise, though it will to many, that most patients with whom Estroff talked and spent time dislike our efforts to provide them sheltered employment, in particular sheltered workshops and to a lesser extent volunteer jobs. In this regard the author is to be commended for sensitively describing the feelings of most psychiatric patients about being categorized with the mentally retarded and the physically handicapped. A lowered self-image can result, as well, from the often clear message that the only work of which they are capable is sheltered (i.e., inferior).

We need to pay close attention to this, constantly reassessing our rehabilitation programs as our patients experience them. At the same time we must be aware that many long-term patients may need to displace their own feelings of inadequacy onto their vocational situation—"It's that workshop that's no good, not me." This, then, paves the way for a face-saving departure and such rationalizations as, "If that's the way they are going to treat me, I'll just say no to all that and live on my SSI."

This is not to imply that all rehabilitation facilities are what they should be; self-criticism has too often been lacking in this field. Moreover, there is a real need for mental health professionals to treat the sheltered employment experience in a way that enhances rather than detracts from their patients' self-esteem. It is crucial that we pay attention to our mode of preparing patients for sheltered vocational activities, helping them to understand their goals and purpose. For instance, "The goal for your having this work placement is to help you get along better with co-workers," or "to help you increase your speed," or "to help you have less trouble with bosses." Just as important is the need to explore with them on an ongoing basis how *they*, individually, can best use the experience.

Added to the negative feelings of patients about workshops is a development with consequences perhaps more far-reaching than the attitudes of mere psychiatric patients; there are rumblings from some in high places in government who complain about the high cost of sheltered employment over and above its limited productivity, and who say that perhaps we should just "pay off" the disabled with welfare and forget about rehabilitation. It is not difficult to see the seriousness of the dilemma and the crisis in rehabilitation which may be approaching.

Without losing sight of the nature and limiting effects of severe mental illness, we still need to be aware of how the mental health treatment system can both contribute to and ameliorate the perpetuation of patienthood and chronicity. Surely we can do better than a system that has rules for "making it crazy," such as those so well described by the author. A beginning is to become aware of this system and these rules. Many, to extricate themselves from all these double binds and contradictory messages, must often extricate themselves from the system itself.

The author observes that being a full-time crazy person is becoming an occupation among many psychiatric patients. She feels that if our society continues to subsidize this career, it is not "humane or justifiable to persist in negatively perceiving those who take us up on the offer and become employed in this way." That is a major thrust of this book. But society seems to fear that without this negative view of those who choose or fall into this role, more and more people will adopt it. How can we lessen that fear? Is there not even some truth in it? What about the almost universal fear and stigmatization of the mentally ill which contributes to this situation? In addition to giving us new insights into the lives of the severely mentally ill in the community, this book highlights and brings clearly into focus some of the important mental health questions of our time.

H. Richard Lamb, M.D.
Associate Professor of Psychiatry
USC School of Medicine

PREFACE

This book grew out of two years of ethnographic fieldwork among some people who have experienced long-standing and severe difficulties in living happily, safely, and productively in an American community. The usual designations for these people, "chronic mental patient" or "chronically mentally ill," will not be used here. This is a time to look at them and their world, and our own, through different lenses. I first formulated what I learned from and with them in my doctoral dissertation in cultural anthropology. The original work remains substantially intact, but I have developed themes and have clarified trouble spots.

Before reading the text, I want the reader to be aware of what this book is and is *not* meant to be, what my own biases, motives, limitations, and weaknesses are, and who helped me personally and professionally along the way. Following this introduction and orientation, the ethnographic material is presented, and I conclude with a theoretical and sociocultural interpretation of the topic and subjects. The literature review and the more theoretical discussions have been grouped to facilitate access to ethnographic material and to prepare the reader to assess my interpretations and conclusions.

With regard to fieldwork methods and tactics, I have tried to be very explicit about what I did, and how and why I did it. In addition, I have attempted to present the various sides of every issue, even when this may have been exasperating or conflicting. I have reflected upon and discussed dilemmas in this book about which I am undecided and ambivalent, and I have preferred to avoid the pretense of simple answers or a solidified position. Overall, I have worked for candor and completeness rather than for polish and neatness, because I believe this is the best way to progress with such a complex topic. If I am taking any position in this work, it is to stress the necessity of carefully considering the individual and sociocultural consequences and the meanings of community life for the chronically psychiatrically disturbed in America.

I should make it clear from the outset that I do not use the word "crazy" in a diagnostic, sensationalistic, or pejorative way. There has already been too much bitter controversy on this point, and I wish to dispense with this as a potential obstacle to confronting much more important issues. I use the word "crazy" in a descriptive and everyday sense, as I learned it from the clients and staff about whom I am writing. Unlike social scientists, some clinicians, and patient advocates, the clients and staff have little hesitancy to use "crazy" to describe self or others. This is not to say, however, that every patient or clinician comfortably embraces the word. There are those who are offended, threatened, and angered by this powerful designation, yet I think we need to examine this very potency and impact. "Crazy" is a word that occurs in everyday discourse, advertisement, music, and literature. For some among us it has very special meaning, not all of which is happy, but which is nonetheless pertinent to our understanding.

Ethnographically, the word "crazy" is used inconsistently but seems to follow some sort of pattern. A distinction exists between "crazy" as *craziness*, the quality or condition of being psychotic or visibly bizarre, of behaving or speaking incomprehensibly, and "crazy" as being *a crazy* or *a nut*, that is, as being a mental patient and client, which is an identity and role. The description and the identity overlap but are not equivalent. I use the word "crazy" in these ways and also to mean nonsensical, perverse, and inexplicably contradictory. A more precise discussion of the term as used in the title and throughout the book is included in chapter 3.

No doubt all who engage in ethnography spend many moments soothing anxieties by going over in their minds what they might have done differently. First and most important, a project such as this should not have been done alone, although there were definite advantages to working by myself. I had more control over rapport, confidentiality, style and manner of interaction with subjects, and direction of the research. Yet these positive factors did not outweigh the costs. A co-worker would have provided more systematic and extensive observation of a geographically dispersed group, not to mention additional time for data collection. My personal biases and subjective perceptions and reactions could have been identified, diluted, and perhaps counteracted.

There was no one in the field situation with whom I felt I could or should be completely disclosive regarding daily observations and personal feelings and reactions. I did not live among the clients on a twenty-four hour basis but had an apartment away from the research site. Contacts and friends in this separate world could not share my roller-coaster experience. Although I had access to my major professor in anthropology and my advisor in psychiatry, because the fieldwork was carried out in the same city where I attended graduate school, a supportive, reality-confirming partner in the field would have eased some pains and increased the acuity of my observations. Each time I touched base with academic types, my feelings of distance and isolation increased. When the psychiatrist suggested we meet more often to discuss the research, I withdrew and did not return for many weeks. In particular, there was no one to whom I could express feelings of anger, frustration, depression, or elation about clients, staff, their interaction, or my own situation. Left unresolved and repressed, these feelings certainly colored and probably distorted ethnographic data. I am still angry about some instances of neglect or insensitivity, and I continue to glow from several potent events. These energies need tapping and channeling. Although Reynolds (Reynolds and Farberow 1973, 1976) takes a somewhat different tack in his fieldwork, we share many reservations.

It is important to remind ourselves of how perilous and personal is the discovery process in fieldwork. All that I report here must have its veil of objectivity removed (Jules-Rosette 1978). Those moments when I felt nearly as desperate, disorganized, and depressed as the clients taught me much that I would never have known had I maintained distance and objectivity (if such exists). Yet I remain unalterably changed by these experiences.

Often, I sat in "my corner" at staff report listening to various persons joke with and support each other, mutually experiencing the roller coaster of daily coping with psychiatric clients and their problems. At those times I envied the sense of belonging, of group support, and of common ground. There is a myth around PACT[1] that mental illness is contagious, caught by drinking out of an unidentified coffee mug. In a sense it is contagious, and perhaps the only vaccination is a serum concocted of companions. For the longer one attempts to enter the clients' world without constant, active, outside reference points, the fuzzier becomes the distinction between crazy and uncrazy, self and other. The more time one spends amid confusion, fear, anxiety, and unhappiness, the more it is highlighted in oneself. Having lost and regained my perspective, objectivity, and confidence countless times during the past years, I would not attempt it alone again.

At the same time, I have few reservations about the validity of this research for this particular setting. I have put forth my *experience* of a world shot through with complexities, contradiction, and distress, but in no way have I meant to suggest that my scholarly perspective and cognitive processes were damaged or undermined. The essence of the anthropological learning process is to experience, discover, and intensely encounter differentness, and then to emerge, reflect, organize, understand, and communicate. These skills, much like those of the therapist, require an awareness of one's own involvement with and responses to the persons and circumstances one is learning about. Yet the process only begins here. It is completed by rigorous data analysis, relentless organization, careful thinking and rethinking, and consultation with other source materials. In sum, while I share my human responses with you, I also communicate ethnographic fact and structured anthropological analysis.

The goals of the project were too global. At this juncture, I could identify, circumscribe, and formulate answerable questions for research. This could not have been done before going into the field. Thus, perhaps more than anything else, I have learned not only what I did not know but what I need to find out in the future. One reaches threshold after threshold of clarity and understanding only to slide gradually into more murkiness, having recognized how very much more one must know to answer the newer, more precise questions.

1. PACT is an acronym for the Program of Assertive Community Treatment, the treatment program that served as setting and provided the subjects for the research. A description of the program is included in chapter 4.

Because of my unique position in clients' and staff's worlds and their intersection, ethical and tactical questions abounded. Would I loan money to a client on a strict money contingency program? Should I spend time with a client on the street who was supposed to be at work when the staff wanted strongly to persuade the person to be at the job? What should I do if the staff were misinformed about a client who was in acute distress? Could I let clients know I attended staff report and parties? The list was nearly endless. Decisions were made on the basis of my evaluation of their consistency with ethical and strategic principles: (1) avoid at all costs undermining or altering the trust of clients and staff in each other or in me; (2) clients come first; (3) evaluate how information would flow were I not present, and "let the system be"; and (4) do not deliberately deceive, misinform, or misrepresent any group or individual—client or staff.

Being female helped and hurt. Over half of the subjects were men. My gender served as an entrée to contacting them and eliciting some interest, but it created tensions as well. Many had never had a female friend, that is, a symmetrical, platonic, heterosexual relationship. This led to some confusion on their part when their sexual advances offended me, and to reluctance on my part in entering situations with them that might be misconstrued. It was often inappropriate to participate with the group as the only female, and as a sexually inaccessible one, at that. In a world where nurses and other female staff were also sexually off limits, this problem undoubtedly maintained some barriers to inside communication. Without question, a male co-worker could have provided a different type of observation and information.

At the outset, I was too timid about spending time alone with clients, especially the men. I clung to group activities and the security of staff presence for a period of time that now seems too long. Because I kept my apartment, I was unable to afford to live in the various hotels and sheltered living situations of clients, and I was unable to participate fully in their activities. The decision to maintain an apartment outside the treatment setting probably was necessary to provide adequate work time and space and a place to recharge my batteries; but I missed some of the quality of experience I might have had. It was too easy to escape the fieldwork setting. At the same time there was no escape, for I was working in the city where I had attended graduate school for five years. Having access to the university and to colleagues, professors, and facilities also had benefits and costs. I had anchors to my former reality, but I had stresses in bouncing back and forth.

Related to the above was the dilemma posed by drug use. At least half of the group used marijuana, alcohol, and other street drugs on a daily basis. Initially, I refused to smoke marijuana and to drink heavily with the group or with individuals for fear of losing accuracy of observations and perception. The refusal created some distance and suspicion on the part of clients. I can recall no occasion when one of them refused a joint or a beer when offered. Still, what does one do in this circumstance? Does one participate to solidify ties with the group, or does one refrain, from maintaining a distance contrary to the desired position of insider? I compromised. At times I participated, though only enough to indicate that symmetry was sought (normals and staff do not share in these activities with clients). At other times I bought a beer for someone, but I drank coffee or a soft drink, saying that I had to drive or giving some other excuse.

I have reservations with regard to the findings of this research. These center on its generalizability, reliability, and sample size. Most of the observations *qua* conclusions are impossible to replicate, yet all need further refinement and rigorous testing. A study of community lives of psychiatric clients in Madison, Wisconsin, has limited general application, because this city has an exceptionally broad range of innovative community mental health services. Also, the clients with whom I consulted do not provide a representative cross section of psychiatric patients nationwide who are being treated in the community. Clearly, the size of the sample precludes sophisticated statistical analysis of questionnaires and other data. In view of this, I feel that the value of what I have done lies in the generation of hypotheses rather than in the confirmation or disconfirmation of any particular theory or hypothesis. I have no illusions about the generalizability of my conclusions or observations for others working in different cities. I hope that similar studies will be done in the future so that comparison can be initiated.

The reader should recognize that this project has never intended or attempted an evaluation of the PACT program. PACT provided me with the opportunity to encounter people for research—a group of psychiatric patients living in a community setting. The program and its staff were for a time potent parts of clients' lives and therefore have been included in the description and analysis. Yet my interest goes beyond the treatment period. Observations and information that I present will not be confined to this time alone. This fact may confound interpretation of some of the statistics, such as those regarding employment. But I have tried to make clear whether an observation refers to PACT treatment or to non-PACT treatment time periods and circumstances.

None of the subjects ceased to receive some form of psychiatric treatment during the research period. My contact with clients was less frequent after PACT discharge or after decrease in active treatment. The new treatment settings and personnel were not studied as intensively as PACT. Although many of my observations and interviews with clients were done within the PACT environment, when all of us were under the influence of PACT, these represent associations in time and space. No cause and effect statements are in order. That is to say, I could not precisely control such important variables as type of treatment received, influences of family, friends, symptoms, and other nearly infinite inputs. If, for example, a client became employed after discharge and began to report that he or she was feeling much better, this may or may not have been related to discharge or to another treatment setting.

If there are correlations between factors, such as type of treatment program or place of residence, these must be isolated and tested further to establish cause and effect. My purpose is primarily descriptive and analytic. Through this exercise I hope to identify possible powerful components of the clients' environment. If these are aspects of the treatment program, then they provide food for further thought and experimentation. This work is meant to supplement and to diverge from the usual program assessment (see Broadhead 1978; Zusman 1976). Responsibility for any tactical, methodological, and personal shortcomings rests with me within the boundaries I have just set forth.

The irony of writing acknowledgments is that, in the process, one realizes how inadequate they are to convey the important senses of appreciation, gratitude, and indebtedness. Because this book is about real people who often suffer a great deal, it is especially difficult to pay proper homage to them and to their willingness to share their lives with me. Most of us never experience the world and ourselves as they do. Nor do we reveal these agonies and fears, these often humiliating intimacies, to others. My debt to the people who tried to teach me about the courage, fear, sorrow, and hope it takes to live with psychosis in our culture is simply unrepayable. So, too, is my debt to the staff members who provided the research opportunity, interest, and honesty essential to carrying out the project. They are an extraordinary group of people and deserve much of the credit for this work. Those who contributed gentleness, wisdom, challenge, and direction know who they are and how very much they gave of themselves.

Anthropological work is an intensely personal endeavor. I have benefited from a wealth of personal resources. My parents and siblings have provided emotional and financial support and encouragement, without which I would have given up long ago. Our joys and conflicts, suffering and celebrations, together and apart, have made this work both easier and more difficult. The courage and need to understand and to learn have come from them as they live in me.

Over the years I have been fortunate enough to participate in creating another nurturant network of caring and sharing. Jennifer Warlick has been a rare and infinite friend throughout, often stabilizing daily chaos during the fieldwork and the writing, always supplying richness and reason and, along with David Betson, sharing with me a place called home. Liffy Franklin and her family have offered me sanity, safety, laughter, and limitless caring. My colleagues and friends in anthropology and psychiatry, especially Emanuel Drechsel, Ronald Diamond, Lorna Benjamin, Andrea Jacobson, James Greenley, and Ronald Kessler have given companionship, criticism, empathy, and intellectual comradeship when these were needed most. A smile and loving thanks go to Kate and Bess for their frivolity and noncontingent affection that constitute vital supplies. Beverly Bliss and Judith Kellner have taught me more about thinking, feeling, and being than any of us can properly measure.

It has been my great pleasure to learn from and to be guided by John T. Hitchcock and Leigh M. Roberts. John T. Hitchcock encouraged me to undertake and to understand a complex and unusual project, literally holding it and me together when both threatened to disintegrate. His friendship, wisdom, extremely hard work, and passion for honest learning are special gifts. He has taught me that it is wise to be curious, to pursue understanding in the face of all obstacles, and to learn as a human being with feelings. Leigh M.

Roberts has taught me about psychiatry, caution, thoroughness, and persistence.

I wish also to thank W. M. O'Barr, Weston LaBarre, Catherine McClellan, Aidan Southall, Louisa Stark, and Robert Miller for their vital intellectual and personal contributions. A rather special kind of gratitude goes to Juanita M. Kreps, who for a decade has been a dear friend, a constant inspiration, and a cheerleader extraordinaire. My students and the members of many audiences to which I have spoken have challenged, stimulated, and enriched my thinking on the subject of this book.

The original fieldwork was carried out while I was a National Science Foundation Fellow. My rethinking, further probing, and rewriting of the manuscript were accomplished within the abundant embrace of the Department of Psychiatry, University of Wisconsin, while I was an NIMH Postdoctoral Fellow. Patsy Jones, Becky Cohen, and Jean Shippy typed parts of the manuscript, often under extreme pressure, and they provided encouragement and assistance beyond the call of duty. I cannot take away the tedium and secretarial stress that I and others cause them, but I can express with gratitude how special are their skills and selves. James Kubeck has made the process of turning a dissertation into a book a pleasure as well as a rich learning experience. Elizabeth Zanichkowsky Wyatt created the index with care and precision.

All these people have come together over time and space, enabling me to love and to work. I am unable to convey the depth and breadth of my appreciation here. My determined belief that life can be a delightful, distressing, and unequivocally worthwhile endeavor has been hatched among these folks—I am committed to creating opportunities for the people in this book to experience themselves and their worlds similarly.

Lake Kegonsa
May 1979

S. E. E.

PART I

INTRODUCTION AND ORIENTATION

1

A PERSONAL VIEW OF CLIENTS AND STAFF

Instead of arranging for passage, visas, fearsome injections, getting out my hiking boots, and packing my trunks, I got in my car, drove for ten minutes to the downtown area of a city where I had lived for five years, and thus began fieldwork. Despite the geographic proximity and lack of exotic contingencies, I am convinced that the experiences of the two years that followed constituted as long, arduous, exciting, and frightening a journey into differentness and newness as that of any novice anthropologist on her first vision quest. My purpose was to encounter and to learn from a group of persons called, in our society (and in some others), mentally ill. These persons are not the sort who have been studied inside psychiatric hospitals by others before me (e.g., Goffman 1961; Kesey 1962; Perrucci 1974; Caudill 1958; Levinson and Gallagher 1964). They are living outside, in an urban setting, and are or were participating to varying degrees in an intensive psychiatric treatment program intended as an alternative to their hospitalization.

A clear-cut, interesting task, I thought. If Goffman and Kesey can do it in an institution, someone ought to try it outside. As is often true of research proposals devised in offices and libraries, the plans, neatness, and deceptive simplicity vanished on the street. I was wrong. Not simple—messy and astoundingly complex; also engulfing and distressing.

When one studies persons grappling with psychiatric disorder and problems in living on the personal, phenomenological, everyday, and cultural level, one is forced to confront all the seeds and sprouts of one's own crazy tendencies; to discover, in fact, a potential crazy self well hidden and shored up inside. In the process of struggling with this work, I have acutely experienced the urge and propensity to flee to psychic disorganization and disability—have felt the lure of craziness in ways that further sensitize me to the worlds of my friends. Thus, for me, the experience has been a curious mixture of personal, intellectual, and psychic turmoil (see Weidman 1970:239–266; Nader 1970:97–118; Henry and Saberwal 1969).

Even then, amid this internal upheaval, I felt drawn by a strange sense of belonging. I recall, with the same discomfort I felt years ago, my first exit from the field. I was to spend four days with my father, who was in Chicago for a convention. This was only six weeks after the start of my research. Though I very much wanted to see him, I was reluctant to leave the field, and I felt a distance and strangeness with him and the new surroundings. I was shaken and resentful that we spent $30 for one meal when I had been living with people trying to eat on $4 for a whole day. The money we spent for cabs, tips, and drinks seemed so indulgent and wasteful. I had already forgotten that some people talked easily and consistently with each other when together. It seemed odd that no one had pressing, paralyzing problems to contend with just to get through the day. I spent those days with my father in limbo—agitated and upset at the disparities, physically sick the tension and exhaustion of trying to integrate these faraway worlds.

During the course of fieldwork I met, learned from, and came to care about people who killed themselves—people who slashed their throats, wrists, and arms, who took massive overdoses of medications, and who jumped out of upper-floor windows. I spent my days and evenings with people who stole, who sold drugs, who ate at restaurants and did not pay. I tried to understand people who perhaps had never held a paying job for more than a few months, or maybe not at all even though their ages averaged in the mid-twenties. I met a number of quiet, lonely individuals who seemed to hunger for companionship and to reject it all at once. I attempted to form relationships with persons who might never have had a friend or lover. And I tried to learn from them what it felt like to be unable to think, or to think thoughts about yourself and others that are racing, agitating, negative, or disjointed. Or what it was like to be high and to envision a different world, believing yourself capable of creating it and living in it with the power to stop time. I tried to understand their ways of perceiving themselves and others and how they acted on those perceptions. Even more, I tried to comprehend their expressed reactions to what was happening to them at that moment in their lives, and what they and others were doing to make it be that way.

Before I went into the field, I had spent approximately three months observing in various clinical psychiatric settings, and I had had secondhand experience with persons having psychiatric difficulties in my own family. Yet I was not prepared by any of this, or by the reading I had done, for actually interacting with PACT clients. At first I asked too many questions, talked too much, displayed too much spontaneous affect, and dressed too neatly. In short order, I learned to slow down—physically and mentally—to dress almost sloppily, and to sit quietly, nearly expressionless, communicating verbally only in spurts. Usually I was unable to engage in prolonged questioning and focused interview, for if I did push for precision and reflection, the responses became, "I don't know," or nothing at all related to my questions.

Clients had a difficult time placing me in their social-interpersonal world because they knew that I was not "like them." As Ben[1] asked one day, "You've never been mentally ill, have you? You've never been a mental patient, have you? You've never been in Mendota,[2] have you? Then what are you doing hanging around with all of us nuts?" Myrtle put it differently. She said it seemed like I was on staff because "you never seem to have any problems." But I also was *not* on the staff. Establishing that autonomy and distinction were essential first tasks for the project. I made a concerted effort never to be directive with clients or to behave like staff in any way toward them, though at first they tried to put me in this position by asking for medications or money. My only response was to refer

1. The names of clients and staff have been changed in order to protect privacy and confidentiality. Those persons who have an intimate knowledge of the PACT program and its clients will undoubtedly recognize the persons described herein. This special information is confined to those who understand the delicacy and personal nature of this topic. Their discretion and integrity are presumed and solicited.

2. Mendota is the familiar name of Mendota Mental Health Institute, the state psychiatric hospital in Madison, Wisconsin.

them to staff or to say I did not know. Clients were constantly curious about my source of income and why I was "not working" or did not seem to have a job. Over time, I explained that I got money from the government (a National Science Foundation Fellowship) somewhat like their Social Security or Veteran's Administration checks. Further, I told them that learning from them was my work—though I had some concern that this would appear too stafflike; that is, working with them was what I got paid for. On those occasions when I had access to information that I knew or was told staff should not hear, I made certain that the clients knew I could be trusted. This process of sharing information and intimacies was tortuously slow from my perspective, but we had to construct relationships sturdy enough to withstand the stresses of crises, relocation, psychosis, and my lack of fit in their world. The confidences and trust were new to all of us and were frightening as well.

The only exception to these rules of confidence was potential, imminent suicide. After an experience during the first weeks of fieldwork with a woman who made two serious attempts, one the day after spending the evening with me, an arrangement with staff was made. If I were with a client, or knew of an immediate threat to life, I could inform one designated staff member of this fear, and staff would investigate or act without mention of the source of information. This system was used only once, and the situation proved to be a false alarm. But I had decided that a client's life was more important than our research relationship.

In the end, I suspect I remain an enigma, a friend, or just another strange person who says she's writing a book about them and their treatment program.

I have shared my home with more than a dozen clients, and I have continued to speak occasionally with them by phone. Some friendships continue while I have lost touch with other clients. I grew to fear them almost never, and to respect them for pushing on despite repeated difficulties, failures, and some successes. In ways, they are a group of strong and courageous people. If I were confronted with their internal and external limitations and anxieties, I am not sure I would want to remain alive. In still other ways, they are hard to cope with continually and can be a demanding, draining, and annoying lot. I have come not to feel guilty for having mixed reactions to them, for I believe they share my sentiments about themselves and each other.

Lest the above appear complete, I must also say that I learned from another group of people in this process: the treatment program staff. Although they were in a different position vis-à-vis psychiatric disorder from the primary subjects, they too became a part of my daily life. Some became close personal friends; others have remained warm work and social acquaintances. They opened their homes, lives, and even staff parties to me. All shared, in remarkably open fashion, the complexities, frustrations, sorrows, pleasures, and rewards of their enormous tasks. I came to respect each in his or her own way, and to admire, in ways which I am unable to fully communicate, their skills, dedication, and capacity for caring in the face of huge obstacles. Often I envied their roles as active help-givers, especially when I shared their sense of concern and despair regarding a particular client. Often I was glad I did not have to invest myself actively in altering the gloomy, seemingly endless series of failures and fears experienced and created by clients.

With surprising flexibility and understanding, they accepted our asymetrical exchange of information. I wanted them to tell me all, yet I censored and withheld from them what clients said and did to preserve confidentiality and trust in my work. Many took an active interest in my work and me, pointing the way, easing the transition into a system where tragedy, fear, and failure flourish, telling me where to look but not what to see, testing ideas and perceptions but not forcing me to see things their way.

An incident that occurred early during the fieldwork period is illustrative. Dorothy, the woman mentioned previously as actively suicidal, tried to stab herself with a knife in the treatment-house kitchen the morning following an evening I had spent wandering around with her. When I arrived at the house that day, I heard mention of the incident, expressed my dismay and reported that she had seemed all right the night before, as I had stayed with her until she went to sleep. One of the staff nurses then said, "Oh well, then it's *your* fault." This was meant to be a joke but was not perceived as such by me. My evident panic and immediate protestation made this clear to the staff, who pointed out that I would have to get used to this sort of thing (both the jokes and the suicide attempts). Still, the painfulness of the remark lingered in the air between me and the nurse. She and another nurse individually took me aside and discussed suicide attempts, mostly in an effort to convince me that only very seldom were the actions of one person responsible for anyone's taking her own life. I was touched and reassured by these conversations but was terribly fearful of seeing Dorothy again. I was also shaken by a sense of massive responsibility and potential for doing harm in this new and unpredictable world. Somehow, the nurse knew that verbal explanations were not enough.

Dorothy was hospitalized and given ECT (electroconvulsive therapy), and I did not see her for approximately three weeks. When I did, she seemed not to recognize me or to remember any of the interaction that had been so potent for me. The nurse who had made the joke casually asked if I wanted to ride out to the hospital with her and Dorothy. I was reluctant, but she urged me to do so. On the way, the nurse took charge of the conversation, and it became clear to me that she was trying to help me adjust to Dorothy's loss of memory and disorientation, and to reintroduce us. I was shaken by Dorothy's condition and felt hopelessly inadequate to interact with her. With the nurse's help, however, including her explanation of the after-effects of ECT (offered after we dropped Dorothy off), a most difficult and discomforting hurdle was overcome. This type of kindness was repeated by almost everyone on the staff in some way.

Contrary to the portrayals of staff as destructive, inconsiderate, power-hungry individuals found in other works similar to mine, I found these people easy to like, almost always genuinely concerned for their clients.

Through this interaction, I was able to see and begin to understand two facets—staff's and client's perspectives and experiences—of a multifacted phenomenon. This was both fortunate and unfortunate. It was fortunate because one biases oneself and needlessly alienates psychiatric professionals by a priori assuming that taking a client's perspective of the treatment process necessitates vilifying staff. Unfortunately, having had a glimpse of both perspectives, I see the profundity of the impasse, the seemingly irreconcilable dilemmas for all concerned.

In sum, both clients and staff surpassed any fantasies I ever had regarding openness and willingness to let me observe and take part in their lives, often under extreme and unhappy circumstances. Nor were they selfish about sharing success and celebration. Many a beer was tipped with clients for a new job, and the happiness associated with personal and professional satisfaction among staff was spread my way as well.

The picture is not at all clear, neat, or simple to comprehend, but I believe that it is more accurate than a one-sided view, or a simple scheme. Over time, it is my hope that I will be able to deal more extensively with these two perspectives and with their interaction, convergences, and divergences. This task, however, is for the future. At this stage, I have chosen to emphasize the client part of the story as I have learned it.

2

DEVELOPMENT OF THE TOPIC AND PERSPECTIVE

> *Conception* is the point at which the social scientist first becomes aware of the alternative systems of thought that are the objects of description. . . . *Discovery* is the full encounter of another thought form in an effort to approach it on its own grounds. . . . *Evaluation* is the process of stepping back to find a bridge between scientific theory and new experience. . . . Through *Communication*, the discoveries of all the previous stages are subjected to translation for a larger audience.
> —(Jules-Rosette 1978:554–555)

THE TOPIC

Living among us are nearly one and a half million persons (Minkoff 1978:13) who are described as chronically and severely mentally ill. For some, community life represents a new challenge after months or even years of continuous or periodic hospitalization. For a growing number of others, the community represents the primary locale of treatment and daily life; these are the new corps of community mental health system veterans who have had frequent but usually brief exposure to inpatient psychiatric treatment. The experiences of literally hundreds of thousands of psychiatric patients in the United States have been dramatically altered during the deinstitutionalization of the past two decades (see Bassuk and Gerson 1978; Mechanic 1978). The philosophies and processes of deinstitutionalization (Bachrach 1978), nonhospitalization, brief hospitalization, and community treatment constitute major human, professional, and social movements whose ramifications are just beginning to be acknowledged and evaluated.

A variety of clinical diagnoses are applied to this group, but by far the largest categories are schizophrenia and the major affective disorders (unipolar [depression or mania] and bipolar [manic-depression]). These numbers and labels, however, tell us precious little about who these people are, what their lives are like, how they experience themselves and others, and what meaning their existence and treatment in American communities rather than in hospitals holds for them and us. It is clear that deinstitutionalization and community treatment express social and professional values and ideals in addition to representing sociocultural processes and movements within our society. The values include: that personal freedom and interdependence are preferable to confinement and dependence; that one is best cared for by people who "care," and that naturally caring people are to be found in local communities; that individual happiness and contentment are good things; and that we all share moral and social responsibility to include and not exclude from our daily lives those who have special and sometimes negatively valued differences (Bachrach 1978:575; Cumming 1968:31; Lamb and Associates 1976; Segal and Aviram 1978:1).

As a process, "deinstitutionalization may be conceptualized as an integrated set of social policies designed to promote a reasonable level of functioning among the handicapped with the fewest possible restrictions on their mobility and social participation" (Mechanic 1978:3). Not only does deinstitutionalization represent a protest movement against the abuses and inefficiencies of institutionalization (Bachrach 1978:576), but it sets in motion waves of change in service delivery and organizations in the entire mental health community. When I refer to community treatment, it is as a part of these processes, in service to these values. In particular, I mean the diagnosis, treatment, and rehabilitation of persistently, severely disturbed members of a given population, *among this same population* (Polack 1978). The major aims of this subset of community psychiatry are avoidance of psychiatric hospitalization and increased gratifying participation in social, vocational, and interpersonal activities of clients in the community.

Although sociological and anthropological research among hospitalized psychiatric patients has helped to stimulate some of the aforementioned processes and philosophical shifts (Dunham 1969:65), analogous research on patienthood in a community setting has barely begun (Manis 1968). This lack of data combined with increasingly polarized and vigorous debate about the wretched and unsatisfactory (Talbott 1979; Kirk and Therrien 1975; Chu and Trotter 1974; Lamb and Goertzl 1971), or improved and improving (Test and Stein 1978*c*; Lamb 1979*a*; Hansell and Willis 1977) conditions of living for these persons in large part motivated this study.

In 1973, Robert Reich described the care and treatment of the chronically mentally ill as a "national disgrace." In 1979, John Talbott (1979:688) wrote that "since then things have grown worse." At the same time, the National Institutes of Mental Health are making a substantial investment in the Community Support Systems program and ideology (Turner 1978; Schulberg 1979) with the belief that community treatment should proceed in the face of multiple sources of resistance (Barahal 1971), stubbornly high hospital recidivism rates for those so treated (Anthony et al. 1972; Rosenblatt and Mayer 1974; Stein and Test 1976), increasing fiscal crises (Sharfstein, Turner, and Clark 1978; Menninger 1978), and the development of serious reservations about the long-term human and medical costs of the antipsychotic medications seemingly essential to community treatment (Gardos and Cole 1976).

Current widespread community psychiatric treatment reflects reductions in inpatient psychiatric treatment facilities and services subsequent to (1) increased attention to and protection of civil rights in commitment proceedings, and the application of the principle of least restrictive alternatives in enforced psychiatric treatment by the courts (Brooks 1974:601-924; Chambers 1978), (2) widespread use of antipsychotic medication, (3) shifting values and treatment modes of the psychiatric system in its struggle with institutionalization and hospital recidivism (Bachrach 1976), (4) economic austerity programs at the state level combined with a federal focus of funding on community mental health centers, and (5) perhaps community tolerance of a widening range of behaviors among its population (Bentz and Edgerton 1971). Of course, community treatment and deinstitutionalization have not occurred in a historical, social, professional, or clinical vacuum (see Williams et al. 1980). I want to delay detailed discussion of these factors, however, until after a thorough exploration of the present research.

My concern in writing this book is to communicate (in Jules-Rosette's scheme) a portion of the cultural and experiential impact of these phenomena upon the lives of forty-three persons who participated in a community treatment program intended as an alternative to their psychiatric hospitalization. I want each of us to discover their worlds and individual lives and to gain a human, sociocultural understanding of psychiatric de- and noninstitutionalization as practiced and experienced in our culture.

THE PERSPECTIVE

However needy this research area appears to be on its own terms, more fundamental and equally motivating were my own perspectives, values, life experiences, and selection of academic-intellectual discipline. An increasing number of social scientists are acknowledging the profound influences of their own experiences, feelings, and essentially nonrational cognitive processes on their work. This rediscovery of the "person in research," now expressed as existential sociology (Douglas and Johnson 1977), phenomenological sociology (Psathas 1973), and ethnomethodology (Mehan and Wood 1975) is indeed welcome, but it seriously neglects old and well-established precedents in anthropology.

Since the beginning, as fieldworkers in powerfully new and strange worlds, we have depended upon and coped with the participation of our social and intrapsychic selves in research. We have counted on our observations and feelings, and, more importantly, have come into often brutal contact with the totality and incomprehensibility of other ways of living and thinking. Many of us have struggled to adjust and translate disparate realities to ourselves, learning amid our confusion and our feelings of being overwhelmingly split between the known and not-yet-known, that we have had to discover and come to understand on experiential and everyday levels (perhaps even to feed and clothe ourselves), not just the intellectual, logical, and rational planes. As Geertz (1973:9, 15) incisively reminds us,

> . . . *we begin with our own interpretations of what our informants are up to, or what we think they are up to, and then systematize those.* In finished anthropological writings . . . this fact—that what we call our data are

> really our own constructions of other people's constructions of what they and their compatriots are up to—is obscured because most of what we need to comprehend a particular event, ritual, custom, idea, or whatever is insinuated as background information before the thing itself is directly examined.

In addition to recognizing the essential incompleteness and second and third order re-creations in our work, we acknowledge the role of our selves in the research discovery and communication process. Douglas (1977:4-5) puts it nicely:

> Our decisions about what is important, and in what ways, are based on what we experience and observe about those complete individuals in concrete situations. Our decisions about how we know these things are based on our experience and our analyses within that experience of how one does, in fact, know the world. . . . *We create truth from within by finding what works, what enables us to understand, explain, piece together, and partially predict our social world. Our knowledge necessarily remains partially relative*, situated, and reflexive . . . (emphasis mine).

Because I believe in what Geertz and Douglas say, I mean to make clear from the outset what I brought to this research and why, and how these factors have influenced what I looked for and learned, and how I have tried to understand and communicate.

For me, the lure of cultural anthropology has been its lack of restriction in subject matter combined with its human focus shot through with curiosity, pursuit of commonsense understanding, and enthusiasm for variety, diversity, creativity, and underlying pattern. This search for comprehension of humanness has led anthropologists to the external and internal frontiers of individuals and groups living on our planet. Within this context, my own fascination has centered on how individuals come to feel, think, behave, and believe both similarly and differently within a given cultural code and environment. Simply said, the intrigue of the individual and his or her distinctness within the boundaries of similarity we call cultural groups has continually captured my attention (cf. Caudill 1973). Among anthropologists there exists a long, albeit ambivalent, tradition regarding the place of individuals and their differences in culture. I wholeheartedly endorse Sapir's (1932:239) position that "the true locus of culture is in the interactions of specific individuals and, on the subjective side, in the world of meanings which each one of these individuals may unconsciously abstract for himself from his participation in these interactions."

It has also seemed to me that if we could begin to understand, accept, and even appreciate cross-cultural human variation through anthropological investigation, perhaps intracultural comprehension of a special form of individual variety (i.e., cognitive, behavioral, and experiential differentness or what we call psychiatric disorder), might likewise benefit from similar treatment. The humanistic, anthropological values I brought to the subject matter dictated that patients have a voice in determining their fates and have access to as many alternatives as possible. Attempting to apply a nonethnocentric perspective to psychiatric disorder prompted me to look not for pathology and sickness but for the sociocultural, meaningful, legitimate aspects of being mentally ill. Logically, I presumed that being mentally ill or crazy was one of many ways of being in our culture. The institutions, doctors, nurses, explanations, treatments, and consequences of psychiatric disorder existed long before any current patient I might see. How was it, then, that some persons in our culture existed within this particular personal, social, and economic niche? Was it perhaps a predictable, understandable adaptation to being diagnosed mentally ill as suggested by social and labeling models of mental illness? Or would I simply observe persons attempting to cope with neurochemical processes that predetermined their behaviors, thoughts, and sociocultural positions as put forth in the medical paradigm? I recognized that psychiatric treatment and even diagnosis represented a form of social control, a value judgment. But many others are concerned with this topic. Lending another voice to the already blaring chorus did not appeal to me, nor did it seem to represent the most productive tactic in the study of persons with psychiatric difficulties. Given the personal and social realities of mental illness in our culture, I wondered what it was like to be on the patient end of it, especially outside the psychiatric hospital. It was more interesting to try to comprehend how persons behaving in these special ways did so, and why, and specifically what impact not being hospitalized had on them. Still further, believing that persons have a right to be different, even crazy, at moments or perpetually, I wanted to know how they could do this in our society. As I became aware of the scope of the deinstitutionalization movement, I began to wonder where all the patients had gone. I began to wonder how people were coping with these changes in their illness experience and whether they were as keen on community treatment as their treators. I wanted to learn about their daily lives, their differences and similarities with other community members, the impact of being crazy on their lives as members of our culture.

As an anthropologist, I had what Sapir (1932:238) has called "the healthiest of all scepticisms about the validity of the concept 'normal behavior' " (see also Devereux 1956). I was interested in trying to apply the same understanding to persons with psychiatric disorder in our culture that has been helpful in comprehending psychotics in other cultures; namely, the contribution of sociocultural convention to the content, meaning, process, and life consequences of experiencing and displaying psychosis.

Finally, I suggest that at a fundamental, theoretical level, psychiatric anthropology constitutes basic social science research of a most urgently needed kind. We have long struggled in our discipline with the painful lack of a fruitful, provocative, and empirically based theoretical system for understanding and predicting human behavior, cognition, and affect. I find the tautologous nature of the prevailing functionalist paradigm shamefully inadequate to participate in the discovery process in the psychiatric area. Our explorations into the extremes of human experience can be conceived of as contributing to basic knowledge of the enormous continuum of human living strategies, capabilities, and limitations. I regard our voyages into the experiential and daily worlds of the psychotic, the developmentally different, the anxious, depressed, and excited as elementary steps toward an understanding of humanness that encompasses, appreciates, and invites differentness in living, thinking, and feeling rather than excluding, denigrating, and eschewing these individual variations. Culture and personality advocates have similarly attacked the individual experience aspect of building cultural theory, but from the other end of the continuum—the expected, more routine, frequently occurring expressions of human existence. My hope is that the calls for renewed commitment to the study of individuals per se and as building blocks for rich and generative cultural theory (e.g., Murdock 1972; Watson 1978) will be heard, especially among those of us who work in the boundary arenas of psychiatry and psychology. The inclination to appreciate and to incorporate psychological, individual dimensions in our work is already operative, I think, and is demonstrated by our choices of topic and approach.

My position should not be mistaken for psychological reductionism. Human sociocultural conduct is not reducible to any simple formula but may be discovered and explored through a variety of philosophical, theoretical, and methodological passageways. The more diversity of approach, conception, and strategy within the discipline the better—for we have more chances for surprise, success, and learning from error and not confusion. My argument is that at least some of us need to work at the foundation level, and psychiatric and psychological anthropologists seem to me to be highly desirable personnel. We can work toward providing thorough, empirical, and adventurous understanding of individual humanness, be it called schizophrenic or Yanomamo.

On reflection, it would seem that psychiatric anthropology, rather than being an exotic subspeciality of cultural anthropology, represents a deeply traditional anthropological exercise. We are obligated to be holistic, relativistic, largely empirical and ethnographic (which represents both strengths and weaknesses), and eventually comparative. Holism is especially required in a field where genetic, neurochemical, and pharmacological factors loom so large. The intimate connections to medicine and to all sorts of illness-experiences urge an integrated view of the biocultural person. A lack of ethnocentrism, indeed egocentrism, is demanded by the intrinsically bizarre nature of our subject matter and subjects. Fieldwork and intimate inter- and intrapersonal experience in the process of inquiry and understanding also seem powerfully present in the psychiatric arena. And in order to learn from our findings regarding the varieties of human flexibility in identifying, experiencing, and coping with psychic distress, we are pushed to compare our findings with others to contribute to generalizable, theory-relevant knowledge. These are healthy, life-giving forces for our work.

My view of psychiatric anthropology is that it represents a multilevel enterprise within anthropology. Our inquiries into the poles of human experience and existence inform and sophisticate fundamental principles of humanness vital to the discipline. Our ethnographic data enrich the store of knowledge and perhaps the eventual appreciation of all types of differentness—and inter- and intracultural. Further, the practice of psychiatric anthropology devotes energy toward comprehending and alleviating marked suffering among our companions. In these times of scarcity of research funds, cries for consumer accountability, and concern for the social and intellectual utility of scientific inquiry, the psychiatric anthropologist engages in a most worthwhile endeavor.

When I began at PACT, I was fishing, looking for leads, surveying the scene. After a time, and in the midst of my own curious culture-contact depression, the search narrowed. The shock of encountering another reality (Berger and Luckman 1967:98) was the key. I had expected that people in the treatment program would be cured or would get better. I did not know that the process and progress would be so slow, so painful, and so laden with failure and setbacks. It occurred to me that perhaps these people were never going to recover in the sense that one recovers from a cold or appendicitis. As time passed, I began to realize that maybe a house in the suburbs, a family, a car, credit card debts, and a full-time job might not be a part of the present or foreseeable future for the people from whom I was learning. The lofty goals of reintegration into the community, satisfactory quality of life (or one like the general population's), and lessening of personal distress and social isolation put forth in the community psychiatry literature seemed far removed from what I was observing. At this point, I became very disheartened—all seemed gloomy and destined to fail. These people were not changing significantly in predictable and reliable ways. And then I began the recurring cycle of pessimism and hope that is probably perpetual if one works in this area (or so I am told by the staff). Little alterations seem like major successes—a spontaneous smile, a good day, a new apartment. Yet, the creeping hopelessness always comes back.

Disarmed by my naiveté about chronic psychiatric patients, I had to backtrack and reformulate. Anthropologically, there was no choice. The ethnocentrism that had precipitated my depression had to go. And the task became to understand how these persons were living, to identify what values, beliefs, perceptions, and special qualities they had that contributed to being able to live this different way. Thus, my values and appreciation for the intricacies of differentness had to change.

Being a long-term psychiatric patient does not seem so awful anymore. Yet it also appears to be a self-other constructed trap. Clients have taught me and have demonstrated the benefits and rewards of this pathway. But they are also not unaware of the costs, negative consequences, and trade-offs to be made. Understanding this seeming contradiction is perhaps the most important and difficult task. From this foundation, our goal becomes one of understanding how the clients and others construct and operate within this reality. Describing this process and that lifeway is the topic of this book.

3

FIELDWORK—TACTICAL AND METHODOLOGICAL ASPECTS

> Exploration is by definition a flexible procedure in which the scholar shifts from one line to another line of inquiry, adopts new points of observation as his study progresses, moves in new directions previously unthought of and changes his recognition of what are relevant data as he acquires more information and better understanding.
> —(Blumer 1969:40)

TACTICS

Before proceeding to more substantive ethnographic material, it is appropriate to outline the actual procedures and principles used to collect and work with the data. How does the anthropologist go about learning to make it crazy?

Traditional approaches to fieldwork include participant observation, structured depth interviews, some use of questionnaires, a gathering of life histories, and a vast array of ad hoc procedures (Edgerton and Langness 1974; Wax 1971; Pelto 1970). This project included all of the above in some manner, but at the experiential and phenomenological levels of learning, obvious obstacles were encountered. The anthropological fieldworker customarily attempts to learn and to reach understanding through asking, doing, watching, testing, and experiencing for herself the same activities, rituals, rules, and meanings as the subjects. Our subjects become the experts, the instructors, and we become the students (Blumer 1969; Maretzki

1973). But if we are studying persons who are crazy (i.e., actively psychotic or living the crazy life), we are restricted in reaching optimal levels of experience and participation in the subjects' world if we are to remain sane.

The proposition that one must become or be mentally ill oneself in order to reach the desired quality of understanding may hold some logical or intellectual merit (cf. Mehan and Wood 1975; Jules-Rosette 1978), but it is patently absurd and dangerously impractical at the personal level. Unlike the enculturation process sought by anthropologists in learning a different culture, the fieldworker in the psychiatric world must constantly guard against passage into a new reality. Completion of such a venture would destroy any value the work might have held and would represent great personal tragedy for the individual scholar. Getting aboard the Eden Express (Vonnegut 1976) is quite a different matter than "going native." Others who have conducted extensive participant observation among psychiatric patients in hospitals report precarious personal states not unlike the one I have alluded to (Reynolds and Farberow 1976; Redlich 1973:315). I can offer no general solutions to this dilemma beyond those put forth in my preface. I can, however, report my own efforts to cope with tactical and methodological problems.

In beginning the fieldwork, it was essential to establish my identity and position in this polarized staff and client social system (cf. Landy 1958). Although such categorization of persons is overly simplistic, as we shall see in chapter 7, at the outset a primary, visible affiliation with clients had to be constructed. They asked me immediately to which group I belonged. This question preceded even asking my name. I made the mistake during the first day of fieldwork of *looking* too much like a staff member (see Pelto 1970:227-230 for a discussion of the importance of dress and impression management in fieldwork). This involved not only my dress, but my affect, manner of speech, posture, and general presentation. I found that dressing and behaving inconspicuously was not enough to separate from staff and align myself with clients. Wearing cut-off or long blue jeans, tee-shirts, and sandals or boots helped, and sitting silently, almost glumly, folded up on the couch in the PACT house, smoking cigarettes, changed the questions from "Are you a new staff member?" or "Are you a student?" to "Are you in PACT? Are you a new client? What are you doing here?"

The answer to the first set of questions was easy. It was no. The second was more delicate. I was not masquerading as a client, but I did not want to leave any room for doubt about my nonstaff status. At the beginning, I simply said I was "hanging around PACT trying to see what it was like." Some clients thought I was setting up a smoke screen around my true patient identity. Others seemed not to care after making sure I was not on the staff.

Staff had been instructed not to introduce me to clients but to let me do this whenever possible. Any questions regarding my status and purpose were to be directed to me. This system worked surprisingly well except for one occasion when a client, who suspected me of being a "spy," had this view reinforced by a staff nurse, who told him she thought I would "probably play both ends against the middle." The belief that I was secretly studying *them* persisted among staff for several months. Over time, I revealed and explained my purpose more straightforwardly to clients. At the present time, all know I am writing about them, and six have read portions of this book, offering several valuable suggestions.[1]

I have underscored this issue because it is important. Although I found that staff and clients at PACT were not necessarily in an adversarial relationship, had I been identified as staff, the utility of my project would have decreased enormously. The information to which I would have had access would not have differed significantly from that already available. In sum, much of my effort for many months was directed toward making a new niche in the system. I cannot be sure if I have succeeded. But I do recognize, as should the reader, that all I have observed and reported here must be evaluated with the success or lack of success of this endeavor in mind.

1. Because the hospital had critically reviewed and accepted my research proposal, and because the clients had already agreed to participate in research associated with the PACT program, I was not obliged to present my credentials to the clients or to seek their "informed consent." Had I approached them from the start with papers and forms, it would have been impossible to establish a productive fieldwork "place" among them. At the same time, professional and personal ethics dictated that I not deceive. Many of the clients were so preoccupied and disturbed about themselves and others that signed forms would not have ensured any sort of honest disclosure. My constant verbal revelations and conduct over two years represents a practical and honest information procedure, appropriate to the field situation.

Virtually all work similar to mine has been conducted in psychiatric hospitals, with the notable exception of Reynolds's study of aftercare facilities in California (Reynolds and Farberow 1977). In the outpatient community setting, one is faced with a different and, in my opinion, more difficult tactical puzzle than in the institutional environment. The architectural embrace of the ward provides a controlled and limited spatial arena for observation. My subjects were scattered over a much larger area than the usual hospital ward setting. The reluctant client could more easily avoid contact with me in the community than in the hospital. Their activities and whereabouts were not regulated by a uniform, predictable time schedule. They were not all in the same places at the same time, as compared with a ward where medications, group therapy, meals, and recreation were often en masse and on schedule. In this sense, the setting within which I worked more closely approximated the village arena frequently encountered by anthropologists. But it was a village without sturdy and visible boundaries, located within a much larger, complicated human and nonhuman environment.

At PACT, evening recreational activities would bring five to fifteen clients together, as would the twice-weekly social skills or assertiveness training classes. These were the only group activities, except for special trips (of which there were two during my project) and holiday dinners or outings (Fourth of July, Thanksgiving, and Christmas). Clients would come to the PACT house at varying times during the day and evening for appointments, to pick up medications and money, to meet with staff before going job or apartment hunting, to do laundry, to apply for city welfare, or for some other activity.

Initially, I made an effort to be at the PACT house at these times in order to identify, observe, and meet clients. As I got to know them better, I used the house more as a base of operations and would go for coffee, a ride, or to someone's apartment or room. Other contact points were around mealtimes at either of the two drugstore and coffee shops on the Capitol Square, or between 3:00 and 4:00 P.M., when the Madison Opportunity Center, where several clients worked, closed for the day. Most clients had access to telephones in their residences, but I did not use this method of communication or even give my telephone number to them until the second year of fieldwork or when clients voluntarily gave their numbers to me. This was done not only to protect my privacy and my place to work undisturbed but to focus on face-to-face interaction. Clients themselves seldom used the phone to communicate with one another but often talked with staff in this manner.

My general approach was to participate *as if* I were a client in as many treatment and nontreatment aspects of clients' lives as was feasible. The purpose of these activities was twofold: to observe clients across the range of their daily lives and to participate in and experience these circumstances myself. At the beginning of fieldwork in July 1975, the major portion of my time was spent in PACT treatment-related activities. As time and my relationships with clients progressed, non-PACT treatment-related activities and meetings increased and exceeded treatment-related interaction. It is important to understand that the clients in this study were admitted to the PACT program at a rate of four to five per month from January 1975 to November 1975. Each received active, intensive treatment for thirteen months from the time of his or her admission.[2] Thus, after approximately July 1976, many members of the group had been discharged, referred, were subject to decreasing treatment contact, or were in various stages of these processes.[3]

2. Although the treatment period was designated as thirteen months, activity and intensity of treatment varied for clients during this time. During periods of relative stability and contentment, a client could decrease contact with the staff or vice versa. When a client became floridly psychotic, extremely anxious, lost a job or a place to live, or was experiencing some other type of crisis, contact with staff might be as frequent as several times per day, both in person and via telephone. The general ideal contact profile sought by staff with clients represents frequent interaction upon admission to the program with a gradual decrease over the treatment period up to the point of discharge. Average contact with staff by clients for the treatment period was three times per week. The range runs from those who had no contact at all for several months because they had left town or discharged themselves, to those who saw staff four to five times per day. Clients who were perceived as becoming too dependent upon interaction with staff were actively "weaned." Others who were fearful or reclusive were actively pursued and were encouraged to form interpersonal relationships with staff and other clients.

3. A follow-up study of the clients in my study, initiated by PACT staff, indicated that half, randomly selected, would receive traditional discharges at the end of thirteen months. This meant that they were referred to another treatment setting and to other therapists. Most often, the referral was to the County Mental Health Center, a day treatment program run by this center, a private social worker with medications from the Visiting Nurse Service, or the University Hospital's outpatient clinic and psychiatric nursing clinic. After discharge, these persons could no longer have any therapeutic contact with PACT personnel. The remaining half of the group were not formally discharged from the program at thirteen months. Their contacts with treatment staff were

Consequently, and because I was interested in continuing observation outside the treatment setting, I tried to apportion my time between those activities and clients that were PACT-related and those that no longer were. Simply put, clients' activities and locations determined my own.

In retrospect, I would characterize the fieldwork and observation as comprising two phases representing polar positions along a continuum. The first dealt almost exclusively with persons actively engaged in receiving PACT treatment and ran from July 1975 to January 1977. The second phase, in contrast, dealt almost exclusively with discharged or semidischarged persons no longer receiving PACT treatment and ran from January 1977 to August 1977.

During the first phase, my schedule evolved into something of a routine. Staff report or cross-shift[4] was attended daily (though not always on weekends or when I had an occasional conflict) from 2:00 until 3:30 P.M. When I was not there, notes were made available to me. When I did attend, I sat out of sight of most staff (with their prior consent and knowledge) in another room, taking down not only reports of clients' activities of the day but also staff remarks, discussions, and descriptions of clients and their predicaments. In

---

put on a crisis-oriented or as-needed basis, with regular medication or problem-solving contacts (usually monthly) set up as the norm. Other agencies and therapists became the primary caregivers in most instances. Thus, involvement in PACT treatment-related activities varies for the group over the fieldwork period. Three persons moved out of the city just before discharge, so their contact was sharply curtailed. The purpose of the projected follow-up study is to compare the adjustment of persons who received the traditional discharge with those who remained in long-term contact with the PACT program. It is hypothesized that the latter group will display and experience superior adjustment and community tenure than the former.

4. Cross shift refers to the fact that from 2:30 P.M. to 3:30 P.M. the morning and evening (or "A.M. and P.M." as they are called) shifts overlap. The A.M. shift runs from 7:00 A.M. until 3:30 P.M. and the P.M. shift from 2:30 P.M. until 11:00 P.M.. The purpose of this meeting is primarily information exchange. In this fashion, the P.M. shift knows how a particular client's day has proceeded from the observations of the A.M. shift. Some planning and alteration of individual treatment programs is also done at this time, but the major planning time is at 8:00 A.M., when the nursing and professional staffs meet to go over the notes about clients left by the P.M. shift from the night before. The professional staff (the social worker, clinical psychologist, recreation therapist, and psychiatric unit chief) usually does not work during the evenings, so these meetings are their chances to coordinate with those members of the nursing staff who do. The meeting also serves as a forum for infrequent group discussions of general treatment issues, introduction of students, visitors, or new staff, the customary celebration of staff birthdays with a cake, and farewell salutes to rotating students or staff who are leaving the program.

this manner, staff were quasi research assistants who saw clients in numerous settings, all of which were physically impossible for me to observe during the day. At these meetings, I was able to get clues as to clients' possible whereabouts and as to their condition that day as perceived by staff. Verbatim quotes from clients often were included as a part of report, so I was able to gain indirect information in their own words, or at least to have some sense of what they were saying to staff.

Though these meetings were a valuable source of information, I did not share this knowledge with clients. I let them tell me about events or circumstances from their perspective and in their own terms, though I might have had prior knowledge. At times I was able to listen to staff's interpretation of events or feelings that I had observed or had been aware of prior to the meeting. Attending report but keeping the information to myself served the dual purpose of gathering two perspectives of the same situation and protected my nonstaff image with clients. On rare occasions I would suggest to staff that a circumstance of some gravity existed with a client, but as a rule I did not participate actively in report.

At no time did I tell a client that I attended these meetings. When two asked me this directly, I denied my participation. Had they known I had access to these sessions and to the information, my position with them would have been severely compromised. I also wanted to avoid the inevitable problem of having to refuse to share information with them regarding what staff had said about them or other clients. The withholding of this information and denial to clients represents the only covert aspect of the research. Even the logistics of attending report became complicated. I slipped out the back door of the PACT house after the meeting to avoid encountering clients who were out front waiting for report to end, or I went upstairs to avoid revealing that I had been in the house when no client was allowed to be there. On occasion, it was impossible to disengage from clients I was chatting with on the front porch before cross-shift, so I skipped the meeting. Or, if the weather were cold and we were inside before the meeting, when clients were asked to leave or to go upstairs, I did the same. Though I was then and am now extremely uneasy regarding this arrangement, no other feasible solution presented itself.

Undoubtedly, the content of staff report, particularly the color and flavor of descriptive remarks made by staff about clients, was at first affected by my presence. After the first few weeks, however, most came to accept me as a part of the furniture. At the orientation meeting, when I was first introduced to the staff to explain my project,[5] I asked them to ignore me, to pretend I was invisible. Though they joked with me about my nonexistence, all eventually followed my instructions and requests. I had some indication of this as each new psychiatric resident who rotated through the program seemed to display some preliminary discomfort at my eavesdropping. One, in particular, consistently sat where he could see me during the

5. The following is the written introduction to staff that I asked them to read before we met for the first time (I include it here because it was extremely helpful in setting the tone for our working relations):

Memorandum

To: PACT Staff

From: Sue Estroff

Re: Research Project

What follows is a brief description of the research I will be doing with PACT III clients for the next eighteen months. Though the focus of this research will be on the clients, each of you is necessarily involved to varying degrees. Because of this, and due to the nature and length of the project, I wish everyone concerned to be fully aware of what I am doing and why. I hope that you will feel free to comment, offer suggestions, and ask questions when I meet with you on July 1, and at any time during the research period.

On the surface, the plan is quite simple. I am a cultural anthropologist and wish to observe the way of life or culture of the PACT III clients. With the growing trend toward community-based treatment and nonhospitalization of persons with mental problems, research has begun to focus on the community in which the treatment takes place. Not only is the community considered a complicated component in the treatment process but so is the interaction of patients with the multitude of factors and persons which make up communities. We know a lot about the way things work on hospital wards, for they are relatively controlled environments that can be studied with some precision. But, life is so complex, even in the quietest neighborhood, that very little systematic investigation of patients in the community has been done. The research staff collects a particular type of invaluable information about the clients, yet there is much we don't know about their daily lives. For instance, who are their friends and what type of influence do these persons have? Or, what situations inherent in the Square area community are particularly stressful or helpful to the clients? What is it like to live in this particular setting trying to cope with internal and external problems that exceed those of the rest of the population?

My goal is to try to understand what community life for persons such as the clients is like. I hope to do this by observing them over a period of time across the broad range of circumstances and activities which comprise their treatment program and lives. I want to look at things from their point of view, as if I were a client in the program. In order to do this I must not only observe but participate in as many aspects of the clients' daily schedule as possible. Most anthropologists can virtually move in with the group they wish to study and, by living with these people, come to understand how and why they behave as they do. I obviously cannot do this with the PACT clients, but with your cooperation perhaps I can approach the in-depth, informal kind of contact required to do detailed and accurate ethnography.

My research design is flexible and in some ways informal. I will be asking clients to complete self-report adjustment scales for me, but the rest of my activities will consist

meeting. When an off-color, derogatory, or "staff humor"[6] remark was made, he checked my reaction, shrugged his shoulders, or asked if I had made sure to record the remark.

Usually, after report, I sought out various clients on the street, in coffee shops, or at a rooming house where several lived, or I met someone with whom I had made prior arrangements. After repeated disappointments when people failed to show up for prearranged meetings, I learned to come early, to stay late, and then to seek them out if they never appeared. Often they had forgotten, and I had to swallow my chagrin at being so unimportant to them when they were so precious to me. I tried to make my anger a learning experience, understanding why they did not want to come, why I felt so put down. At times, I found people just sitting, knowing we were supposed to meet, but "not feeling like it." When I told them it really mattered to me, some seemed surprised and pleased but clearly unaccustomed to their friends' expecting that they would be reliable in such matters. On other occasions, early in the research, the clients deliberately avoided seeing me because they thought I

---

of observation—hanging around with them, going to work with them, following them as an informal observer through their routines. I intend to monitor their use of both informal and formal community supports, and to tap their perceptions of what is bothersome or stressful about their lives. That is, in essence, what I am about. We hope that by gathering this type of information we can provide a program of treatment that is sensitive to and appropriate for the particular community in which it takes place and the client for whom we are all concerned.

It is critical that the clients not view me as a staff person of any kind. At the same time, it is important that you understand my role as a neutral observer. If the research is to succeed, I must form friendly, nonobstructed working relationships with as many clients as possible. This will probably involve trading favors (within definite limits) and participating in activities with them that you would not. What I do, and how I do it, in large part depends on the individual client involved and their reaction to me. Your help in learning how best to deal with these people will be enormously appreciated. I also need your assistance in gaining the status of a nonstaff and nonclient person. It is a precarious position, but absolutely necessary. You should treat me more as a client (or simply ignore me) when they are around than as a colleague or researcher. At the outset I will probably need some help in orienting myself to the program and in locating/making contact with clients. However, it is clear to me that the smooth working of the program has top priority. I will avoid any disruptive role at all costs. I will not act as an infiltrator or an advocate for the clients with you or vice versa. If I get caught between individuals or groups the project will suffer.

In general, I simply request that you be honest and communicative with me about my behavior as it affects your work. As time goes by we will undoubtedly work out the best means for accomplishing all our tasks in the most productive fashion.

6. The subject of staff humor is fascinating and could be pursued with enthusiasm. It seems that in the face of bleakness, little or no therapeutic progress, and constant exposure to bizarre thoughts and inexplicable behavior, staff develops a particular type of

was "nosy" or was really on the staff, wanting to talk with them about other appointments they had failed to keep.

There were two general lessons here. The first was that if a client felt upset, preoccupied, tired, or whatever, this was a legitimate reason not to appear and required no notice or explanation, especially if he were *not* meeting staff. The code among clients seemed much more ad hoc and convenience oriented in terms of spending time with each other than any I was accustomed to. At times when I was anxious or feeling especially uncertain, I was glad the person did not show up. I felt obligated to go because of the research and my previous code of conduct, but as I became enmeshed in their world, I understood more about why a casual dinner or cup of coffee loomed so large and foreboding. Second, I suspected that being important to others as friends and companions was new to them—indicating a set of meanings for friendships and interpersonal relations that differed from mine.

At least three times per week I ate dinner at a small lunch counter frequented by several clients because they could use their city welfare vouchers for food, or at one of the drugstores on the Square. After the meal, I returned to the PACT house to wait for the evening activity or to catch up on notes before 7:00 P.M., when clients would begin arriving. Monday evenings were free nights for me, because the men's recreational group met then and I could not attend. Tuesday evening was taken up with a female clients' group, led initially by staff and then by community volunteers. Wednesday and Thursday offered social-skills classes. Though clients attended only one of the two groups, which had different foci and

---

humor which may seem perverse or even cruel to the outsider. But it serves to channel hostility and frustration into a relatively harmless arena, functions as a release of tension, and also brightens up the gloom. An example will be helpful: One evening after a social skills class in which clients were assigned to decide upon outside activities to be enjoyed with a friend, Jack and another client not in my research group went to the apartment of Alice. Alice was known for her generosity regarding sexual favors. Jack and Alice went to bed in front of the other client. When they attempted to have intercourse, Alice was so anxious and vaginally constricted that they were unable. Jack reported the incident to Dr. C and he shared the information at report. After listening carefully, one staff member deadpanned, suggesting that it was "one social skills assignment that didn't get screwed up." One-liners were also in abundance. For example, one staff member told me, "The only difference between staff and clients is that clients get better." At another time, the staff decided they were all "human nutcrackers." "What we do around here is crack nuts."

skill levels, I was able to participate in both. Friday, Saturday, and Sunday evenings I attended group recreational activities that consisted of softball, tennis, or miniature golf in summer and, in the winter months, bowling, movies, going to a particular root-beer stand, shopping center, University Union, or other such place to eat. During weekend days, I often attended a breakfast with clients and staff that served as a time for staff to encourage clients to plan activities for the day. Many clients slept late on these days, so I usually wandered around the PACT house or nearby clients' neighborhoods in the afternoon. After the activities, I usually returned to the PACT house to write up the evening's notes and to observe the later night activities of staff. At this time, medications were taken to various clients, phone calls were received from some who might be upset or might need information regarding the next day's schedule, and notes were made for the morning shift. Frequently, I went for a drink with various staff after the office closed at 11:00 P.M.

The above schedule was kept for approximately one year. As an increasing number of my subjects were discharged, more time was spent in prearranged or spontaneous activities with one client in his or her apartment, in my own home, or while out for a meal. New clients were being admitted to PACT continually, and though I was in contact with them, they were not the primary focus of the research.

During February and March 1976, I took fluphenazine for six weeks. Fluphenazine (trade name: Prolixin), was the antipsychotic medication that most of the clients were receiving during the time I was working with them. The decision to take the medication was a difficult one, and it caused much consternation among my family, friends, and colleagues. Interestingly, the psychiatric professionals had the most reservations, not the social scientists. Those staff members whose opinions I sought strongly advised against it, saying they would never take medications. However, because these medications represented such a substantial and meaning-laden part of the clients' world and experience, anthropologically it seemed logical and worthwhile. The medication was prescribed by a physician with whom I had agreed that I would accept legal, medical, and financial responsibility for my actions in taking the drug. I also had a complete physical examination by another physician prior to taking Prolixin and had obtained his consent to proceed. The prescribing physician monitored my course with the drug, offering his around-the-clock availability if I should need assistance with side effects. His helpfulness and willingness to allow me this experience were greatly appreciated. A brief summary of this episode is found in chapter 5 which investigates the general subject of medication.

During December 1975, I worked for two weeks as if I were a PACT client at the St. Benedict's Center workshop directed by PACT staff. None of the sisters or staff at St. Benedict's knew that I was *not* a client. Other PACT staff were eager to gain an inside perspective on the setting, and clients never thought to tell the sisters otherwise. This represented a unique experience, for at no other time during fieldwork was I in a situation where the persons in authority did not know my identity or the purpose of my presence. I did not have the opportunity to work at Goodwill Industries or the Madison Opportunity Center, the other sheltered workshop settings in which clients worked. My St. Benedict's experience is included in chapter 6, which discusses the subject of work among clients.

Miscellaneous fieldwork activities included simply dropping in at clients' apartments to chat for a time, on four occasions double-dating with two clients and a male friend of mine, taking clients shopping or giving them rides in my car, playing pool or poker, barhopping, taking an overnight camping trip with the women's group, visiting clients if they were hospitalized, and attending two court proceedings involving clients. I also met six sets of clients' parents, four of these in the clients' homes. With the group from PACT, I attended the funeral of one client who took his life.

I used a formal questionnaire to gain a different perspective on the lives of clients in the community. Social adjustment scales utilized in research with psychiatric patients in the community are plentiful (Weissman 1975), but to date none has been developed which pleases even a majority of researchers in the field. I selected the Community Adaptation Schedule (CAS) (Burnes and Roen 1967; Roen et al. 1966) because it required completion by clients themselves[7] and because it focused on aspects of their lives not ex-

7. Weissman and Bothwell (1976) report results from use of their Social Adjustment Scale Self-Report as comparable to information obtained both from direct interview and from relatives of the test subject. Further, they noted the advantages of self-report scales as follows:

(1) Supplements interview assessment and represents another source of information for research.

tensively explored in the research instruments utilized by PACT. The questionnaire is included in the appendix.

The CAS focuses on three modes of response: (1) actual behavior or fact, (2) feeling or affect, and (3) perception or belief. Each of these areas is scored separately but can be integrated into a total descriptive profile of the subject. The CAS offers a diachronic view, including questions regarding the past as well as the present and future (Weissman 1975:362). The schedule consists of 156 items and can be completed in forty-five minutes to one hour. In prepublication tests, the CAS proved capable of distinguishing between patient and nonpatient but did not sort respondents on the basis of socioeconomic class (Roen et al. 1966:41). Thus, the scale was particularly well suited for my subjects, who were all psychiatric patients but who represented various socioeconomic backgrounds.

With the advice of the clinical psychologist at PACT, I modified the CAS. Some of the language was too abstract and complicated and was simplified without significant alteration of original meanings. In addition, a number of questions that indicated no particular time period were changed to specify either the present or a period within four weeks of completing the scale. My data reported from the CAS are drawn entirely from the baseline results, that is, from each client's scores at the time of PACT discharge or change in active treatment status.

It is difficult to convey my discomfort in asking clients to complete the questionnaire. I feared irreparable damage to the rapport I had worked so hard to attain. Six clients, with whom I had worked extensively and whom I considered friends, steadfastly refused to answer the questions. None refused because they felt it was too probing or personal. Three insisted that their concentration was inadequate to the task. Some others felt inconvenienced and thought that, without pay, it was not worth the effort. Some consistently forgot to complete it when it was left with them. The remainder of the group complied surprisingly easily. I explained to them that this would help with my writing, would provide information un-

---

(2) Discrepancies between self-report and interview measures may give an indication of cultural bias on the part of the rater or misperception of norms of behavior by the patient. These differences then may not indicate poor instruments but may inform us about cultural or perceptual differences between the client and researchers (or nonclients).

solicited by PACT, and would give us (them and me) a measure of their progress and improvement over time and without the input of the PACT program.

Thirty-five of the forty-three subjects completed the baseline CAS in a variety of settings. Sixteen took it in their rooms or apartments, six in restaurants, five in bars, one in my car, four outside in parks, two in the University Union, and one in a Lutheran facility for alcoholics. Those who could do so wrote the answers on the answer sheets. Others preferred that I record their responses. Five clients completed the task without my being present. The remainder worked with me in order to accomplish the job.

My fears regarding the impact of the CAS on rapport had been unfounded. Perhaps more than anything else, it highlighted to clients my membership in another, outside professional system and diminished the suspicions of some that my writing about PACT was just a story to cover my real status as a patient. Results of the CAS have been included under relevant topics throughout the book.

When I refer to data, I mean primarily volumes of field notebooks filled with verbatim and reconstructed conversations, my own thoughts and feelings, descriptions of events and individual behaviors, synopses of discussions, and miscellaneous information collected from a variety of sources. The other materials I used were notes made by clients (some solicited and some unsolicited) and staff, CAS responses that were computed, coded, and scored, some transcribed tapes of in-depth interviews with staff members, and veritable mountains of newspaper clippings, books, and scholarly articles. I created a file for each client that contained essential information such as demographic, admission, and discharge facts. In addition, these files contained medication, employment, and personal histories as well as current status—all as reported to me by the clients.

Working with these materials was a messy, exasperating, and complicated procedure. I began by reading all the field notes and raw materials repeatedly until I knew what was in each volume and where it was, creating a sort of mental map and table of contents. Then, as the structure and order of presentation of topics became clearer, I literally surrounded myself with data. I made concentric circles of important pages of field notes, articles, books, and drafts, and I perched in the middle of these to think, sort, and combine. Each of these circles became a chapter, but only after it had become a shambles. Days were spent shuffling and grabbing, realizing a whole section needed rewriting and so beginning again, or rescuing all from numerous disasters with the paws of muddy dogs who assaulted me for attention. Always there was the attendant panic of the lost quote or description and the fatigue that made me wonder if I had really heard it and had written it somewhere, or if I had just hoped a client had said or done it. I remember questioning the truthfulness and honesty of all my anthropological ancestors as I *wished* persons had said or done things that would have confirmed a pattern I felt was there, would have exemplified a point I wanted to make.

METHODOLOGY

The preceding scenario, describing the circumstances and manner of data collection and analysis, does not represent a complete explication of methodology. Following Blumer (1969:24-60) and Jarvie (1967), I believe that methodology encompasses more than tactics and techniques. Inherent to method are one's philosophies, assumptions, and values regarding the subject, and these articles of faith dictate the manner and means by which the subject is pursued (cf. Tead 1958; Gouldner 1970). They determine the questions one asks of a phenomenon, and the standards of proof one levels and exacts in reaching an answer and deciding upon a satisfactory explanation (see Jarvie 1967:16 ff. for discussion of this idea).

During the research period, I collected an enormous amount of data in search of satisfactory explanations. I have selected for presentation those examples from this data that I have come to understand most thoroughly and have been able to utilize most effectively in organizing and systematizing important aspects of psychiatric patienthood in a community setting. Some topics and issues I have treated only briefly, such as community attitudes and responses to the mentally ill, the subjective experience of psychosis, friendship among clients, and staff's views on numerous issues. My goal has been to present the scope of each issue, to highlight its significance for clients, to present observational and empirical data pertinent to the subject, and to integrate this into some semblance of a comprehensible whole. It would be dishonest to assert that I have understood it all. I have not.

Although this is a study in cultural anthropology, it is not an exercise in identifying and explaining the intricacies of culture. Culture possesses a special and powerful meaning, even though it represents many things to many people (see Bohannon 1973; Geertz 1973). My own definition is well stated by Kluckhohn (1976:42), who asserts, "Culture is a way of thinking, feeling, believing." I would add only that its aspects must in some way be patterned, shared, learned, or learnable within and among a group of people, and these aspects must have some visible behavioral correlates. In this study, I have not presumed that culture exists apart from these individuals or that all clients share ways of thinking, feeling, and believing that can be identified as a "culture of being 'crazy'." There may well be a culture of schizophrenia (or more precisely schizophrenics) (Ludwig 1971) or mental illness. *Perhaps this culture, or what I believe to be an adaptation secondary to an individual's psychotic experiences within the American cultural context, is what is so impervious to treatment intervention—not the disease or disorder itself.* At this time I am not prepared to make this claim more strongly or to demonstrate conclusively that a culture exists within and among clients.

There are clear, observable similarities in behavior and experience within this group, but these are outnumbered and outweighed by diversity and variation. We lose little by appreciating these differences instead of confining ourselves to tracing only the similarities. Significant exceptions exist for almost any characterization one might make of the group except that, during the time I have known them, only four have demonstrated the ability or the successful desire to make it, without craziness, outside of the mental health system. Is the question of chronic mental patienthood a question of culture? We must remember that the group was brought together by circumstances other than those which usually unite cultural groups. These people were brought together by others on the basis of diagnosed or recognized similarities, that is, their symptoms and their problems in living. The clients clearly contributed to this convocation by displaying symptoms, experiencing problems, and sometimes asking for help. But these behavioral similarities do not allow us to presume underlying *cultural* patterns before the fact. In a sense, we are in search of culture. If we do not find it, perhaps we will still learn along the way.

We must also take into consideration the relatively short span of time in the lives of clients represented by this study and by their participation in PACT. We have but a few lines of a novel, several frames of a feature-length film. Although this is true of any ethnography, it is particularly important to remember here because we are investigating processes (i.e., psychiatric treatment) that are *meant* to alter persons and that are in turn altered by persons over time. Treatment per se is predicated on or seeks to facilitate the occurrence of change. Illness and craziness are not static but dynamic, active life phenomena. There may be weeks or years of stabilization, but months of depression may subtly or dramatically evolve into feeling better. Some may argue that chronic mental illness is by definition less of a processual, moving circumstance than the more acute or neurotic disorders. There is certainly truth to this, but it is a mistake to presume that chronicity implies stability or even progressive regression.

The persons from whom I have learned have demonstrated that there are few simple patterns in this regard. Depending upon a multiplicity of factors, such as age, length of illness, type of disorder, prior life adjustment and lifeway, quantity and quality of interpersonal networks, to name just a few, the course and content of the persons' patienthood varies. We are perhaps observing the formation, reformation, and struggling of individuals to form acceptable identities—acceptable to them and others. Often these are in conflict. Each person is in the process of trying to cope with, understand, integrate—or perhaps forget—self, symptoms, socioeconomic situation, and relationships with others. In sum, it is most critical to recognize the fluid nature of a subject that has necessarily become captive in my words.

Simultaneously, we must realize that however powerful an experience being in PACT treatment may have been for clients, it was but an instant in a lifelong scenario. Simply, our view is skewed by the time limits of research if the goal is a generalized, valid view of community psychiatric patienthood for the long-term client. This became clear when, in the course of collecting data beyond the treatment period, Agatha presented this problem. At the time of her final interview, she was working at a competitive job in a nursing home, living independently at the YWCA, and enjoying some relief from symptomatology including auditory hallucinations that had distressed her quite a bit. Just three weeks later, she had cut her arms with a razor blade, was hospitalized, lost the job, and was acutely symptomatic again. Thus, caution is in order all around in putting the data and my conclusions into proper perspective.

If I have revealed a propensity for elasticity and lack of rigid experimental design, it is intentional. Blumer (1969) has explained the rationale for this approach nicely: ". . . the complete scientific act, itself, has to fit the obdurate character of the empirical world under study; therefore methods are subservient to that world and should be subject to test by it." I have tried to let the clients determine priorities rather than the grant-funding agency, or the dictates of a particular theory regarding psychiatric treatment, deviance, culture, or the like. I have tried to let the clients determine what was important to learn and to understand. In addition, I have sought answers to questions regarding community psychiatric treatment in a manner that reveals my presumptions about the crucial problems involved. These assumptions are subsumed by my conviction that an individual's perceptions, beliefs, feelings, experience, and behaviors constitute the most important unit of analysis and understanding in any contemporary social scientific endeavor (see Murdock 1972:22-23). Based on this premise, I have formulated questions and sought answers regarding clients' experiences in living with psychiatric problems and the life consequences of these misfortunes. The questions asked reflect my belief in inherent rights to equality, dignity, and freedom for all human beings, regardless of how they live. This endorsement explicitly excludes those whose values and lifeways deny these same rights to others. To my way of thinking, clients' needs, wishes, values, and sensibilities rank as high in priority for research and planning as the nonclient community's rules and wishes, or the requirements, goals, and values of the treatment system and its personnel. I cast no aspersions on those whose techniques and orientations differ. In fact, I welcome the range of variation in philosophy and approach found among researchers in this field. As Mehan and Wood (1975:226) remind us, "The truths of science are argued, not revealed." Ultimately these methodological-theoretical decisions are a matter of faith and belief, no matter how they may be embellished with logic, data, and the apparatus of science.

SUMMARY AND RESTATEMENT OF THE TOPIC

Until this point I have engaged in laying foundations. I have presented an introduction to clients and staff and my working relationships with them to orient the reader to the subjects of the research, and I have discussed the development, rationale, and personal-intellectual aspects of the topic. Also, I have explained the tactics and methodological features of my approach. Because an anthropologist is his or her own most important research tool, I consider the preceding material very important. These factors must be available for evaluation. At this juncture, I will restate the topic, define the boundaries of the investigation, and outline the remainder of the book.

If there is a central question I seek to answer, it is that posed in the title. How does one live in the community if one is a self and/or other-identified crazy person? To answer this question involves exploring how one provides food, shelter, clothing, money, and other resources necessary to sustain life. These are subsistence strategies and constitute a basic level of analysis. But in seeking to answer just this deceptively simple question about the clients, complexity increases. Even at the subsistence level, the clients are enmeshed in a complicated system oriented to psychiatric disability—a system in which their identities or roles as crazy people are the means by which they "make it" or survive. An answer requires more than a description of daily activities, use of time, space, and resources, type of knowledge, and access to information. It demands exploration of an essentially ancillary process: the construction, reconstruction, and elaboration of a psychosocial identity. *Clients*, with identified deficits in living skills, interact with *staff*, who recognize and seek to alter these deficits, or with *community members*, who do not seek to change the deficits or the identity directly, but who exist mainly as markers for differentness or sameness in clients' eyes.

A second level of meaning in the title acknowledges this process, referring to the tautological idea that clients, because they are diagnosed and perceived as crazy, make or produce craziness. That is to say, our ideas about craziness stem not only from culturally conditioned beliefs about mental illness but from the behaviors and thoughts of persons so defined (see also Devereux 1956:19). A mutual molding process exists between clients' behaviors and our ideas about craziness, shaping our images as effectively as do medical, social, or historical precepts. This is a much-neglected perspective in many sociological theories of deviance, and it is overemphasized in many clinical-medical paradigms. Designation, creation of mythology, labeling, deviance amplification—whatever one chooses to call it—does not occur in a vacuum. It is not a one-way process, and it is not well served by the combat metaphors of enemy and victim so prevalent in the literature.

At still another level, and with another meaning, clients' interaction with staff for example, can make for craziness despite the fact that the purpose of treatment is to change from being crazy to not being crazy, or to being less crazy. If the craziness is not being eliminated, it is somehow being maintained. "Crazy," as I use it in this case, means *nonsensical, perverse, and contradictory*. This meaning of crazy refers to the fact that certain processes and factors, while intending alleviation of psychiatric disorders and suffering, may perversely be stabilizing, maintaining, and perpetuating them. So when I say that we are exploring the ways of making it crazy, we must distinguish and then synthesize the different levels and meanings.

"Crazy" has two meanings: one refers to pathology, psychosis and psychiatric symptomatology; the other refers to interpersonal and sociocultural circumstances, processes, and conditions that are nonsensical, perverse, and contradictory. Clients make it crazy by surviving with their symptoms and their negatively different behaviors. They also help to define or make craziness. In addition they make it crazy by maintaining this pathology, which seems nonsensical and perverse given the negative meaning of the pathology in their lives. Nonclients, that is, all the rest of us, make it crazy in our roles as definers and perceivers of mental illness. We also make it crazy, or contradictory and nonsensical, by contributing to the perpetuation of circumstances that we have already defined and evaluated as wrong, bad, or unfortunate.

Those who adhere to the medical model of psychiatric illness primarily attribute the deficits and problems in living to the nature, symptoms, and course of a disease. Those who locate the sources of illness within social and labeling processes attribute these problems to the sociocultural and psychiatric treatment system and to others who enforce and reinforce the idea of illness in clients' lives. My position is that each of these factors contributes to the process—clients, staff, clients' families, community members, significant others, neurochemical factors, and genetic predisposition—virtually everyone and everything, including myself, are potential contributors. We all make this lifeway a crazy one, not only by defining it as pathological but by contributing to its perpetuation with this very act of treatment *qua* definition. I hope to clarify this interpretation by examining the intricacies of the actual processes as I have observed and recorded them.

An awareness of these factors provides a lens through which to perceive the remainder of the book. Clients, PACT and other features of their world are described within an organizing matrix of data on time, space, and resources. The topics of subsistence strategies and medications are discussed with reference to the experiences of the clients. The manner in which clients categorize persons in their world is presented, followed by a look at those clients who have made it minus their craziness.

After the above descriptions and discussions, a theoretical and interpretive framework is introduced and a detailed review of relevant anthropological and psychiatric research is presented. In these chapters I attempt to interweave elements and viewpoints deriving from anthropology, symbolic interactionism, labeling theory, and deviant identity formation. Another thread in the fabric consists of the systems theory concepts of amplifying deviation and maintaining feedback (Buckley 1967), morphostasis and morphogenesis (Maruyama 1963), and schismogenesis (Bateson 1958). Within this explanatory structure, the process of making it crazy is elaborated. Observations are made regarding the identity trap created by clients and others in the process of treatment and living in the community as a psychiatric patient. Community treatment is reevaluated from this perspective, and the institutionalization syndrome is reexamined in its new clothing. The book concludes with reflections and questions for further research on the interaction of cultural factors and chronicity, especially with regard to problems in living such as those encountered in my fieldwork.

PART II

ETHNOGRAPHIC MATERIAL

4

CLIENTS AND PACT—A DESCRIPTION

> Everything is significant if you know how to read it. . . .
> —Hall (1973:98)

The following pages discuss our primary subjects and the most important components of their environment during the research: the PACT program and staff, other clients, and the community setting. A demographic profile of clients is provided, including pertinent aspects of their psychiatric histories and clinical designations. Staff composition is outlined, and the PACT treatment modality and philosophy is discussed. Important features of the setting are described and the clients are characterized according to their conceptions and use of time, space, and information.

CLIENTS

Forty-three persons comprised the group of clients studied for this project. All were admitted to treatment in the PACT program between January and November 1975.[1] Two took their own lives during treatment and the research period, but they were included in the study until the time of their deaths. There were twenty-eight

1. Fifty persons were admitted to PACT between January and November 1975. Five persons, who discharged themselves after brief involvement in treatment, refused to participate in my study. One person stayed in treatment but refused contact with me, and another was excluded from treatment because it was discovered that he had not met

males and fifteen females in the group. The average age of the women was twenty-eight years; the men were slightly younger with an average of twenty-six years. Thirty-seven had never married, five had divorced, and two married while in the program (a woman married a man she met while in Mendota and a man married a nonclient girlfriend). Of those who had been previously married, four had children, though none had custody.

Part of the client profile was predetermined by the admission criteria utilized for this Phase III research group. Admission criteria for the clients was as follows:

1. Presentation for admission at Mendota Mental Health Institute, or referral from a private physician, local hospital, or mental health agency in the Dane County area.
2. Poor employment history, especially within the past six months.
3. Primary diagnosis must not include alcoholism or organic brain syndrome.
4. Client must not be imminently homicidal or suicidal.
5. Single or divorced marital status.
6. Age between eighteen and sixty-five years.
7. Client must reside in the Dane County area or have significant other or family in the Dane County area.
8. Client must possess psychiatric symptomatology and difficulty ordinarily requiring hospitalization.

Regular admissions to Mendota Mental Health Institute accounted for eight clients, and thirty-five were referred to the program by therapists in the Madison area. Two clients were involuntarily committed by the court to participate in PACT treatment and one other had PACT treatment established as a condition of probation. Another who was near discharge was ordered by the court to receive medications and treatment from PACT. The remainder were voluntary patients.

---

admission criteria. Two persons, who were, in effect, not actively participating in treatment during the research period, are included in my project. One of these clients left the program after three months and the other after six months.

The group's background of previous psychiatric hospitalization was diverse. Three clients had no prior psychiatric admissions, though the average number of admissions for the entire group was 5.36, averaging 21.34 weeks of total hospitalization per person. The range in number of psychiatric hospitalizations varied from one to fifteen. Eight persons had been admitted only once before being in PACT; seven had more than ten inpatient episodes. These statistics provided me with important information about the duration and intensity of recognized psychiatric difficulty experienced by the clients prior to my encounter with them. It was difficult to generalize about these backgrounds because of the evident variation in experience with psychiatric treatment, but very few were novice patients, and most had lived with problems long enough to warrant their description by clinicians as long-term or chronic clients.[2]

Before and during the research period, I chose not to be aware of clients' clinical diagnoses unless they told me about these themselves. My rationale was that a particular psychiatric label was of little or no value in the project and might, in fact, bias my observations and interpretations. I wanted to look beyond and behind the diagnostic label. I was interested in learning whether clients were

2. The idea of chronicity is pervasive, although it is imprecisely defined in the psychiatric literature on community treatment. Definitions vary from clinic to clinic and from staff to staff. On one level, chronicity refers to the length of illness and/or hospitalization (Sanders, Smith, and Weinman 1967:75), but the terms "chronic psychotic" and "chronic patient" also imply a cluster of psychiatric, social, behavioral, attitudinal, and interpersonal characteristics (see Ludwig 1971). PACT staff described clients as "looking chronic" or "looking like a chronic." Being a chronic psychiatric patient also indicates that the person will probably require medications and/or psychiatric care for decades, if not for a lifetime.

Recently, Minkoff (1978:12) has attempted to refine definitions of chronicity along three axes: illness, disability, and institutionalization. He proposes three distinct subcategories:

1. *The chronic mentally ill:* based primarily on *diagnosis*, that is, schizophrenia, manic-depressive disease (bipolar affective disorder), alcoholism, organic brain syndrome, senility, mental retardation, and some addictions and personality disorders.
2. *The chronic mentally disabled:* based on "partial or total impairment of instrumental role performance . . . the extent of disability is related to the *degree of social inadequacy*, the *extent of symptomatic impairment*, and the *need for external structure, support, or treatment* . . . greater chronicity of disability is associated with greater *duration of disability* and *more continuous disability*." (emphasis mine)
3. *Chronic mental patients:* based on *institutionalization* or the *duration*, *continuity* and *number* of psychiatric hospitalizations.

While I do not agree that the tautology presented in the first category holds true, these distinctions represent an improvement on previous vagueness. If we use Minkoff's categories, the people involved in PACT treatment are those described in category 2, the chronic mentally disabled.

aware of their diagnoses, and, if they were, how important these might be in their perceptions of their problems.

It is instructive and informative to note the diagnoses made for the clients by the PACT service chief and the nursing and professional staffs (see table 1). The major psychoses and personality or character disorders are heavily represented, particularly the various subcategories of schizophrenia,[3] and the clients fit the general de-

3. The state of the art of psychiatric diagnosis and the validity, reliability, and utility of such labeling provokes consistent controversy and discussion both in and out of the profession (see Carpenter, Strauss, and Bartko 1974). Although the topic cannot be covered here with precision, the following definitions suggest the fundamental meanings of these terms. The interested reader is referred to the American Psychiatric Association Diagnostic and Statistical Manual of Mental Disorders (1978:C:1, E:1, K:1) for more detailed descriptions.

SCHIZOPHRENIC DISORDERS

The essential features of this group of disorders include: disorganization of a previous level of functioning; characteristic symptoms involving multiple psychological processes; the presence of certain psychotic features during the active phase of the illness; the absence of a full affective syndrome concurrent with or developing prior to the active phase of the illness; and a tendency toward chronicity. In addition, the disturbance is not explainable by any of the Organic Mental Disorders.

As defined here, at some time during the illness a Schizophrenic Disorder always involves at least one of the following: delusions, hallucinations, or certain characteristic types of thought disorder. No single clinical feature is unique to this condition or is evident in every case or at every phase of the illness. By definition, the diagnosis is not made unless the period of illness has persisted for at least six months.

AFFECTIVE DISORDERS

The essential feature of this group of disorders is a primary disturbance of mood accompanied by related symptoms. "Mood" refers to a prolonged emotion that colors the whole psychic life, usually involving either depression or elation. The disorders grouped here include those which in other classification systems are grouped in various categories, including Affective, Neurotic, and Personality Disorders.

Affective Disorders may be either Episodic or Chronic. The term "episodic" denotes a period of illness in which there is a sustained disturbance clearly distinguished from previous functioning. The term "chronic" indicates a long-standing (at least two years) illness, usually without a clear onset. The disturbance in mood and related symptoms may be sustained throughout the period or may be intermittent. Individuals with Chronic Affective Disorders may have a superimposed Episodic Affective Disorder, in which case both diagnoses should be given.

The Neurotic Disorders (Neuroses) are characterized by anxiety. They produce symptoms experienced as subjective distress from which the patient seeks and desires relief. The patient is aware of his disturbed mental functioning.

Personality Disorders feature deeply ingrained, inflexible, maladaptive patterns of relating to, perceiving, and thinking about the environment and oneself. These patterns are of sufficient severity to cause either significant impairment in adaptive functioning or subjective distress. As pervasive personality traits, they are exhibited in a wide range of important social and personal contexts. Personality Disorders usually manifest themselves in childhood or adolescence and persist throughout adult life, although they often become less obvious in middle or old age.

TABLE 1

CLINICAL DIAGNOSES

Diagnosis	Number of Clients
1. *Schizophrenia*:	
Latent type	5
Chronic, undifferentiated	8
Paranoid type	7
Simple	3
Schizo-affective	4
Residual	2
2. *Affective disorders*:	
Manic-depression, manic type	1
Manic-depression, circular type	1
3. *Neurosis*	
Anxiety neurosis	2
4. *Personality disorders*:	
Hysterical personality	1
Passive-aggressive personality	1
Inadequate personality	2
Other disorders	6
Total	43

SOURCE: Data provided by PACT research staff.

scriptive category of chronic mentally disabled.[4] These classifications are not imperative for ethnographic purposes, but they provide a reference point and a basis for identification and comparison with the psychiatric and social science literature.

4. Test (personal communication) suggests that the clients included in my project are not representative of the median chronic psychiatric population in the United States. According to Test, they represent the lower end of adequacy, competence, and adjustment. Test's remarks underscore the importance of the broad perspective. One of the difficulties encountered in the psychiatric literature on community treatment is a lack of comparability of patient populations. A key problem at present is identifying which patients are helped most by which type of treatment program. Unless the characteristics of one's client group are specified, this task is impossible. For our purposes, it is necessary to acknowledge the poor psychiatric prognoses of the clients included in my pro-

PROGRAM FOR ASSERTIVE COMMUNITY TREATMENT: PACT

The treatment program in which all subjects participated is a clinical and research unit of the Mendota Mental Health Institute designed as an alternative to psychiatric hospitalization. In the program's words: "The mission of the PACT program has been one of investigating and implementing community treatment alternatives for those individuals who have been chronically involved in the traditional mental health system and, for all intents and purposes, have been treatment failures" (MMHI Manual, #8.301, Nov., 1976:1). The program assesses that its clients "exhibit gross coping skill deficits when living in the community and have been pathologically dependent upon family and institutions" (ibid.).

The treatment focuses on five major areas: (1) *Vocational and work-related skills*—job application and interview, job attendance and performance, communication with employers and supervisors; (2) *Activities of daily living*—grooming and personal hygiene, cooking and housekeeping, locating and obtaining a place to live, budgeting, shopping for groceries and clothes; (3) *Social and Recreational activities*—learning group assertiveness for social and interpersonal skills, learning group sports; participating in community organizations, attending group entertainment events such as concerts, movies, and plays; (4) *Family*—working to establish a less disruptive and debilitating dependency between client and family, providing family therapy, monitoring and controlling contact between client and family, teaching family how to relate to client with the PACT philosophy; and (5) *Medications, psychotherapy, and nursing care*—administering as needed.

The treatment modality at PACT is based on principles of social learning theory (Paul and Lentz 1977), with widespread use of contingency programs, with role playing and role modeling, and with provision of time structure and emotional support. Little intensive individual psychotherapy is utilized, though various clients meet

---

ject. The PACT clinical staff has described their typical client as follows: ". . . this patient is unemployed and has had a chaotic job history, is deficient in basic social skills, is highly dependent on his family and psychiatric institutions, is single, and is inexperienced in independent living" (PACT Staff 1977:1).

with the psychiatrist and psychologist for problem-solving and "talk" sessions. The staff uses a learning and doing approach that emphasizes the client's responsibility for his or her actions and life situation. In this context, the staff works on behalf of the client at his job, at his residence, on the street, or with other community agencies, serving as advocate, coordinator of services, and provider of direction, feedback, and emotional support.

The PACT philosophy and method are based on years of experience, of trial and error, and of failure and success in treating persons with long-term, complex problems in living. The techniques used in the program seek to alter the clients' life patterns of repeated defeats and psychotic experiences which often result in hospitalization. The client is taught, however firmly, that he or she *can* manage the details of daily living in a community setting. Because staff views the client as excessively reluctant and anxious rather than as actually deficient in capability, they try to motivate and encourage clients with many means—persuasion, example, contingency, control, sympathy, caring, instruction, and practical advice.

There is often a silent testing of wills. The client may be convinced that he or she cannot cope. Staff may believe to the contrary, or vice versa. Staff may "re-parent" a client, attempting to resocialize a person they consider insufficiently knowledgeable or effective in his or her social and interpersonal environment. By encouraging and fostering an initial dependence on staff, the program moves to influence, to redirect, even to control and to demand changes in the clients' behavior. Although clients may perceive the actions of staff to be controlling and demanding, they also acknowledge that such attitudes move them toward taking responsible direction of their own lives. PACT may represent the clients' best opportunity to achieve relative independence. By virtue of their being in PACT, most other means can be assumed to have failed. Even if a client must be provoked into action, or has acted only out of defiance toward staff, the staff views this as a positive step if it means a move in the direction of independence, self-determination, and achievement.

PACT has won national acclaim for its innovative treatment approach and for its marked success in maintaining clients in the community with minimal use of inpatient hospitalization, at a cost equal to that of hospital treatment, and with some indication of positive self-esteem and adequate quality of life among clients.[5] Much of this achievement derives not only from the ingenious research and clinical design of the program but from the exceptional versatility, independence, and dedication of staff members. They manifest a sense of pride and commitment, and most vow that they are "community converts" who would never work in a hospital setting again. Some of this euphoria fades over time. Nearly half of the staff who were there during my research have left. Only one, however, has returned to an inpatient psychiatric setting.

The PACT professional and nursing staff consists of a psychiatrist, who is the unit or service chief, a psychiatric social worker, a clinical psychologist, an occupational-recreation therapist, six registered nurses, eight client-services assistants, and a ward clerk. The nearby university provides rotating psychiatric residents, psychology interns, and students of social work, nursing, and occupational-recreation therapy who, after training and initiation, supplement the basic staff.

Duties among staff are distributed on the basis of professional training, informal expertise, and availability. For example, medication type and dosage are determined by the psychiatrist and the nursing staff. Clinical résumés for medical records are written by the professional staff. Almost all other duties are performed by client-services assistants who often write the most detailed nursing notes about clients. They solve problems with clients, meet with agencies and employers, and direct activities. All participate in family therapy sessions, called "family meetings." A client customarily is assigned to a team of primary staff, although all staff members work with each client. Some staff, through special interest, have assumed such duties as monitoring clients' money programs or employment possibilities. After change in active treatment status, one staff member typically follows one client. Each staff member becomes quite versatile, performing whatever duties are necessary to implement treatment goals. The ward clerk serves as secretary, receptionist, and keeper of money records for both clients and staff.

5. PACT received the Gold Award from *Hospital and Community Psychiatry*, a journal devoted to the subject (25:669-672). Numerous publications and presentations have been made about the PACT program. Pertinent references are Marx et al. 1973; Stein, L. I. and M. A. Test 1975, 1976, 1980.; Test and Stein 1977*a*, 1977*b*, 1978*a*, 1978*b*, *1980*; Weisbrod et al. 1980.

In addition to this clinical group, a separate research staff is maintained. These persons are responsible for data collection and for analysis of the various studies undertaken by the clinical program.

THE COMMUNITY

As a resident of Madison for eight years, I have found this city of 200,000 to be a rich, busy, and friendly place, distinguished by oppressively long, cold winters (six months' duration with temperatures at times below −20°F), and short, glorious summers marked by local festivals, fresh produce, fourteen hours of daylight, and hordes of hungry mosquitoes. The community is diverse but usually harmonious, bringing together the scholarly corps from the University (40,000 students and a faculty of 2,300), the bureaucrats and politicians in state government, and the members of the community at large, representing business, service, and professional interests. Local politics are largely progressive and are hotly debated, intent upon brewing new schemes and themes for improving community life.

Madison's geography is shaped by its two large lakes, Mendota and Monona. Its demography is determined by the massive University of Wisconsin and the State Capitol, the two largest employers in town. These factors combine to attract a young (average age 18–24 years) and transient population. The PACT clients can blend superficially into such a setting in terms of physical appearances, unconventional time schedules, and lack of financial resources.

The PACT program is headquartered in the central city area of Madison in an old house serving as both office and meeting place for staff and clients. The clients' spatial world is centered in the area near the Square and PACT house, which encompasses both the "student ghetto" areas of town and whatever old and shabby housing one finds in the city. Inexpensive rental housing in the Square area near PACT (see map) is a scarce and sought-after commodity; indeed, over half of the housing units in Madison are occupied by renters. In Madison, the areas east of the Capitol are the older, blue-collar neighborhoods. The West Side, surrounding and beyond the University, includes newer upper-class neighborhoods that house the families of professors and other professionals. The city is very

1. YWCA
2. YMCA
3. Community Center
4. MOC
5. PACT
6. Church
7. SRO Hotel
8. SRO Hotel
9. Lunch Counter
10. Lunch Counter
11. Lunch Counter
12. Rooming House
13. Bar
14. Bar
15. Goodwill Industries
16. City Welfare Office
17. SRO Hotel
Lake Mendota
Lake Monona
University Ave.
State Street
Johnson Street
Wisconsin Ave.
W. Washington Ave.
E. Washington Ave
Main Street
Monona Ave.
N

spread out; because most clients do not drive, it is easier for them to inhabit the downtown area.

As a university town, Madison attracts people from various backgrounds, adding a cosmopolitan flavor to its basic ethnic character. Ethnic origins in this upper midwestern region are predominantly German and Scandinavian, and this factor imparts a characteristic heartiness to customs in food, drink, and religious and social networks. At the University, Madison plays host to a significant international community as well as to sizable groups of transplanted Northeasterners and West Coasters. Outside the University, the town includes small but organized groups of American blacks, Native Americans, and Spanish-speaking persons. Few members of these minority groups are involved in the substantial mental health professional community that distinguishes Madison.

The systems of help-giving and psychiatric care in Madison have remarkable scope for a community of its size. A recent study (Greenley and Schoenher 1975) listed ninety-two help-giving organizations. Of these, twenty-five are oriented to psychiatric counseling, including five hospitals, each of which maintains a psychiatric ward. In addition, the community's private practitioners include numerous and varied psychiatric professionals, such as psychiatrists, psychologists, nurse clinicians, social workers, and other counselors. The Dane County Mental Health Center boasts a wide range of progressive services, with a staff of 100, that serves over a thousand clients per year. The Mendota Mental Health Institute, the University of Wisconsin Medical School's Department of Psychiatry, the Graduate School of Social Work, and other graduate programs in counseling and psychology contribute to a broad psychiatric work force that is well informed and intellectually active. Thus, in the area of mental health care, Madison is atypical of most communities its size and of many larger cities as well.

SPACE, TIME, AND SHARED INFORMATION

At this point, it will be useful to examine general features of the clients' world and their interaction with the staff and the treatment program.

Space

It is important to understand the clients' use and perception of space because the spatial dimension provides significant information and messages to people about themselves and their relations with others. Hall (1966:105) has observed that "man's feeling about being properly oriented in space runs deep. Such knowledge is ultimately linked to survival and sanity. To be disoriented in space is to be psychotic" (see especially Hall 1973:11–21; Hall 1963:422–445; Henry 1964). It is necessary to know what type of space clients occupy, how they use it, and what this analysis signifies about clients' self-perceptions. It is important to understand how these self-perceptions are learned and how they shape the clients' sense of social place in the community setting.

Admission to the PACT program nearly always means a change in residence or type and location of living space for clients. Of the people I studied, seventeen had left their parents' homes, several for the first time, eleven others had left the hospital, and the remaining fifteen were in a temporary living situation or were living in their own apartment or room. In most instances, entry into the program had resulted in a decrease in the quality and size of living space for clients. During treatment, several factors tended to concentrate clients in the central city area near the PACT house: choice, PACT influence, economic constraints, and problems with landlords who were reluctant to accept such people as tenants. Clients moved so frequently that they often greeted each other by asking, "Where are you living now?"

More than half of the group lived or had lived at the central YWCA or YMCA, though by the time of discharge or change in active treatment status, most had moved to apartments or rooms in houses. Madison does not have the numerous "board and care" homes found in many other cities (Reynolds and Farberow 1977).

During the course of treatment, eight of the women lived in the same halfway and three-quarter way houses, though not all at the same time. The names of these residences describe the transitional placement on the way to fully independent living. The halfway house provides more guidance, communal activity, and supervision for residents than does the three-quarter way house. At the halfway house, women prepared and ate meals together, participated in group discussions and housekeeping chores, and abided by rules set by the fulltime houseparents. The women shared bedrooms and bath facilities when the house was at capacity. Most clients learned to enjoy the halfway house, though their adjustment was often confounded by those same psychiatric and life difficulties that had precluded more independent living. At one time during the research, when some thoroughly involved houseparents were in residence, several of the women became actively engaged in the large family atmosphere (see Glasscote et al. 1971*a* for general information on halfway houses).

The three-quarter way house was next door to the halfway house. It consisted of several two-bedroom apartments, usually occupied by four women. Three women "graduated" to this residence from the halfway house. Here, the women were responsible for all household chores. There was no time schedule or formal communal activity, and minimal supervision was provided. The women also shared bedrooms and bathing facilities. These apartments were furnished, and the State Division of Vocational Rehabilitation often subsidized a resident's rent. Because of departmental funding and the emphasis on work, the halfway house instituted a policy that residents had to be out of the house during the workday.

The only such facility for men was a home for very disabled veterans, where one male client resided. Consequently, most of the male clients circulated between the YMCA, three inexpensive hotels, apartments, and a rooming house that had been receptive to PACT clients. Most of the men started out at the YMCA. During treatment, the attempt to move toward more spacious and independent residences was made by staff and clients. In the recent past, the YMCA had gained a reputation as a place for the down and out, including a large number of discharged and community-treated psychiatric patients. A recent survey of living arrangements of discharged Mendota Mental Health Institute patients revealed that "the largest single provider of housing to adults with mental health problems is the YMCA, which houses 18.7 percent of the clients referred" (Ossowski and Martony n.d.). The resident manager of the YMCA estimated that thirty to forty of the nearly ninety YMCA residents were persons with severe mental health problems (Balch 1976).

Within the past four years, six residents attempted suicide by jumping off the YMCA building. One of them was one of my subjects. He survived the jump and later moved into an apartment with another PACT client. Under pressure to alleviate the obvious mental health hazard at the YMCA, the management hired a social worker to help counsel depressed and anxious residents.

Clients reported mixed feelings about the YMCA. Most agreed that the atmosphere was depressing if not oppressive to them, and they attributed this to the concentration of persons with psychiatric difficulties and to older men who are "crabby and don't have anything to do except sit around and complain and wait to die." Nonetheless, many were reluctant to move, for they appreciated the low rent, the convenient location, and access to friends or acquaintances. As Walter explained, "I really should move out of this dump. But I'm afraid if I do I'll get lonely. At least there's always somebody around to talk to or sit with." Steven echoed these sentiments, complaining that Herb, Harold, and Alf never came to visit him when he moved out of the YMCA and into an apartment. "You guys really let me down. You never came to see me. And when you did, all we did was watch TV." PACT staff developed a close working relationship with the Y management, helping to arbitrate landlord-tenant problems on occasion. To date, all but one client have moved from the YMCA, largely with the help of the Special Living Arrangements program that was instituted in part to disperse this concentration and to provide more positive living space for community psychiatric patients (see Ossowski and Martony n.d.).

The YWCA was a different place, though it too recently lost a resident, a former PACT client, who jumped from the ninth floor to her death. The resident manager of the YWCA worked closely with PACT and other mental health agencies, and she saw herself as a folk part of the treatment system. She maintained contact with PACT staff, who recognized her as an important community resource for housing. The manager estimated that 15 percent of the YWCA residents had "emotional problems" or were "people that really need help." However, she worked to keep the number down, saying, "We're not a halfway house, you know. This week I've got all I can handle. A doctor called this morning wanting a room for a gal right away. I asked if he were calling from the psych ward. When he said yes, I told him I just couldn't have anymore right now. I have a responsibility to the other residents, you know." Women who lived at the YWCA learned that the manager's power over their tenure and conduct there was to be reckoned with and respected. Many felt she was too involved and knowledgeable about them. Dorothy felt constrained and under surveillance while living at the YWCA and also thought it a lonely place. Alice concurred and complained about the small rooms. Others seemed to enjoy living there for the same reasons that the men liked the YMCA. One client has remained at the YWCA, and one was recently evicted, much to her dismay.

Living space available to clients could be graded on a ladder. The bottom rung, used only for temporary shelter, included the local Rescue Mission and a boarding house nearby that catered primarily to vagrants, persons who revolved in and out of jail, and alcoholics. Several clients stayed there for a few days at most, and only when all other options were closed. The next rung on the ladder included three old and inexpensive hotels near the PACT house, used by clients who were evicted from or unable to live at the Y's or other places (see map, p. 000). Fifteen clients lived in these hotels at some time during treatment. One hotel in particular was viewed by most clients and staff as housing a collection of strange outcasts who had little or no place else to go. Ben and Sadie rather enjoyed these surroundings, often entertaining other residents with stories of their hospital adventures or demonstrating their "craziness" in the lobby by talking nonsense, gesturing, or otherwise behaving bizarrely. Most clients disliked living in these places and were glad to move up to either of the two Y's.

Comparable to the Y's in status and facilities was a rooming house that had boarded eight clients (a maximum of five at any one time). Only one female client lived there. A few university students also lived in the house, but the majority of the residents had portfolios similar to those of our subjects—men or women with little money, no jobs, and psychiatric difficulties. Better still, in staff's view, were apartments or rooms in more respectable houses that were less patient populated. Clients also valued such apartments, but as a rule they preferred to live in proximity to fellow clients, to places to eat, and to resources such as PACT. Three women in particular did not fit this pattern. They much preferred apartment dwelling, choosing not to associate with other clients, especially in a living situation.

We have some measure of clients' feelings about their living space from CAS questionnaire responses. At the time clients answered the baseline questions, the residential breakdown was as follows:

YMCA	*Apartments*	*Rooms in House*	*Parents' Home*
7	8	9	5
3/4 Way House	*YWCA*	*Sheltered Living*[6]	*Hotels*
3	1	4	3

When asked how they felt about where they lived at the time, client response was varied; half were satisfied and half were not. But twenty-seven of the thirty-five who answered the questionnaire indicated that they would like to move. Twenty-three thought their living circumstances needed improvement. Twenty-one indicated that they interacted with their neighbors seldom to never, but twenty-five reported liking these people. Ten clients had unfriendly feelings toward their neighbors. Twenty-nine answered that they considered few if any neighbors to be personal friends. Twenty-four felt they lived in friendly neighborhoods; eleven felt they did not.

Though these responses are difficult to interpret because no clear patterns are evident, a paradoxical trend is apparent. Clients expressed satisfaction with their living circumstances but at the same time perceived them as needing improvement. They also would like to move. It appears that one-third of the group were not comfortable with their neighbors.

In general, clients were restricted to inexpensive housing by their budgets and by location preferences. Spacious housing in the central area of town was expensive because of the large rental market from university students and state employees. Of the group of forty-three, only four clients owned cars. The majority relied on public transportation or, more commonly, foot travel. PACT provided occasional transportation to appointments or in moving, but staff avoided and resented "being a taxi service." Those clients who

6. By sheltered living I mean that one person was in a facility for alcoholics, one was in a residential facility for the disabled and handicapped, one was in a nursing home, and one was hospitalized.

owned cars often had no money for gas, or they found themselves with numerous parking tickets because they had forgotten where their cars were, or because they could not be bothered with finding legal spaces.

Very few clients cooked their own meals, though many had access to cooking facilities. Most ate at the coffee shops and lunch counters around the Square. Some did this because they had vouchers from various sources for meals in these places, though the main gathering place was so heavily patronized by clients that the management stopped accepting vouchers because they created such confusion for the waitresses.

Clients, as a rule, lived with or near each other in and around the Square. Six sets shared apartments. They often did so by choice, but the choice was not always theirs. Few could find roommates outside the client population, and those who did were not able to maintain the relationship for long. Moreover, clients encountered problems in attempting to move out of this part of town because many landlords were reluctant to sign leases with a person who had few, if any, references, was unemployed (as most were), or was receiving some form of public financial assistance. At least five clients were openly discriminated against in this manner. Other landlords were accustomed to this population, which they regarded as a viable clientele in the rental market. Since these landlords usually rented to PACT applicants, this further contributed to patients' spatial concentration. Many clients could not afford security deposits for apartments, and several had established such poor tenant histories that even the old hotels refused them.

The Special Living Arrangements program helped to eliminate discrimination against clients on the basis of their disabilities, but, at the same time, it was another factor that served to concentrate them in the same apartments. Annie refused to utilize the services of the program when she desperately needed them. She said, "I don't want to live with somebody who has emotional problems. They told me they would try to help but that I'd have to share with somebody like that."

The clients were able to use and occupy living space that was affordable and was tolerant of their often nonexistent housekeeping skills and sometimes strange behavior. Because of the latter problems, eviction was not uncommon for individuals in the group.

Even in one of the old hotels, Andy, for example, had a difficult time of it because the desk clerk felt "people like him shouldn't be out here with the rest of us." After losing that room and several others, he ended up in a small motel near the outskirts of town, epitomizing his marginality to the community.

Except for the scarce and rather spartan living space utilized by clients, there were few places and spaces they could use in comfort or freedom. Many were not comfortable sharing space with large numbers of people. During treatment, none were allowed to go to their parents' homes at will, but only at specified times. If this rule were broken, parents were asked to tell the client to leave, to lock him or her out, or if need be, to call the police to remove them. Staff felt that clients had abused the good will and resources of their parents and families. They also wanted them to learn to cope without "escaping" to home. In favorable weather, a dozen clients paced or wandered the streets and public places such as shopping centers, parks, or the University Union. The severe Wisconsin winters drastically curtailed outdoor walking for almost half the year. During the winter many clients sat and stared, smoked, paced indoors, or watched television. Others stretched cups of coffee or beers for hours. Some ran away. As if to explore new space and leave behind the constraints and meaning of the old, six clients simply left town for periods of time, some traveling as far as California. Each of these was ultimately picked up and returned by a legal or a psychiatric institution.

Space at the PACT house was controlled by the staff. It was not a place where clients could go to sit or to chat informally with others. The need for a drop-in center, a place for clients to socialize or simply sit, was acknowledged by staff, but there was really no room at PACT. The rules for use of space in the house by clients varied with the time of day and the number of staff present. For example, during the day when many staff were working, clients had to wait for appointments or medications in the small lounge or in a front entryway. Any client who had been in the house for more than several minutes was asked his purpose. If he had no acceptable answer, he was asked to leave. The staff workroom was off-limits to clients, as were the upstairs offices and the kitchen-medications room unless the client was authorized or accompanied by a staff member. In the evening and on weekends, clients were more free to relax and move about in the house, though they were never permitted behind the receptionist's desk, where money was often kept.

Some of these rules were established to protect clients' confidentiality, as medical charts were often out for staff use and clients were curious. The house was locked during daily staff report for this same reason. Clients were often annoyed and angered by this rule, but staff held firmly to their need for client-free space so that they could speak freely with one another. The house took the brunt of several clients' rage at being excluded or told to wait, and each person who kicked in the railing or door was held responsible for these acts.

The only spaces over which clients had even occasional control were living space and mental space. Living space was under the ultimate control of landlords and of others who often paid the rent. Mental space was often intruded on by medications and psychotherapy. On the whole, however, the clients' inner, mental space, being relatively infinite, was more under their control and was perhaps more attractive than any form of external space. Some clients felt that they had no place to go and that they did not belong anywhere, though such people were in the minority. Nonetheless, access to positive, self-controlled space remained a problem for clients.

Time

Because most clients did not work at conventional jobs, or did so only briefly, their concepts of time and their use of it differed from most other persons'. There was no work versus leisure time distinction for a majority of the group. Staff felt strongly that clients encountered more personal and psychiatric problems when their time was "unstructured" or offered few foci around which to organize. Clients were given written schedules to follow for a week at a time. During active treatment, clients were kept busy with appointments at PACT or with assigned tasks such as doing laundry, shopping, going to the library, seeking employment, or finding a place to live. Many were engaged in work programs at various stages during treatment, and with the evening and weekend activities described previously. One social skills group assigned members to plan and execute a recreational activity with other persons.

In general, near the end of active treatment and after discharge, many clients spent much of their time sitting, either alone or together, watching television, smoking cigarettes or marijuana, drinking beer, and listening to music. The day might be marked by medication doses, appointments with help-giving professionals, or the arrival of mealtimes. Many reported that they were bored or had nothing to do. Others never mentioned this problem and seemed content with possessing large quantities of solitary, silent time. Spanky expressed one response: "You know, I don't have to be anywhere at any certain time except at the mental health center. It's nice to just feel you have to do something at a particular time." Wally, on the other hand, filled his days with television, beer, cigarettes, and fantasies.

An alternative chosen by ten clients was to attend vocational school. All of these academic endeavors, except two, ended prematurely when the person lost interest or when the work became too difficult.

Clients' use of time was influenced by their lack of money. Most did not have enough to spend in relation to the amount of free, unencumbered time available to them. Movies, drinking, and other entertainments often were not feasible given their limited budgets. They made use of the free tickets to many community special events that PACT was able to obtain.

Those clients who did work were separated in and by time and space from other clients. This form of separation was stressful to some who preferred companionship to vocation, or relaxation to conventional productivity. For others, it was a comforting indication of their competence and fit with the larger community. Other clients, who might appear to have nothing to do, came to perceive each day as a unit of time and as a task unto itself. They slept for long hours and routinized eating, sitting, and walking here or there to accomplish an errand, to keep an appointment with mental health professionals, or to visit a friend. Many of the men participated in evening sports activities, such as volleyball or softball at PACT, and, after discharge, at the county mental health center. Also, after discharge, clients usually spent time with their families on weekends.

Two of the women worked at handicrafts periodically. Ten of the clients played guitar and sang, and another four painted, though infrequently. In general, the group had few hobby interests.

Two were deeply involved in religious groups, spending much

time engaged in classes and other religious activities. Another attended Alcoholics Anonymous meetings on an almost daily basis, not only because of drinking problems but because it provided something for her to do, a group to which she could belong. Two others belonged to a group of ex-psychiatric patients called Recovery. Recovery is part of a national organization that meets weekly as a group discussion for members, emphasizing self help and problem solving.

Usually, however, when clients spent time and shared space with other persons, it was with other clients, family, or PACT staff and mental health professionals. Only five spent time with one or more "outside" or nonclient friends. Clients were with each other out of choice and because few others, save older persons and students, occupied the same space and had similar time orientations. PACT has had a program of community volunteers who have developed one-to-one relationships with clients, but on the whole these have not been long-lasting contacts. Of the group of forty-three clients, two had relationships with volunteers that exceeded several months. These contacts diminished usually because the client and/or volunteer lost interest. Less often, the pair were mismatched vis-à-vis interests and personalities and could not establish a basis on which to interact in comfort.

Moore (1963:38–39) has suggested that a person's perceived scarcity of time may be taken as an index of his integration into society. If he is correct, the clients' possession of great chunks of solitary and "free" time indicates a lack of integration into an otherwise busy and overscheduled world.

Information

Understanding the type, content, and flow of information among clients, and between clients and staff, provides insight into the social interaction and internal workings of this system. As a group, the clients had access to specialized information in very few areas: the subjective experience of psychosis, taking psychotropic medication, being a patient in the mental health system, and persuading others to assist in one's life tasks. Two could be called skilled workers in conventional employment. The rest did not possess individual knowledge or skills beyond simple vocational tasks. Several were well read in psychological subjects, and a group of eight men knew quite a bit about street drugs and barroom behavior. Although it was available to them, clients had little information about their legal rights as disabled persons, or even as ordinary citizens. Several were evicted unfairly and were threatened with civil commitment and did not know that their fears were unfounded.

The sharing of information within the client group is difficult to systematize. Although most did not discuss this with staff, hospital experiences as well as contacts with the police were boasted about. Ben and Harold held a "crazy contest" one afternoon on the PACT porch, each claiming he was the "craziest bastard" the other could possibly have met. Ben told us how many days he had spent in seclusion while in the hospital, and Harold countered by saying the staff had thrown a party for themselves when he was discharged from the VA hospital.

A surprising number of clients knew each other from concurrent stays in various hospitals, from high school, or from working in the same sheltered workshop. Two brothers and one mother and daughter were in the program simultaneously. Thus, clients shared a special kind of information about past hospital experiences and about one anothers' conduct in earlier treatment situations. No hard and fast rules about "squealing" to staff existed. On occasion, even friends would report if a client were not taking medications or going to work. At other times, clients protected the whereabouts of another who was avoiding staff. If there were any underlying pattern, it was this: a client would be referred to staff if he were experiencing difficulty beyond the ability of friends and other clients to help, or if he were exceeding the limits of tolerance for craziness within the group or between individuals.

Clients apparently had a code among themselves that dictated "keeping your crazies to yourself," especially with each other and outside normals. Two examples are instructive. Humphrey often mumbled obscenities in mixed company, naming genitalia and voicing crude sexual propositions. Customarily he kept his voice low. If he were asked to repeat what he had said, he would smile and refuse to do so. At a party at Cy's apartment one evening, I was the only female. The situation seemed near to getting out of hand. Humphrey's obscene remarks to me drew the attention of the rest of the group, and he was asked to stop. He complied with the request. I was very glad, because of my embarrassment and because of the escalating tension among the others present. On another occasion, a group of eight clients were swimming at a local park for a weekend evening activity. Charlotte wandered away from the group and invited herself to a nearby family picnic. Dorothy was concerned that Charlotte would embarrass herself or the group and urged me to retrieve her. When I refused, Dorothy took up a post near the family so that she might keep an eye on Charlotte. With beer and sandwich in hand, Charlotte soon approached Dorothy and me. She was followed by a woman from the picnicking group. The woman asked us if Charlotte were a friend of ours. Dorothy replied that she was. We were then asked, "She's having some problems, isn't she?" Dorothy replied, "No, of course not!" With that, the woman gave us a knowing look, said, "Oh, I see," and returned to her picnic.

Staff knew much more about individual clients than clients knew about each other or, sometimes, about themselves. Clients were legally entitled to read their medical records, but only two did so. The information processing and exchanging system among staff was more highly developed and systematic than that among clients. A number of clients disliked knowing that staff talked about them or made notes of their problems and conversations. Without question, staff possessed qualitatively and quantitatively more information about clients than vice versa, for they had more control. Also, staff were better informed about the resources and facilities available for clients.

Clients were relatively passive participants in the information system. After listening to hundreds of hours of "conversation" among clients, I am convinced that primarily incidental and mundane information was exchanged verbally. Nonverbal messages were sometimes more richly informative. Facial expression, dress, personal hygiene, body posture, rigidity, or withdrawal said nearly all that was necessary. For example, clients customarily did not remove their coats when with others, even in warm, close rooms in the winter. Agatha pointed out that coats provided comfort and protection, and she suggested that, if one's mind were busy with other things, it was easier not to forget a coat and lose it if it were left on.

The information about each other that clients seemed most interested in related to jobs, places of residence, sources of income, and types of medication taken. This curiosity may have stemmed from an interest in borrowing money, or a wish to ascertain the person's psychiatric status or availability of resources, such as living space or a television. Many times these questions were asked in front of staff and may have been for their benefit, reflecting a client's presentation of treatment program values (see Braginsky and Braginsky 1973; Braginsky, Grosse, and Ring 1973).

The staff usually did not share with one another in detail the content of one-to-one sessions with clients. Often such facts as attendance at work or compliance with medication were discussed with little focus on the subjective feelings a client may have expressed. There were exceptions to this practice, but usually the staff charted (wrote about) these contacts in greater detail than when they discussed the information with each other. Clients perceived this as well. Sam observed that "Staff doesn't really care how you feel. They just care about what you do."

Staff members customarily did not share personal information with clients. Staff's home telephone numbers and addresses were not given to clients. Clients could not receive other clients' numbers or addresses from staff, who directed them to the client in question. Clients could address staff members by their first names and most did so. The service chief and psychiatric residents were addressed as "Doctor" by most clients, unless a one-to-one therapeutic relationship developed in which first names were used.

Five clients indicated that they were aware of their clinical diagnoses. Ben called Steven his "schizophrenic brother." Doc explained that he was a manic-depressive and a schizophrenic, "Schizophrenia means you have split fibers of the brain." At another time he said, "You know, I'd be a pretty dynamic guy if I weren't psychotic." With some trepidation, Herb explained that at one time he "had schizophrenia" and had feared he was a "manic-depressive, but I'm just a little crazy sometimes." In general, however, diagnoses were not talked about within the group.

Clients and staff also communicated information nonverbally to each other about themselves and their relationship. Staff members dressed in street clothes, not uniforms (though the former has become common practice even in psychiatric institutions), to convey casualness, informality, and a lack of rigid distinctions between themselves and clients, and to fit appropriately into the community surroundings. The service chief and psychiatric residents were the only male staff members who wore ties. Otherwise the dress was rather informal, though blue jeans were frowned upon by the professional staff. Clients often dressed in soiled, ill-fitting, and ragged clothes. Often they did not bathe, launder, or attend to personal hygiene with regularity. The women clients seldom wore dresses and almost never wore shorts in the warm weather. None of the men ever wore a suit or tie. Jeans were the customary garb, as is true among many persons of similar age and social position in our society. But the usually disheveled and soiled nature of dress, along with a customary lack of attention to style and matching of colors and prints, gave the clients a subtly distinctive appearance. Even though there were no uniforms and institutional garments to express staff-client (or client-community member) differences, these differences were nonetheless visibly communicated. In addition, staff had the prerogative of passing judgment on clients' appearance, but the opposite was not true. The staff was concerned with teaching clients acceptable grooming habits, and at times required that a client return home to bathe or to change clothing before going to work or to a job interview.

This relative inattention to personal appearance and hygiene among many clients was an interesting feature, open to multiple interpretations (see Largey and Watson 1974). Clients seemingly expressed their solitary nature, their lack of interest in or ability to interact closely with others, and their general sense of alienation and isolation by ignoring culturally expected personal habits. The American concern with masking or eliminating body odors, for example, was in general not shared by the group. Several of the male clients gave off rather pungent smells and continually had to be persuaded to bathe. On occasion, clients were jokingly asked to raise their arms for odor checks by staff before going on an activity. Others took poor (if any) care of their teeth. Often, food that was spilled on clothing or self was left where it landed. In these ways, clients appeared different from staff and from the majority of the outside community.

Physical contact provided another mode of exchanging nonverbal information. Between staff and clients, there was very little touching. On occasion, a staff member might embrace a client to reassure him or her, but this was rare and almost always in private. Public touching between staff and clients was nearly nonexistent, probably because both groups prefered it this way. Staff and clients touched and shared personal space more freely and more often with members of their own respective groups. Staff nurses and clients shared the most physical contact, because the former gave the latter injections, but this was also done privately. Thus, physical and intimate boundaries were maintained between the two groups. The information conveyed by these practices and appearances confirmed and enhanced the differences between staff and clients, and constituted another means by which staff were in an authoritative and controlling position with clients.

5

MEDICATIONS

Cans't thou not minister to a mind diseas'd,
Pluck from the memory a rooted sorrow,
Raze out the written troubles of the brain,
And with some sweet oblivious antidote
Cleanse the stuff'd bosom of that perilous stuff
Which weighs upon the heart?
—Macbeth, Act V, Scene 3

In exploring the subject of psychoactive medication, termed "meds" by clients and staff, a brief orientation to the medications most often prescribed for the group is offered, as well as an overview of the benefits and drawbacks of their use from a research and clinical psychiatric perspective. The focus is not only on clients' feelings about taking meds but upon attendant side effects and their significance in the clients' world. A commentary on my experience with meds is also included.

To the outsider, medications represent one of the most striking and distinct aspects of the psychiatric world, especially among clients. One hears a strange, new vocabulary of chemical names, observes small, brown packets of pills passing from staff to clients, or notes the disappearance of a client and nurse into the PACT kitchen for a shot. Only one of the forty-three subjects took no medications during the research period. Three took meds for very short periods of time on a trial basis. Although taking meds represents one of the obvious similarities within the group, clients differ in their experiences with medications, in their compliance with taking prescribed amounts, and in their attitudes and feelings about being "on meds."

Of the thirty-nine persons who were consistently receiving meds, twenty-seven were prescribed primarily fluphenazine decanoate, hereafter referred to as Prolixin (trade and common name).[1] Six received Prolixin along with lithium carbonate,[2] hereafter referred to as lithium. Three received lithium without Prolixin or other phenothiazines. Two people received, as their primary medication, phenothiazines other than Prolixin. Specifically, they were taking thioridazine (trade and common name: Mellaril) and haloperidol (trade and common name: Haldol). One person received methylphenidate (trade and common name: Ritalin) for a short period of time. These frequencies represent the antipsychotic medications received for the majority of time during research. The other medications prescribed, in order of greatest frequency, were benztropine mesylate (trade and common name: Cogentin), fluzepam hydrochloride (trade and common name: Dalmane), diazepam (trade and common name: Valium), and trihexyphenidyl hydrochloride (trade and common name: Artane). These and other medications received are listed, with frequency of prescription, in table 2 (p. 88).

OVERVIEW: PHENOTHIAZINES AND COMMUNITY TREATMENT

Psychopharmacology, in various forms and amounts, has been practiced for some time among a substantial number of cultural groups (Torrey 1972:66-67; Szasz 1974; Kiev 1964:14-15). Western psychiatry began its latest and largest pharmacological revolution nearly three decades ago with the discovery of the marked antipsychotic

1. Fluphenazine is a member of the family of phenothiazines, which in turn are known as neuroleptics, major tranquilizers, psychotropic medications, and antipsychotics (see Lehman 1975:27-45 for complete chemical and generic information; also Shader 1975:11-14). Prolixin is the trade name for fluphenazine, which is marketed by the Squibb Pharmaceutical Company. The decanoate ester is an injectible, long-acting medication. I use "Prolixin" to refer to fluphenazine decanoate because it is the term used by clients and staff.

2. See Jefferson and Greist 1977, *Primer of Lithium Therapy* (Williams and Wilkings Publishing Co.); and F. N. Johnson, ed. 1975, *Lithium Research and Therapy* (N.Y.: Academic Press), for information on lithium carbonate.

effects of the phenothiazines, in particular chlorpromazine (trade and common name: Thorazine) (Greenblatt 1978). The demonstrated efficacy and the extremely widespread use of these medicines results from and supports the prevailing Western belief systems about the nature of schizophrenia; namely, that it involves neurochemical processes, probably influenced by genetic predisposition, expressed differentially depending upon intrapsychic, sociocultural, and interpersonal factors (see Hokin 1978; Snyder et al. 1974; Meehl 1973; Henn 1978; Szasz 1976; Fabrega 1975).

Since the early 1950s, approximately twenty phenothiazines have been developed and marketed with such great success that in 1966 Brill reported sales worth more than $38 million (Tissot 1977:90), accounting for 9.5 percent of all drug prescriptions written in the United States (GAP 1975:274). The depot or long-acting, injectable phenothiazines first appeared in 1964 (Simpson and Lee 1978), and Ayd (1975:499) estimated in 1975 that they were being taken by at least 400,000 persons globally. The phenothiazines, in particular the long-acting types, have been credited with helping to salvage (even if partially) hundreds of thousands of lives, with opening psychiatric hospital doors, and with promoting the growth and viability of community-based treatment (Shagass 1971; Davis 1975, 1976; Tissot 1977).[3]

Literally tens of thousands of research papers on psychotropic drugs have been published (GAP 1975); our focus, however, is on the use of the phenothiazines in the treatment of long-term psychiatric outpatients. The most convincing data comes from double-blind research on phenothiazines which indicates that, without exception, more patients have experienced relapse when taking placebo than when taking phenothiazines (Davis 1975, 1976; Ayd 1975). In a comprehensive review of this research, Davis (1975:1244) demonstrates that "698 patients out of 1,068 patients who received placebo (65 percent) relapsed, in contrast with 639 patients out of 2,127 who received maintenance antipsychotics (30

3. There is some disagreement as to how much responsibility phenothiazines have in the current deinstitutionalization movement. It is clear that attempts to treat markedly mentally different and suffering persons outside the hospital antedate widespread drug use in this and other countries (Caplan and Caplan 1969; Tissot 1977). However, the temporal association between introduction of the major tranquilizers and significant decreases in hospital census is indisputable (see Davis 1975:71, 1976; Greenblatt 1978).

percent)." Nearly unqualified agreement exists among reviewers of the phenothiazine literature, as exemplified by Davis (1975:1239), who says, "... there is overwhelming statistical evidence that the antipsychotic drugs prevent relapse in schizophrenia."

Recently, however, increasingly frequent and serious questions have been raised about the effects of these drugs on the quality of life adjustment of patients. Following one of the most elaborate and methodologically sound studies of phenothiazines in community treatment, Hogarty et al. (1975:6) noted, "at no time did placebo-treated patients appear better adjusted than drug-treated patients. Clearly, the real difference between drug and placebo was the ability of the drug to prevent relapse; it is nearly impossible to detect differences in adjustment between drug-treated and placebo-treated survivors." Important questions about who these placebo survivors are, and how and why they manage without drugs, remain unanswered.

Gardos and Cole (1976, 1978) have critically reviewed outpatient maintenance phenothiazine studies. They suggest that although at least 40 percent of outpatients seem to benefit from antipsychotic medications, at least 50 percent "would do well without medication" (1976:34). Chandler (1978:246), reviewing medications in a representative sample of residents of aftercare facilities in California thoroughly examined by Aviram and Segal, suggests that, among the most ill, "... the use of high levels of antipsychotic drugs actually depresses residents' levels of integration." More disturbingly, she reports (1978:248) that "for the healthiest portion of the sample, drugs work against the patient's ability to negotiate his or her needs through the operator and the facility."

In response to this and to other suggestive data (e.g., Carpenter, McGlashan, and Strauss 1977), it is essential to identify those persons who are drug responsive—in all spheres of their lives, not just in terms of clinical symptomatology and rehospitalization—differentiating those who are not drug responsive and who are potentially poorly served by being medicated. May and Goldberg (1978:1144) aptly define the current dilemma in their extensive review of factors predicting patient response to pharmacotherapy in schizophrenia: "Despite the dubious and conflicting evidence cited above, it is nevertheless difficult to believe that all patients benefit from drugs.... We may speculate that there are probably two subgroups who perhaps ought not to receive drugs. The first is a subgroup who do well in the community without drugs and the second a subgroup who do poorly in general and are not helped further by the drug. The trouble is that at present we have no certain way to identify either group."

When we examine specific studies of the use of long-acting phenothiazines, particularly Prolixin, with outpatients, again the data are positive and replicated in study after study. Prolixin has a conclusive and impressive record in reducing clinical schizophrenic symptoms such as agitation, delusions, and disordered thinking (see Ayd 1975; Groves and Mandel 1975; Zander 1977 for comprehensive reviews of research). Although its initial use a decade ago was among psychiatric inpatients, ". . . by 1974 the majority of patients receiving depot fluphenazine[4] therapy were outpatients . . ." (Ayd 1975:492). One can safely say that Prolixin has become a drug of choice in community and outpatient psychiatric treatment (Fink 1971).

The clinical efficacy of the drug has been incontrovertibly established. Hogarty et al. (1973), for example, report that in their sample of 374 schizophrenics living in the community, relapse rates for a group receiving placebo were twice that of groups receiving phenothiazine medications. Hirsch et al. (1973), in a comparable population, found that 71 percent of those receiving placebo experienced psychiatric relapse as compared with 17 percent of those receiving Prolixin. In an interesting and very pertinent study, Stevens (1973) reported that placebo takers constituted more of a "social burden on the community" than Prolixin-treated patients by behaving more noisily, aggressively, attending to delusions, and generally disrupting family relationships.

As clinical experience with these drugs increases, more sophisticated questions are being raised about appropriate dosage levels, type of phenothiazine, and fit between type of patient, drug, and treatment program (see May and Goldberg 1978; Linn et al. 1979). Goldstein et al. (1975) investigated individual differences in response to treatment with fluphenazine enanthate among first-break, young

4. Prolixin decanoate belongs to the class of depot fluphenazines. "Depot" signifies that the drug is injected into the muscle ("intramuscularly" in medical parlance), usually an arm or hip, which serves as a slow release point, or "depot," for the drug over a period of time.

schizophrenics. They combined and contrasted low and high dosages of drug therapy with the presence or absence of family-oriented social therapy. Preliminary results indicate significantly more treatment failures in the group with low dosage and no social therapy. But patients in the group with high dosage and social therapy fared worse than patients with high dosage and no social therapy. These data suggest the hypothesis that first-break schizophrenics benefit from low doses of phenothiazine combined with family-social therapy. In other words, more treatment is not necessarily better.

In a collaborative study involving ten day-treatment centers in seven states and 162 male schizophrenic patients, Linn et al. (1979) compared day treatment with phenothiazines (DTC) with phenothiazine treatment alone (ODM). There were no statistically significant differences between the two groups two years into the study with regard to time spent in the community, time spent in hospital, number of readmissions, percentage surviving in the community, and cost of treatment. Differences were apparent, however, in the area of social functioning as assessed by project social workers. DTC subjects showed significant improvement over ODM subjects. DTC subjects also scored higher on measures of attitudes toward hospital and people. None of the centers and neither of the treatment conditions significantly altered patient attitudes toward self, family, or "me-as-I-would-like-to-be." Again, it is clear that while drugs can help prevent clinical relapse, supportive care is needed to improve psychological and social conditions. Neither drugs nor day-treatment care are enough to combat the negative experience of self reported by these patients.

McClelland et al. (1976) report that clinically there were no significant differences between chronic patients treated with very high doses of Prolixin and standard doses of the same drug. The group on very high dosage manifested slightly more side effects, but these were not statistically significant. These results differ from studies in France and the United States (Rifkin et al. 1971), indicating some advantages to very high doses for patients who are otherwise treatment refractory. The question of dosage level for subgroups of these patients remains to be answered.

Several researchers have worked at determining which type of phenothiazine is most effective for long-term patients. In France, Simon et al. (1978) compared standard neuroleptics and an oral phenothiazine (pipotiazine palmitate) with Prolixin. An outstanding feature of this research was that instead of simply comparing relapse rates, the authors used scales rating symptom and adjustment, combining this with subjective clinical analysis to evaluate the patients. All the patients tended to improve over eighteen months, but no significant differences were found among the three medications. Rifkin et al. (1977 *a* and *b*) found that for the seventy-three outpatients in their study comparing oral and injectable Prolixin and placebo, 68 percent of the placebo patients relapsed as compared with only 10 percent of the Prolixin patients. Among patients considered to be "chronic," the results were even more marked; 75 percent of the placebo patients experienced relapse as did 6 percent of the Prolixin patients. These researchers expressed concern with what they considered to be a high rate of toxicity and incidence of side effects with the decanoate (injectable) as compared with the hydrochloride (oral). In a later study, Quitkin et al. (1978) compared Prolixin with penfluridol and found that 10 percent of the patients taking either drug relapsed. The same high incidence of toxicity and side effects was not reported, but the authors could provide no explanation for the difference. This same research group (Kane, Quitkin, and Rifkin 1978) has found, however, that of the two injectable forms of fluphenazine (decanoate and enanthate), the decanoate produces significantly fewer extrapyramidal side effects.

Prolixin, in particular, has gained widespread use not only because of its clinical efficacy but because it is less expensive, less time-consuming, and more reliable than most other phenothiazines (Ayd 1975:498). The injectable Prolixin is less costly because the actual dosage is less than in the oral form, requires less staff time to administer, and is thought to indirectly result in fewer relapses (often measured by rates of hospitalization) because injection ensures that the drug is taken. The injections can be given every two to four weeks as compared with oral medications, which are customarily administered daily. Compliance with medication is thus not dependent on the patient's daily follow-through or on the staff's daily delivery. It can be administered quickly (2-3 minutes) and infrequently. As recent advertising for Prolixin has indicated, the drug saves time, money, and people.[5]

5. See any psychiatric journal (e.g., *Archives of General Psychiatry*) for this advertisement. It is instructive to note the order of priorities the company uses for marketing.

It would appear that Prolixin is the current drug of choice for treating schizophrenic outpatients. But two major problems exist with the drug, problems that may well be interrelated; namely, noncompliance and side effects.

NONCOMPLIANCE OR DRUG DEFAULT

A number of studies reveal that from 24 to 63 percent of psychiatric outpatients do not take the medications prescribed for them in the desired amount or, at times, not at all (Van Putten 1974:67; Groves and Mandel 1975:873). These rates, however, fall well within the range for all medical patients with chronic conditions requiring maintenance medication. Blackwell's (1972) review of fifty studies of drug default yielded estimates of from 25 to 50 percent noncompliance. In view of the evidence on relapse, it is clear that default represents a substantial dilemma for long-term patients, their physicians and the community at large. As Van Putten (1974:67) has written, "The reluctance of patients with schizophrenia to take their prescribed phenothiazines is the bane of the psychiatrist. Readmissions are commonly precipitated by drug reluctance. . . ." Patients persistently are not taking a medication that has demonstrably beneficial clinical effects.

An array of factors appears to be associated with noncompliance. These factors include the following: multiple medications; multiple doses; lengthy treatment; prophylactic treatment; side effects; youth; lack of interested or available significant other; lengthy illness; and outpatient status (Blackwell 1972; 1973). Positive physician characteristics and a supportive doctor-patient relationship seem to result in improved compliance along with such factors as the patient's belief in the efficacy of the drug, the specificity of instructions, clear and accurate information about the drug, and availability of the physician. On the part of the physician, a friendly, reliable, and generally concerned demeanor, and gentle interpersonal persuasion seem to support better compliance rates (Cartwright 1974; Klein and Davis 1969).

Many explanations for noncompliance among psychiatric patients have been offered. These include: paranoia focused on medications; hostility and aggression transferred to medications; a tendency for patients to adjust their medications downward in accordance with self-identified needs; side effects; lack of encouragement by significant others to take medications; severity of disorder; acceptance of medications forcing the patient to admit to illness; medications symbolizing the patient's lack of control over his own life, symbolizing external domination identified with estranged authority figures; and the wish to be crazy (Van Putten 1974:68; Van Putten et al. 1976). These explanations and speculations suggest that compliance problems center around three areas: interpersonal and power struggles between patients and staff or authority figures; physical and clinical/psychiatric factors; and the attributed significance of medications for patients' view of themselves and their psychiatric problems.

Two recent studies (Hogarty et al. 1979; Schooler et al. 1980) have called into serious question the importance of compliance in preventing relapse and enhancing social adjustment. Schooler et al. (1980) compared the community tenure and adjustment of 290 schizophrenic patients at four hospitals who were randomly given injectable and oral Prolixin. They assumed that those patients in the oral Prolixin group would comply less well than those in the injectable Prolixin group, whose actual medication ingestion could be carefully monitored. Even though the study is seriously flawed because no measures of compliance were taken for the oral Prolixin group, the results are interesting. The investigators found no significant differences in relapse rates between the two groups, nor were any differences in social functioning apparent at the end of one year. Both groups showed decreases in primary schizophrenic symptoms, such as thinking disorders. Emotional withdrawal and blunted affect, however, worsened for all subjects. Hogarty et al. (1979) also compared relapse rates and social adjustment for 105 schizophrenic patients randomly assigned to receive oral or injectable Prolixin and high or low degrees of social therapy (ST). After one year, no differences were found between those patients receiving oral and injectable Prolixin, but those patients receiving injectable Prolixin and social therapy appeared to survive with some greater frequency. Hogarty et al (1979:1292) conclude, "Schizophrenic relapse, then, at least in the first year postdischarge, is not adequately explained by drug non-compliance." These investigators did find that patients receiving injectable Prolixin scored significantly higher on anxiety and depression scales, and that the patient's self-report of distress and symptoms was the best predictor of relapse. The results of these studies are in part unexpected, given the prevalent beliefs about medication forestalling relapse. Questions raised about the subjective impact on the patient of taking these drugs are welcome, and I will return to the subject in concluding this chapter.

It is interesting that none of the studies on drug default report having simply asked the patients why they did or did not take the medications, and why they liked or disliked them. Ratings of attitudes and compliance have been carried out by staff or other researchers (cf. Zander 1977; Van Putten 1974; Van Putten et al. 1976). In the process of this research project, I asked clients about their feelings regarding medications after it became clear to me that a significant part of their lives involved meds. A controlled, rigorous experiment was not undertaken. Though the data may not be systematic enough to warrant either comparison with other studies or generalization, it may serve to raise questions or to suggest alternative explanations.

SIDE EFFECTS

It has been estimated that the long-acting phenothiazines, which include Prolixin, produce temporary side effects in from 19 to 50 percent of their recipients (Groves and Mandel 1975:895; Ayd 1974). And it has recently been reported that Prolixin produces significantly more of these side effects than the oral form of the drug, fluphenazine hydrochloride (Rifkin et al. 1977 *a* and *b*). Specifically, Prolixin *decanoate* was associated with 35 percent more severe akinesia (the appearance of blank, indifferent facial expression), apathy, depression, indifference, subjective feelings of deadness and lack of energy, and slowing of motor response (ibid.; cf. Van Putten 1974 re akinesia).

The side effects most frequently associated with phenothiazines come under the general descriptive rubrics of extrapyramidal symptoms (EPS) and pseudo-parkinsonian symptoms (PS). EPS are further categorized as (1) *Akathisia* (called by clients the "Prolixin Stomp"), general restlessness and jitters, a jiggling or bouncing of the legs when one is seated, or a shifting back and forth from foot to foot when standing; (2) *Akinesia*, a lack of spontaneous facial expression, feelings of weakness, fatigue, diminished speech, interest, and emotional responsiveness; (3) *Tremor*, usually the PS category, shakiness of the hands or limbs; (4) *Dystonias*, possible neck stiffness and spasms, facial grimacing, other involuntary muscle movement, and oculygyric crises or uncontrolled rolling of the eyes up and into the head, eyes becoming fixed in that position (see Swett 1975); (5) *Other parkinsonian symptoms*—(called by clients the "Mendota Shuffle"),[6] rigidity of limbs, poverty of movement, gait and postural disturbances; (6) *Tardive dyskinesia*, relatively rare, usually irreversible, involuntary facial contractions and movements of the tongue, jaw, and mouth not unlike puckering and pursing the lips, flicking the tongue (cf. Van Putten 1974:468-469; Ayd 1974: 279-280; Ayd 1975:495-496 for side effects in general.)

Tardive dyskinesia was first reported as being neuroleptic-induced in 1956 (Jeste et al. 1979) and since that time has caused increasingly serious concern about the long-term use of phenothiazines and other major tranquilizers. Although studies of incidence are flawed by variations in diagnostic criteria and the masking of symptoms that often occurs while persons are taking phenothiazines, it is reported that from 0.5 to 56 percent (Tepper and Haas 1979) of patients who take neuroleptics develop the syndrome.

Past surveys completed in inpatient settings have profiled the at-risk dyskinetic patient as being female, over fifty-five years of age, using neuroleptics for over two years and having prior organic or brain damage (Tepper and Haas 1979). Two recent studies of tardive dyskinesia among schizophrenic outpatients reported 31 percent (Chouinard et al. 1979) and 43.4 percent (Asnis et al. 1977) incidence rates. Chouinard et al. (1979) found more tardive dyskinesia among older, treatment-resistant, longer-hospitalized patients who were taking fluphenazine. Asnis et al. (1977) reported that age, sex, and years of neuroleptic use were *not* associated with higher rates of tardive dyskinesia. These researchers expressed surprise at the relatively high incidence of tardive dyskinesia among their subjects who were young, were neuroleptic users of short-duration and were not chronically hospitalized.

Until recently it has been thought that tardive dyskinesia was irreversible, untreatable, and essentially homogeneous. Success with reversibility has been associated with early detection, low dosage,

6. George Surman (personal communication) informs me that this side effect is called the "Camarillo Shuffle" at the Los Angeles County Hospital, and the "RGH Boogie" at Riverside General Hospital in California.

short-term drug taking, and drug-free intervals. Jeste et al. (1979) have suggested that there may be two types of tardive dyskinesia: reversible and persistent. The reversible type is associated with younger patients with fewer drug-free intervals than the persistent type, which is associated with an older group with more drug-free periods. This conflicting data merely highlights the need for more research to identify accurately who is at risk for tardive dyskinesia and how the syndrome can be reversed if not prevented (see also Gardos and Cole 1980).

Increasing attention is also being directed to various depressive and withdrawal syndromes associated with the phenothiazines. Investigating what they call "akinetic depression," Van Putten and May (1978) have found that among the 30 percent of their patients who developed akinesia, depression was also present. The depression decreased after administration of medications to counter side effects. Another study of pharmacologically induced depression in patients who were taking Prolixin (Floru, Heinrich, and Wittek 1975) substantiates that side effects may be associated with so called postpsychotic depressions. Withdrawal from antipsychotic medications has frequently been associated with relapse. Gardos, Cole, and Tarsy (1978) suggest that actual withdrawal symptoms may mimic psychotic decompensation and may result in erroneous or premature resumption of drug therapy. Arguing that between 17 and 75 percent of patients may experience some withdrawal effects, they urge a sufficient time lapse before drugs are reinstated so that clinical decompensation is accurately distinguished from withdrawal symptoms. Most of this data is suggestive and not conclusive, but it is encouraging in its specificity and sensitivity. The future will no doubt bring welcome refinements in our knowledge about and control of the deleterious side effects of psychopharmacology.

Medication in the form of Cogentin and Artane is prescribed for many of these PS problems, but these can cause their own side effects, such as blurring of vision and dryness of the mouth (see Zander 1977).

LITHIUM

Lithium carbonate was taken orally in pill or capsule form as primary medication by three of the clients in my project, and in conjunction with Prolixin by six. I will not review the long, illustrious, and controversial career of lithium salts here (see fn. 2 for references), but will summarize briefly. Lithium has been used primarily for treatment of mania (cf. Takahashi et al. 1975; Cade 1949), although Greist et al. (1977) indicate that the drug has been tried as treatment for thirty-six different disorders, ranging from gout to numerous psychiatric conditions. Recently, it has gained some popularity as an effective medication for depression, primarily the bipolar type (depression coexistent with mania in the same patient) (see Mendels 1973, 1975, 1976 for reviews of these studies). Currently, lithium is being considered as an impressive agent in reducing impulsive aggressive behavior (Sheard et al. 1976) and in the treatment of schizophrenia (Alexander et al. 1979).

Proponents of lithium are highly enthusiastic about its actual and potential merits, even though the drug is highly toxic in uncontrolled or excessive doses (Freedman et al. 1977; Vacaflor 1975). Persons who take this drug must have blood levels drawn routinely to monitor the amount of lithium in their systems. Around PACT, this procedure is called a "lithium level." Clients customarily have lithium levels taken weekly when starting the drug, gradually decreasing to bimonthly or monthly monitoring. This procedure serves to alert the staff, through evidence from the blood sample, when a patient is taking less or more lithium than s/he should.

Noncompliance

Even with monitoring, it is difficult to ascertain the regularity and consistency of patient compliance. At least three clients in this sample stopped their doses periodically, and some figured out how much lithium to take the night before the blood test to reach the expected level. If the amount of research undertaken and reported is any measure of concern with a problem, relatively few studies of lithium address the issues of noncompliance and default.

Side Effects

Lithium produces side effects that include the central nervous system abnormalities, such as confusion, convulsions, or coma produced by toxicity (Freedman et al. 1977). Among its additional side effects, nausea, diarrhea, general gastrointestinal distress, and hand tremor are the most common (Mendels 1976). Cogwheeling (muscle rigidity with jerking movement) (Shopshin and Gershon 1975) and one case of attendant myasthenia gravis (Neil et al. 1976) have been reported (see also, Vacaflor 1975).

PROLIXIN AND LITHIUM: AN ASSESSMENT

The use of phenothiazines and lithium as a significant part of treatment for those psychotic persons in our culture who enter the mainstream treatment system has benefited mental health personnel, patients, their significant others, and society at large. Increasing concern is being expressed by all groups about the consequences of this treatment over both the short and the long term.

Lithium appears to be a remarkably effective medication for mania and probably for depression, but it is dangerous unless carefully supervised, and questions regarding its safety are still being raised (Freedman et al. 1977; Jefferson and Greist 1979). Both Prolixin and lithium are clinically proven effective medications, but patients frequently develop unpleasant, often visible side effects and many do not take these medications as prescribed. These drugs have contributed to significant decreases in the expression and experience of the most extreme, painful, and disturbing symptoms of psychosis. It is time to assess carefully the sociocultural correlates of this achievement, attempting to understand the place of these drugs in the lives of the chronic mentally disabled.

The Mechanics of Medication

At PACT, the service chief, a psychiatrist, had primary responsibility for the prescription and management of medications. Psychiatric residents training at PACT also prescribed and monitored the drug treatment program. The registered nurses on the staff administered and recorded medications, on occasion recommending changes in dosage or type. Clients were usually referred to the service chief with questions and complaints regarding drug treatment. Other members of the staff might attempt to persuade a client to take medications, or facilitate the delivery of meds. No one on the staff was entirely divorced from this recommendation and delivery system.

Medication was given to clients in three forms: (1) injection; (2) daily doses of oral medications; and (3) "self-service" oral supplies for periods ranging from one day to a week or more. The nurses administered the injections of Prolixin in the kitchen, which was the only downstairs room at PACT with a closed door. Drugs were kept locked in a cupboard in this room. By customary procedure, patients came to the PACT house to receive their meds, announcing "I'm here for my meds," each obtaining a small brown packet containing pills if these had been "set up" (ordered by the service chief, prepared by the nurses.) If an injection were required, an available nurse would take the client into the kitchen, close the door and, amid some chatter, administer the shot. Injections and pills were also dispensed at the client's residence, or if he were avoiding staff, wherever he was located. Nurses sometimes gave shots to clients while in the back seat of the state vehicles driven by staff, or they sometimes took to the streets with syringe and injection in hand to deliver meds. Several reluctant clients were paid for coming in to PACT for their medications, though staff did not like to engage in this type of contingency program.

Oral medications such as Cogentin, antidepressants, antianxiety drugs, sleeping pills, and lithium were administered in daily or self-service doses, depending on the reliability of the client in taking meds and his or her history of medication abuse. Daily doses were given to those clients who had been known to "stockpile," saving doses of oral meds and thereby posing an overdose threat. They were not given large enough supplies to injure themselves and received the daily or sometimes multiple daily doses. Unreliable compliers also received daily doses and were asked to swallow the medication in the presence of staff. Most received self-service medications to alleviate side effects. These were handed out whenever it was convenient or before or during various client activities at PACT. Sleep-inducing medications ("sleepers") were sometimes delivered by staff to clients late in the evening.

Clients refused meds in a variety of ways. Some chose the path of least resistance and simply avoided staff by leaving their rooms or by not coming to the PACT house when scheduled. Others openly declared their intentions, though this made them more susceptible to persuasion to change their minds. The most successful mode of refusal was to express powerful fears regarding the drugs, declaring a willingness to go to great lengths to escape. When staff perceived that they might lose leverage or contact with a client because of meds, they temporarily decreased the emphasis. Some refusals took on a repetitive, ritualistic character. The client would express the same negative feelings, staff would repeat the same arguments for taking the medication, and eventually the client would comply.

Upon discharge from PACT, a number of clients took Prolixin injections from the local visiting nurse service. Others received meds from the agency or therapist to whom they were referred. No client ceased receiving meds throughout the research period, though some have since gradually decreased their doses.

The PACT staff, with two or three exceptions, believed firmly in the efficacy of medications. Each staff person was interviewed at length during the course of the research. Two of the questions involved meds. Staff were asked if they thought meds were essential to treatment and if they felt a person who refused meds was choosing to remain crazy and not get better. The response of one of the nurses (B) was representative of the position expressed by a majority of staff members:

A. Do you think medications are helpful and/or necessary for effective treatment? And do you think that patients who refuse meds are choosing to be ill?

B. Well, first of all, I think meds are, can be, an important part of a patient's treatment. Certainly the kind of clients that we work with, 80 percent of the cases, require medications and fairly high doses of medications, too. I think the way in which they're useful is that they're a portion of the whole that helps the person get healthier. You can't teach someone to cope with certain things if they aren't organized, if their head isn't organized. You can, you know, "behavior mod" somebody till you're blue in the face, and if their head is racing around, they aren't going to benefit from that treatment or probably any other treatment method. I think medications play an important part. I don't think that they're always necessary. I don't think that just because someone is deemed to have a problem that, you know, medications necessarily follow. I think we're a very medication-oriented society, whether it's for a backache or a headache or whatever. We look at that as being the ultimate treatment, a pill. And it certainly by itself is not. It's only a part of the whole, and that's the way I view it, and I would tell patients the same thing.

That it does not take control out of their hands. In fact, if anything, it affords them more control to do as they please.

A. What about heavy doses of medications as a trade-off, say with tardive dyskinesia or other kinds of side effects? Do you feel that patients ought to have that information available to them?

B. Yes. Yes, I do. I think they ought to have the information, but it's sort of like when you go to the doctor and he says, "I'm going to give you this antiacid, but just bear in mind that you probably will be constipated. You may be nauseated, but you won't have a stomachache."

A. That's a choice of symptoms, really.

B. Really, it is. And I think the tardive dyskinesia, though it's really a very grotesque kind of side effect and limiting, in that sense, because it's visually, it's disturbing to others. I think that for a person to be able to converse back and forth with somebody, to perhaps hold a job, that seems to me a small trade-off to cope with that symptom. And, of course, there's stuff being done every day to try to alleviate those kinds of side effects with the drugs that we're using.

A. Then, how would you feel about somebody who deliberately refuses meds? Do you think that they're making a choice of maintaining their symptoms?

B. Well, it brings to mind one particular client, which, of course, I won't name, but I think with this person we've all felt anyhow that his performance, his ability to cope day-to-day, would be tremendously enhanced if he were to accept the medication, which he won't do. And a lot of us have viewed this as sort of an insanity on his part, that he can't see it. And I, you know, after a while, after listening to him, I really felt that he knew very well that he didn't want to accept the medication, was saying so in a very sane, controlled way. And I think, in his case, it was purely an example of not wanting to give up the symptoms. I think that, more than the fear of brain damage and all the other things that patients frequently will verbalize to you. It's a comfortable thing to be living with the symptoms for him. And I don't think that he wants to be free of them. And, yes, there are times when that makes me angry, when that frustrates me to the hilt because I can't, there's no way I can present to him what his life might be like with medication. With the medication and the same kind of input and ability to really learn different behaviors, as maybe a result of being more organized. There's no way to present that, except verbally, from one person to another. And I don't think that for him, that he, you know, he's afraid to change his behavior.

All agreed that meds were important if not imperative, for they had seen too many "miracle cures" with meds not to believe in them. They agreed that there was a strong, though often subtle, pressure at PACT to take meds, followed by an often unspoken, punitive attitude toward clients who had consistently refused meds in the face of stubborn psychoses. The attitude was that if the person refused, then s/he must pay the consequences.

Three staff members were less committed to medications than the others. These persons expressed feelings that clients should be able to decide for themselves about meds without pressure from staff, family, and others. Furthermore, they thought clients had reasonable fears and reservations regarding medications, fears that were shared by staff. None said they would take meds themselves. One of these staff members with reservations about meds said:

> Yeah, I think medications are helpful and, I don't know about being necessary for effective treatment. I know one thing, that if I had side effects from Prolixin, no matter how crazy I was, I would not take it. Because it's my body, and I would not want to end up with tardive dyskinesia, and they look more bizarre than the craziness does. But if I could take it without the side effects, you know, that would help me. But I think that a patient or a client should be able to choose.

Another staff member (B) expressed a somewhat different perspective:

> B. Truthfully, I don't like meds.
>
> A. Why?
>
> B. For one thing, I don't understand them. There are a lot of questions in my mind about what, you know, what are the long-term effects. We're just starting to see a lot of the long-term effects—especially on women, and I think they're a necessary evil. They do serve a function, you know, helping someone to organize themselves that are in acute distress. I think a lot of professionals overprescribe them and don't review them as much as they should.
>
> A. Do you think that in general people tend to overmedicate in the community setting? I mean, you clearly don't have the controls that you have in the hospital.

B. Yeah. I think generally people were overmedicated all the way around, and in the last ten years. I think, you know, people are medicated better in the inpatient setting than they are in the outpatient—especially, how can a doctor really, uh, control someone's medication when they see them for forty-five minutes, you know, every two weeks?

A. Or when there's a chance, statistically, that they're not going to be taking all of them. Okay, so you're apprehensive about meds. Okay, do you think that somebody who refuses is, in any way, saying, "I prefer my symptoms to compensating"?

B. Yeah.

A. Does that, in any way, change your attitude, commitment, desire to work with that person?

B. I don't think it changes it. I think I have to reevaluate it. I think there are times when a person needs meds, and it's nice, you know, it would be good for that person to give meds a trial run, maybe to try a small dose for a short time until they became organized, and then try to reduce them, you know, to a point where they don't have to take them anymore. But I think that's just been programmed into them.

A. Okay, let me ask you if you agree with this. I think there's kind of an unspoken code around here, that if it's a group decision or a person who knows—if it's the doctor's decision, that a person needs meds and they would be helpful, and the person refuses those meds, there's a real silent kind of coercion and a pulling back upon refusal to do so. A pulling back of some of the, maybe enthusiasm—real soft stuff—warm support about getting better, that the person might have gotten. The person isn't a good patient. Now, I don't think it's cruel, I don't think it's unusual, you know, whatever, but that leads me to believe that most people here think meds should be taken.

B. Yeah, I think that's because most people have operated in a manic environment, whereas I think I have been somewhat lucky in seeing, you know, people treated without meds successfully. It takes a hell of a lot more work and a lot more structure. And I don't think it would be too applicable to the community—mainly because, since we work for the state, [there] wouldn't be enough money.

A. Or not enough manpower.

B. Yeah, I think you'd really have to work one-on-one, and be really flexible in meeting client's needs. Uh, I think we do a fairly good job, when we do use medications, of, you know, evaluating the effectiveness and things like that, although—some people, I really question, should they be treated in a community setting with medication?

One medication that I do believe in and, I think, it's just because I think it is a biological or genetic thing.

A. Yeah. Okay. It's interesting, too, because patients—I talk to them about the same thing about their feelings about meds. And there's a real division, real clear. People on lithium love it. People on Prolixin hate it. Some of it has to do with side effects, but I've never heard any of the people in my group on the lithium say, "I hate it, I don't want to take it," and so forth, except those people who, on occasion, enjoy getting high, and purposely don't take it.

B. Yeah, I'm sure. I am somewhat envious of those people. They have the choice of enjoying something.

A. Yeah, really. But I've never heard anybody. I've heard people being neutral about the phenothiazine, but I've never heard anybody, you know, take it like the gospel, like they have lithium.

B. Yeah, I've never really experienced it.

A. The side effects are unpleasant. You know, I can tell you that. There's no question about it. Uh, and I've also heard very few people get on Prolixin and say it really helps.

B. Well, I have heard it.

A. Some people have said that?

B. Yeah, and I'm sure that's just for staff to hear.

BEING ON MEDS

For purposes of discussion, clients are divided into three groups: (1) the phenothiazine or Prolixin group; (2) the Prolixin-lithium group; and (3) the lithium group. This is done not only for convenience but because clients distinguished themselves vis-à-vis meds in this manner. Those in the Prolixin-lithium group most often identified themselves as lithium-takers, with one exception. As is evident in table 2, other medications were taken by the group, but Prolixin and lithium, followed by Cogentin, are the most important for our consideration.

Attitudes and behaviors toward meds among clients have been classified here as positive, ambivalent, neutral, and negative. If these categories seem neat, it is because they are somewhat artificial. Ac-

TABLE 2

MEDICATIONS PRESCRIBED FOR CLIENTS*

Phenothiazines	
Prolixin decanoate	33
Thorazine	5
Stelazine	4
Haldol	2
Mellaril	2
Lithium Carbonate	9
Side Effect Medication	
Cogentin	26
Artane	3
Antidepressants	
Elavil	2
Tofranil	2
Navane	1
Sleep-Inducing Medications	
Dalmane	11
Antianxiety Medications	
Valium	7
Librium	2
Antialcohol Medications	
Antabuse	2
Sedatives	
Sodium amytol	2

*Clients may receive up to four different medications at once.

tually, many statements and behaviors of clients regarding meds were difficult to systematize because they changed sometimes rapidly, and were not always internally consistent. The categories have been defined in the following manner:

1. *Positive*—person feels the medication is helpful, with relief from symptoms and/or daily life. Side effects either not mentioned as troublesome, or if mentioned, do not compare to benefits of meds. Always or almost always takes prescribed dose.

2. *Ambivalent*—person has mixture of firm positive and negative feelings regarding meds. Usually positive to neutral about improvement in symptoms, negative about side effects. Person usually takes prescribed dosage; refuses at times (more often than neutrals). Person does not like meds but feels must or should take them.

3. *Neutral*—person has no *strong* positive or negative feelings about meds. Usually takes prescribed dose, though may refuse or avoid rarely. Takes meds because is asked to or told to; believes he needs them. May not think meds help, but also not bothered enough by them to respond actively.

4. *Negative*—person consistently verbalizes strong dislike for the meds and/or the side effects. Complies begrudgingly or under pressure. Often refuses prescribed dose. Blames meds for problems.

In applying these groupings, it should be kept in mind that, on any given day, a client put in one category might have behaved in a manner that more closely approximated a different classification. In an effort to control some of this vacillation, two dimensions were operative in each category; namely, feelings or attitudes stated to staff and to me, and behavior regarding meds. For example, a person might consistently have expressed neutral to negative feelings about meds, but if he also had refused medications frequently, he was classified as negative. Also, in an attempt to systematize the data, clients were classified according to the predominant attitudes and behaviors observed during the research period. As a result, occasional exceptions to the groupings are distressingly evident for any one client. Persons taking Prolixin and lithium are classified and discussed separately according to their feelings and actions regarding each drug.

PROLIXIN: CLIENT ATTITUDE

Positive Attitude—Prolixin

Doc was the staunchest proponent of Prolixin among the group. He viewed the medication as one of the most positive aspects of PACT treatment, crediting it with having increased his self-confidence and his ability to think clearly, and having decreased his silliness. Doc had an explanation for his problems in Prolixin, and he readily incorporated it into his present and future:

> Prolixin will be with me a long time. I've been missing this chemical in

> my body ever since I was little, and that's why I was depressed. Dr. I. [his private therapist] said that's probably why I was depressed when I was younger. Before, I was taking Stelazine, but that's not what I was missing.

Again:

> I believe I was born missing a chemical. I was missing Prolixin. Before they knew that, I was really depressed, and now I'm not. I saw a picture of me with my father when I was about three or four, and I was so glum. That's it. I was missing Prolixin.[7]

Two other patients in the group expressed positive attitudes about Prolixin. Cy had been taking Prolixin for four years. "I used to have a terrible temper and have these tantrums. It stabilizes me. It keeps me from having tantrums."

Christie was uncertain about the utility of meds until she took them. Her positive feelings related directly to symptom relief and to the security of following medical advice: "I'd never go against the doctor. He knows more than I do. When I first came to PACT, I wasn't on anything, and I was against it. But it helps. It does help." During her tenure in the PACT program, Christie took her medications consistently, sometimes in high doses. Near discharge (she was in the complete discharge group) she expressed some anger at the program, saying she was not "going to take any more of your damn meds." Several months after discharge, she stopped taking Prolixin, stating, "I just decided not to have it anymore. It wasn't doing anything for me anyway, and I didn't want it." Since that time, she has begun Prolixin again. Part of the reason she stopped was the winter weather. She did not want to travel to the clinic in the cold for her shots.

7. It is possible that Doc, who takes both lithium and Prolixin, has confused an explanation for the utility of lithium with Prolixin. The biochemical imbalance message is most often given to lithium takers. Throughout this section, the reader should keep in mind that although clients' views may not always mesh with clinical or chemical fact, they are taken as valid and important for understanding the clients' world. As Gutheil (1977) has said: "Physicians have all kinds of fantasies about what drugs do; patients have even more elaborate ones, since their imaginations are not cramped by some knowledge of pharmacology."

Two others who took Prolixin almost fit the positive profile, especially with regard to compliance. But their stated desires to be able to function without it, and their severe problems with side effects, recommended them as more appropriate candidates for the ambivalent group.

For the three clients with positive attitudes, important factors were: (1) self-perceived improvement in symptoms and life circumstances and (2) feelings of comfort and security deriving from a satisfactory explanation for their psychiatric difficulties or from persuasive medical advice. Christie's discharge and postdischarge negative feelings regarding Prolixin reflected, in part, her frustration with not getting better. This frustration was echoed by others who were ambivalent, neutral, or negative about meds.

Refusal of medication when angry or dissatisfied with PACT personnel, programs, or life in general was a frequent occurrence. This was an important behavior, for it revealed the clients' chosen manner of defiance in associating meds with PACT or with others in authority. This means of rebellion was, as were most others available to clients, unfortunately self-defeating. The momentary satisfaction of refusal usually resulted in despair, regret, or life problems when the seemingly inevitable escalation of psychotic thoughts and feelings occurred, attended by severe losses associated with eviction, termination at work, or hospitalization.

Ambivalent Attitude—Prolixin

Seven clients expressed attitudes best described as ambivalent. With unusual precision, Walter wrote the following assessment:[8]

> Pro and Con for Medication (Prolixin)
>
> *Pros*
> 1. Prevention of insidious psychosis
> 2. Keeps me from dramatic mood swings > thinking disorganization
> 3. Possibly improved reception to therapy

8. This is a verbatim transcription of an unsolicited written statement prepared by Walter. He had read fairly widely in psychiatric literature, and this was reflected in his vocabulary. Three other male clients also engaged in this type of study.

Cons

1. Physical manifestation of Prolixins [sic]
   a. increased nervousness
   b. uncontrollable tremors
   c. mood changes due to A and B (cycle of 2 wks.)
2. Physical man. from Artane
   a. dryness of the mouth
   b. lightness of body causing upset stomach
3. Difficulty in concentration
4. Difficulty with excessive motor nervousness, shuffling feet, and moving digits of hands.
5. All of the above contribute to the feeling of despair, anxiety, and restlessness.

Walter's insights reveal not only his physical and psychic experience with Prolixin and Artane but also his emotional responses (1.c., 5.) to the drugs. He recognizes the therapeutic effects of Prolixin, but this does not change his negative response to the side effects and to the impact on his feelings. More importantly, we see the secondary result; namely, the despair attached to the side effects. Walter attempted to return to school three times, but he felt that he could not sit still long enough to study and that his concentration was impaired by meds. Internal factors other than meds may have contributed to this circumstance, but the significant fact is that he perceived it otherwise. He was unhappy that the same substance that helped him to remain compensated also presented obstacles to his ability to function.

Another facet of ambivalence stems from feelings of dependence on Prolixin. Agatha sums it up: "I don't like them [Prolixin and Cogentin], but I wouldn't be without them." Her feelings about meds were initially extremely positive. She began on Mellaril. After she cut her throat, she was switched to heavy doses of Thorazine and later to Prolixin. Discovering that Prolixin made her "feel like superwoman," she wanted more medications, thinking they would solve many internal problems. While on Prolixin, Agatha attempted to shoot a co-worker with a 30-30 rifle. She was then hospitalized and her Prolixin was greatly increased. After this incident, she related the following:

> Maybe I ought to let someone else tell you. I was crazy, out of my mind. I just couldn't pull the trigger. I bought a gun and tried to shoot

> this lady. I kept telling them to give me more Prolixin. I either had to kill myself, or kill this lady, or get more Prolixin to get the voices to stop.

Four days earlier she had said:

> I'm horrible. The ultimate bummer has happened. I have these four voices in my head telling me I'm a mind fucker, fucking no-good, horrible person. They're telling me that right now. They're the voices of these four girls at work. Do you know where I can get some Secanol. That'd do it. I could just die, and then I'd get out of this.

After her release from the hospital three weeks later, Agatha slowly began to feel better. She was hearing fewer voices, less frequently, but she was concerned at having the Prolixin decreased to one-fifth of the dose she had received in the hospital. She feared the voices and felt she continually needed more Prolixin despite the fact that "the medication makes me forget things, short-term, and I can't read because my eyes are blurred from the Cogentin. I hate that, because I love to read, but when you consider the alternatives . . ." She found it necessary to use a magnifying glass to read for months, but she did not mind the side effects as much as what she feared might happen if she were to stop taking meds. Her ambivalence, then, derived from compelling feelings of dependence and an acknowledged need for the medication.

Agatha continued to take Prolixin during the years after my fieldwork ended. In the winter of 1979, a minor fall on the street severely damaged the vasculature in her leg. Two arterial transplant attempts failed, and the leg was eventually amputated. I marvel at her courage and steadiness in the face of yet another ominous obstacle in living, but I continue to wonder what role the years of taking substantial doses of phenothiazines and Cogentin played in the loss of her leg. It seemed like such a routine fall. It seemed so unfair that she suffer yet more pain. It seemed remarkable that the veins and arteries were so fragile and unable to heal. Agatha now lives in a nursing home. I keep wondering about the costs and benefits of taking Prolixin.

Gail is another client with concerns about Prolixin:

> I feel very insecure without my medications. I get very anxious. I suppose if I'd grow up, I wouldn't have to take them at all. I could get along without the Prolixin if I'd just be mature and face my problems. But I rely on it. I get very scared without it. I'm afraid to try it without meds. Dr. C. told me it was my decision whether or not to take them.

Three months later Gail reported that her Prolixin had been decreased, but "I couldn't make it, so it is up again." During this later interview she denied having related the above maturity hypothesis, addressing herself to her lifelong need to maintain drug therapy. Gail did not directly equate the meds with reduction in psychiatric symptoms, as did Agatha. But when her life was going well and she felt confident, she would call the PACT psychiatrist to ask if the Prolixin should be decreased.

The fact remained that Prolixin would, in effect, always be a part of Gail's life, whether or not she continued its use. She had developed tardive dyskinesia. When talking to her, I noticed that she pursed her lips frequently, almost rhythmically. She never discussed the tardive dyskinesia with me, so I have no information about her reactions to this circumstance.

The remainder of the ambivalent group had neutral to positive feelings about the impact of Prolixin on their thinking and feelings, but they strongly disliked the side effects. Alice occasionally avoided or refused her Prolixin. She variously felt that she didn't need the drug, that it did not help her, or that she should take it. Although Alice experienced marked stiffness and eye-rolling (oculogyric crises) from Prolixin, she frequently forgot to take her Cogentin, (which would have reduced these symptoms). Regarding Prolixin, she said: "I refused my meds and [the PACT psychiatrist] talked to me. I told him I didn't want to take them anymore. I'd like to get off it altogether. I don't like the side effects. He told me I needed it. He said I always get into trouble off it."

Alice reported that the eye-rolling was embarrassing to her and made her extremely uncomfortable. "I feel sick. My eyes hurt. I have to take my Cogentin and lie down for a while. It happened in a bar once, and I had to go to the bathroom and stay there." PACT staff felt she could control the eye-rolling, and they adopted a policy of ignoring it. When her Prolixin was increased, her hands shook noticeably. I asked if it bothered her, and she responded, "Well, no.

Not unless it bothers other people. Most people I know have it, too. I try to hide it when I meet a neat guy."

Rod takes chlorpromazine (Thorazine) as well as Prolixin. "It takes me quite a long time to wake up in the morning. The medication makes it very difficult for me to get going before noon or when I've had enough coffee. I don't like that, but there doesn't seem to be an alternative."

Prolixin created real conflicts for clients. The trade-offs were significant, considering the possible social and interpersonal consequences. Persons who accepted their need for the drug and took it seemed destined to encounter personal and social obstacles because of the side effects. From a psychiatric perspective, the choice was clear, though PACT staff were aware of the cost-benefit formula and the value nature of their options. They felt that the positive influences of the medication were worth the price. These clients seemed to agree, but their perspective was different, for they were the ones who suffered the consequences and reaped the rewards. Gail balanced the security of Prolixin with the visible contortions of her mouth; Rod balanced his internal fears and delusions with his slowness, lethargy, and nonworking days.

In understanding medication as a permanent aspect of clients' lives, it is foolish not to consider at what price clinical improvement and community tenure is maintained. The embarrassment, the feelings of dependence, the despair, and the restriction of activity have consequences not only in terms of self-image but in terms of clients' ability to interact with persons to whom meds and side effects are strange or stigmatizing. It is important to evaluate the social and cultural costs of medications and their possible perverse effects for these clients.

Neutral Attitude—Prolixin

Persons were considered neutral in attitude if they offered little or no comment regarding Prolixin, if they customarily took medications, refusing or avoiding them only on occasion, and if they reported no strongly positive or negative convictions about Prolixin. Tendencies toward ambivalence and negativism existed within the group, but nearly consistent compliance and an acknowledgment of some (if minimal) benefits made a neutral classification most appropriate. This benign label will seem realistic to those who recognize the problems with Prolixin, but who feel it is the best option currently available within the psychiatric system.

Abe provides a representative illustration. He expressed interest regarding his meds, often discussing them with the PACT psychiatrist. Seldom did he refuse them, but when he told me he was "feeling much better these days," he credited a gradually decreasing dosage of Prolixin. "I can hardly tell I'm on it anymore. I mean, it's a stabilizer for me, but I think after a while you build up a tolerance for it."

Ben, though a bit more negative than Abe, had remained on Prolixin for over two years. He had entered the PACT program after a tempestuous stay in Mendota Mental Health Institute, where he had been incontinent and had spent many hours in seclusion because of assaultive behavior. After PACT, he lived at home without further hospitalizations. Prolixin constituted but a small part of his life. "It doesn't do a thing for me. I take it because they told me I have to. I don't know. I just have to take it. It makes me nervous. It doesn't do anything." Ben exhibited the Mendota Shuffle, shifting back and forth from foot to foot when standing. His brother, Steven, was also in the PACT program and experienced marked side effects. Their parents were initially negative about medications, but they eventually made compliance a requisite for either son to live at home.

Tim had also taken medications for several years. He reported that this had been against his will during his stay in Winnebago State Hospital. He was admittedly difficult to interpret, for his thinking and responses to questions regarding medications were what staff would have called "crazy" or "loose." When asked about Prolixin, Tim (B) responded:

B. It doesn't affect my head at all.

A. Then why do you take it?

B. Because the body has to suffer. And so, if I take it, then my children will be immune, and their children will be immune. I get a shot every two weeks. It doesn't feel like a thing.

The latter half of the response is, of course, idiosyncratic, but the acknowledgment of bodily suffering refers to side effects. The mention of children is contradictory, for Tim disliked women and had fantasies of cutting them up with knives.

Eleven clients expressed neutral feelings about Prolixin. The above examples imply that although Prolixin may have helped clients, in the opinion of others, often clients spoke as if they did not share this evaluation. But they continued to take the drug. The desire to "make it" without Prolixin was manifest throughout the group. When their lives were stable and going well, clients sometimes experimented by openly asking for meds reduction or by covertly prescribing a decrease. Characteristically, members of the neutral group would not go to great lengths to avoid or to refuse Prolixin. They could be rather easily persuaded to continue. Still, not one person in the group would have taken the drug if they had not felt they must. These clients were as much convinced of this fact of life by their own experimentations without Prolixin as they were by other persons. As Humphrey said, "Yeah, it'd be nice without it. But my screws come loose if I don't have it." His acceptance was reinforced by staff, his family, and others, as was true of most in the group. Like those in the ambivalent category, they wished they did not need Prolixin but were resigned to its place in their lives. They had side effects, regrets, and hopes, but they had few perceived alternatives.

Negative Attitude—Prolixin

Eleven people comprised a decidedly and vociferously anti-Prolixin group. Three felt so strongly about the medication that they had to be forced by court order to take it. Another was pressured by the conditions of probation to take Prolixin. Two of the four became less negative after the order, but their resistance and fears remained. Underlying the attitudes toward Prolixin among this group were fears about the drug, resistance to perceived control by others, strong dislike of side effects, and a reluctance to acknowledge the need for psychiatric medications and the existence of psychiatric problems.

Stanley had spent several years "running away from meds," as he put it, before the PACT staff filed a court petition for protective services to force the medication issue. The application was made by staff after all efforts to convince Stan to take Prolixin had failed for almost ten months. Throughout his initial tenure in PACT, Stan had spent a great deal of his time mute, often curled up in a fetal position during group activities, or wearing an Air Force parka zipped all the way up so that only a small, round, furry hole framed his face. For a while, he wore over his eyes and face a hat he had found in a garbage can. Staff frustration with his behavior ran high, but he steadfastly refused the overtures of one psychiatric resident after another—even those who had offered him "an attractive selection of pills." In amazement, he thumbed through the medications encyclopedia (Physicians Desk Reference) with another client, saying he was "checking out the arsenal."

Stanley's persistent fears about Prolixin changed after his involuntary introduction. He alternately reported that it helped or that it made no difference. When he was asked why he had been so fearful, he said:

> Well, I saw all these other people on it. They looked dead, I mean all shakes and not around here at all. I know what it can do. I hate the crazies. Crazies are like terrible pain. It's like this pain you can't get away from, and it makes you crazy, or just running around not caring what you do. Sometimes I get the crazies. But it's okay to be crazy. Crazy is like bright colors and gay. I mean, I didn't want to be all straight. I thought it might make me get lost, you know?

These fears of becoming "dead," or of "losing" aspects of self thought of as special, were true for at least two of the others with negative feelings. Note that Stanley emphatically did not wish to have the "crazies," or psychotic episodes. He did not, however, wish to lose his ability to be "crazy," his license for eccentricity, flights of fancy, and fun.

Bitter, persistent complaints about side effects typified this group. Martin was also ordered by the court to take Prolixin, but this did not stop his constant complaints and condemnation of meds:

> That damn Prolixin. I couldn't think clearly on it. I wasn't myself when I had so much of that. They [PACT staff] wouldn't listen to me when I told them how I felt. They'd say, "You look natural to us." My

> back hurt. I couldn't sit still. Hell! I couldn't do nothing. My legs half up in the air. They're too heavy with that medication. I think you should be able to change doctors if you want to. I didn't like that. You should be able to have another opinion about medications. It didn't help me a bit.

Annie took Mellaril, another phenothiazine. She blamed the drug for her inability to concentrate and for her tiredness. At the same time, she had demanding expectations of its performance for her. "It better calm me down or I'll have to get something else. These damn medications. I don't know. They're supposed to help you, but all they ever do is mess you up. All those people look like zombies on drugs." Annie did not identify herself with "nuts and mental patients, you know, people with emotional problems." She constantly made negative remarks about her co-workers at a sheltered workshop and about her boyfriend, Doc, who was also a PACT patient. Despite her denial of psychiatric problems and social patienthood, Annie spent most of her time among persons with psychiatric liabilities, and she continued to condemn them and their "crutch" medications.

Unfortunately, her negative feelings about meds and her refusal to take them contributed to her eviction from the YWCA, where she had lived for over one year. The resident manager there felt very strongly that Annie needed meds. When Annie's giggling, talking to herself, speaking on the hall telephone loudly, and appearing in her underwear in the halls began to bother other residents, and when she refused to take her meds for fear of "becoming a drug addict," the manager gave her notice. This was after the manager, who viewed herself as a volunteer part of residents' treatment teams, had had several conversations with Annie's therapist and had tried to convince Annie to take her meds.

Alex, Sadie, and Robert viewed meds as attempts by others to control them. Robert saw PACT personnel as "drug pushers" and felt that he was still being controlled by a Prolixin injection given him two years ago. Off medications, Robert was eventually committed to Mendota Mental Health Institute. Alex had an infamous history of legal problems, some due to a lack of impulse control. Nonetheless, he feared and disliked Prolixin. This fear did not extend to various street drugs, such as amphetamines, uppers, and downers. He said he felt "much, much better when I get that shit out of my system. You never know what they'll give you. I don't trust those people." Paradoxically, Alex seemed to recognize the necessity of meds where others were concerned. Referring to Robert, he said, "Now, there's somebody who really needs to take their medications." Sadie viewed herself and her life as infinitely more interesting when "I'm not taking that death drug." Unfortunately, what Sadie preferred to Prolixin resulted at times in her thoughts being expressed as in the following written note:

in a pee pee pee is a
see see see in a tee tee te is a de de de
in a rr rr rr is a key key key

Side Effects—Prolixin

A systematic appraisal of the incidence of side effects throughout the group suggests the following observations. Drugs countering side effects are not administered prophylactically. The PACT service chief dispenses Cogentin and Artane for side effects only when and if they appear. As is evident in table 2, twenty-nine persons received these drugs. Of the thirty-five persons taking phenothiazines primarily and predominantly, 85 percent developed side effects of some type. One person experienced oculogyric crises, and three others developed tardive dyskinesia as diagnosed by staff. One person limped so badly that he was hospitalized for neurological tests. The tests determined that the problem was a side effect. Stanley's "Prolixin Stomp" was so loud during the review hearing for his medications commitment that his lawyer had to ask that he try to stop. Most of the side effects experienced and displayed by the group were of the stiffness, shakes, and gait disturbance type (akathisia).

Taking Prolixin—A Six-Weeks' Journal

My six-weeks' experience with Prolixin hydrochloride (oral Prolixin) was instructive in that I did experience some of the minor side effects: shakes, stiffness, and flat facial expression. The feelings I had confirmed for me what clients had said. Excerpts from the diary I kept while on the drug are illustrative:

> On 2/17/76 I began to take fluphenazine or Prolixin. After discussing the matter with various medical and nonmedical people, I decided to proceed with the weight of the opinion, plus my own inclination. Of those I discussed taking the drug with, those persons who were somehow emotionally involved with me—i.e., family and close friends, most were opposed to it.
>
> We all agreed that the drug affects different people differently, and that I did not have the psychosis most of the PACT III clients had when they began the drug. In addition, it has been clear from the outset that I could draw no general conclusions from this venture—that it would be a purely personal, experiential project. My reasoning has been mostly anthropological: as a participant in a system so pervaded by this particular drug, I felt I should at least try it. I was hoping to experience some of the side effects so bitterly complained about by clients, and so obviously displayed by them. This physiological experience I did think I could share to some degree.
>
> Without question, I was somewhat ambivalent and apprehensive about beginning the meds. I had been warned of possible side effects and medical problems, but the most anxious part of it was the unknown. No one could tell me with any assurance what I would experience, how it would affect me.
>
> I started on a dose of 2.5 mg. per day. I had decided to begin taking it upon return from a three-week vacation in Florida after a complete physical examination. On return, with the go-ahead from my physician of many years, I indicated to the doctor here that I was ready to begin.
>
> He thoroughly explained the possible side effects to me—most of them having to do with muscle and nervous systems. There are three basic groups, the names of which I have forgotten. I'm not sure if the speech he gave me is comparable to what he tells clients or not. But I felt a sense of foreboding—as if these things would probably happen to me and I would in some way be temporarily debilitated. I had the sense of a little bit of humiliation—i.e., that I would shake or shuffle in the same way as I have so often seen clients do with no capacity to control this. The main thing I disliked was feeling that others would see me and perceive me in this vulnerable or drug-induced condition. I wonder if clients feel this kind of initial embarrassment over a potential source of self-exposure to lack of control of bodily function.
>
> A couple of my friends said they did not want to see me if I were "messed up by the drug," others merely expressed concern and/or disapproval for my "experiment." I do not view this experience as an experiment, for it lacks the controls and reliability of a true clinical

experiment. I view it more as something I *should* do to get a fuller cognitive picture of what it's like to be a part of this particular client system.

2/17 The first day of taking the drug was uneventful. I was attending a conference on Advocacy for Reintegration, and sitting and thinking all day. I could not tell except for some minute nervousness that I was taking anything. I suspect I was looking for more than was there. I slept well.

2/19 I was interested to see how things would go at the seminar. I could detect no change in my thought processes. No problem sticking to topics or in thinking about intangibles. I felt a bit paranoid, wondering if others could tell. Felt a bit impatient and argumentative, but may have been because the seminar was so unfocused and rambling. Also because I had things to do after, which I wanted to get to.

I am sleeping okay; a bit more tired than usual.

2/20 Wasn't very hungry and did not sleep well 2/19 P.M. Felt dry and queasy—as if I had a hangover. Feeling flat and a bit self-contained. Shaky. Got an audit letter from the Department of Revenue and I shook noticeably. First time had uncontrollable shaking of the hands and arms. Felt lousy and strung out all day. Had headache and no appetite. Went to bed early. Explained to friends I was taking the drug. They a bit sceptical. I was very talkative at dinner.

2/21 Feel better today, not so tight and shaky. Head a bit foggy. Saw a male friend off and took a couple of naps. Feeling edgy and a bit as if on thin ice.

Not able to sit down to write comfortably. Hands feel odd holding a pen. Begin double dose tomorrow and I am a bit sceptical, though I am back to not feeling the drug much. Others perceive thick speech and some muscular discoordination. Some minor cogwheeling.

2/22 Rested most of the day. Took 5 mg. for first time. Definitely feel as if I have less energy, but feel mentally nervous. I don't know why—perhaps due to tension with a friend about taking the drug at all.

I began to menstruate and this may account for some of my nervousness the previous two days. I always experience some hyper-inside feelings prior to my period. Have begun to shake my legs a bit—it feels natural and comfortable to do this. Limbs feel a little tight and light.

2/23 In my head I feel directed toward attaining goal of normalcy—I feel I'm fighting the drug rather than letting go and seeing how it feels.

Shaking my legs still—getting lots of negative comments by friends for doing this.

2/24 Went to group at the Union. Felt some need to move around a bit. Shaking legs quite vigorously. The shaking is intentional but feels necessary to relax and stay sitting down. I feel a bit forgetful and preoccupied but don't know with what.

It is increasingly difficult to write and sit still. Pen feels uncomfortable, and hand not sure about writing. Haven't got the patience to sit. I am also smoking more heavily.

In ways I definitely feel different taking the drug, in others I am not at all impressed by differences it makes in my head. The side effects are not as marked as I thought they'd be. I am told I am less spontaneous but I don't feel this way.

I began to feel ambivalent about taking it when I felt so bad that one day, but now I'm still interested and liking it a bit.

Enjoyed the music at the Union but I do feel more comfortable with one or two people than with a whole group. Time moves a bit slowly for me, and I have some difficulty waiting for things.

2/25 Feeling okay and getting used to feeling on edge. Some minor cogwheeling in my left arm.

At social skills I had a very hard time sitting through the session. Constantly changing position, restless, impatient for the thing to be over.

I feel the need to flee almost, to move constantly from stimulus to stimulus—maybe I'm so slowed down in my head I need more movement outside. Don't know.

Feeling rather irritable and feeling a bit vulnerable. I know my affect is flat but I don't feel flat. I am processing and receiving information okay, but probably not reacting to it. In some ways I am hypersensitive—especially to criticism from friends regarding my behavior.

Feel kind of like I want to move from one thing to another physically, but am tired in my head. Sleeping a bit more, but I suspect I am sleeping to hide some from the small discomfort I am feeling.

2/26 Had a very long, hard day of it. My thinking seems unaffected by the drug. I am able to focus on and deal with ideas and thoughts intensely without the impatience I felt at social skills.

Feeling a bit dry and shaky when excited (i.e., about post doctoral program) or under stress.

Very irritable and impatient with the seminar again. I feel angry that others are tangential and move slowly. Would like to stand or pace and would feel more comfortable.

Rushed from seminar to Social Skills. Dreaded sitting through it. Definitely shaking my leg.

My face feels flat but I am receiving and perceiving as much as ever—perhaps just not openly responding.

I think I am smoking more for something to do with my hands. Any type of movement is relaxing or natural to me. I feel tired at the same time but also tight and light.

I am usually lighter and more shaky in the evenings when tired. Feel a bit racy and unable merely calmly to discuss things. Feel like I should keep conversation moving and go from subject to subject.

All in all, for the first week, I feel as if part of me is racing and part is slowing down. In some ways stimulus is too much and I prefer to be alone or asleep; in other ways I crave it. Not feeling very uncomfortable or that ambivalent about taking it. Still interested in how I'm feeling.

2/27 Not much change.

Napping and sleeping a little harder. Met with [my doctor] and he said I could take it all at bedtime. No Cogentin needed yet.

Anxious and shaky about site visit. Went well. Had no trouble thinking or answering questions. Felt visibly shaky before, but did not shake during interview.

Weather is awful, but I'm not having any trouble driving.

Still feeling a bit as if things are moving slowly.

Having a hard time sitting down to do notes and take notes at report.

Having a hard time coordinating walking on ice.

At times I feel inappropriately brash, but at others very self-contained. Discussed taking drug with resident and friends—they seemed unimpressed.

3/2 Did forget my gloves however. Doing a few more forgetful things than usual. Did not want to sit around and gab though as I should have wanted to do. Always feel the need to move and go when things are winding down. Still feeling irritable—not much tolerance for lapses in conversation. Got impatient with a friend for taking so long. Feel the need for physical activity.

Not having trouble remembering what people say, i.e., for notes, but do feel a bit foggy in retrospect. Feel a little distracted but don't know by what. It's easy for me to fall asleep once I do get still. Feel generally a bit tighter, however.

3/3 A.M. Went to see friends. A bit worried they wouldn't want to see me. Though close friends, I felt as though I had little to say. The feeling of self-containment grows. Conversation did not seem very stimulating to me and I usually am very involved. As if there were a glass barrier between me and others—emotions subdued and flat if there. Am thinking things through but not necessarily reacting strongly in positive ways.

It is harder than usual for me to wake up in the A.M. and I am sleeping sounder (not hearing phone which is unusual). Very shaky in the mornings.

3/4 Felt *very* light and loose and shaky when I got home. A bit discoordinated. Conversation racy and animated, but part of me feels flat. Like I'm functioning differently on different levels.

Nothing seems to move fast enough, but at the same time things feel a little loose.

3/6 Having some lower back pain—fairly constant. Still pretty constipated. Feel as if no position is comfortable to settle in except sleep. Consequently very hard to relax and talk with friends.

Did not want to meet friends late for drinks. Made excuses. Increasingly want to be quiet and alone.

3/7 Feel a little stiff and disoriented, but focused on one or two things at the same time. Antsy to get from one event to the next. But not really getting into the event. Find I am hesitant to make decisions—hurrying along without paying attention to detail as I normally do. Discomfort with work and writing continues.

3/18 It is harder than usual for me to wake up in the A.M. and I am sleeping sounder. Very shaky in the mornings. Thoughts are more focused, less racy. Scared that might mean I'm a little crazy.

When I stopped taking Prolixin after six weeks at a dosage of five milligrams per day, the side effects continued for approximately two weeks. More important, I experienced what my physician called a "sympathetic discharge." This meant that I had a difficult time cognitively and emotionally adjusting to *not* taking the meds. Anxiety, self-doubt, distress, suicidal thoughts ran rampant. Taking Cogentin helped a bit. For all its lack of precision and lack of generalizability, the venture into Prolixin provided a very personal and instructive means of learning. By the time I stopped the Prolixin, I was very thankful I did not have to take it forever, for my ambivalence toward it was getting stronger each day.

For clients, Prolixin held a variety of meanings. The medication evoked mixed feelings, neutral to negative, about self and others identified with the drug. Clients struggled to evaluate the role of Prolixin in their lives, accepting or rejecting their need for it and weighing its costs and benefits. In a sense, the choice was not theirs to make. Medications played a pervasive role in their environment, coloring their relationships with mental health professionals, with their families, even with their landlords. Except for staff, almost everyone with whom they associated when in treatment was also taking medication. Compared with an in-patient setting, clients had abundant opportunities to escape meds, in terms of available time and space. But the web of persuasion surrounding the clients was powerful. Those who chose to try it without meds ran known risks, to be learned firsthand. Despite this, the persistence of their negative or ambivalent feelings and their attempts to erase meds from their lives reveals a paradoxical dilemma of patienthood, even in the community, that deserves attention.

LITHIUM AND LITHIUM-PROLIXIN: CLIENT ATTITUDE

Negative Attitude—Prolixin; Neutral Attitude—Lithium

Six persons regularly received Prolixin and lithium; one customarily received lithium only, adding Prolixin when he periodically became psychotic. With the exception of Doc, noted earlier, those in this dual category felt much more positively toward the lithium than the Prolixin. Herb provides an example: "I'd like to get off meds completely. I'll probably have to take them for the rest of my life, the lithium anyway. I don't mind the lithium. It's that Prolixin—makes me nervous; makes me shake."

Steven echoed these sentiments: "I take my lithium faithfully, but I just won't take that Prolixin. It makes me feel awful, like I want to get outside of myself. It doesn't help my head at all, and it just makes my muscles feel wrong." Steve had one of the most negative attitudes toward Prolixin coupled with the greatest need. Frequently, when he refused Prolixin, PACT staff would remind him that he always got crazy without it. Usually he agreed and eventually took the shot, but not without expressing his despair and frustration. His longest run without Prolixin during the research period was six weeks. Six months in the hospital followed.

The Prolixin-lithium group had negative attitudes toward Prolixin because of side effects and no perceived benefits. Herb explained that he would take the lithium, as long as it did not "mess me up like Prolixin."

Positive-Ambivalent Attitude—Lithium

In contrast to the Prolixin group, the lithium takers expressed positive attitudes toward the drug. But this did not mean, as it did among positive Prolixin takers, that they consistently complied. In fact, periodic noncompliance, resulting in a manic episode or "high," was characteristic of the group.

Steven, who earlier proclaimed faithfulness to lithium, expressed it this way:

> You know why I have to take lithium? It's so I won't get high. Society does that. Society can't get high, so they don't want me to; they can't understand. Being high is like physical heaven on earth. I can get so high. I'll have that all my life. They can't take that away from me.

His periodic ventures without meds all ended in tumultuous psychotic escapades, arrests by the police, and stays in the hospital. George and Dorothy experimented less often, but when taking lithium, they also missed the ability to get high. Dorothy, however, did not miss her depressions and suicidal feelings. George, like Dorothy, paid for his own medication after discharge from active status in PACT. At times he did not take his lithium because he had spent all of his money elsewhere. PACT would have helped each to purchase or obtain meds, but this alternative was not explored until each had lost enough control to have caught the attention of roommates, family, or staff. The expense was a problem for Steven as well, who spent nearly $50 per month for medications.

Dennis is enamored of street drugs, such as marijuana and hashish. He respected the lithium, calling it his "happy stuff." He sold or gave it to friends on occasion, reporting that they "really get off on it." Dennis had a very negative attitude toward phenothiazines, which he took before his PACT admission, calling them "death drugs." "Prolixin is used for physical control by shrinks. It slows your body down, but your head is still going 1,000 miles per hour. Lithium is different. It mellows you out. I've taken up to eight [tablets] at a time. I get bitchy and irritable when I don't take it. I mean, you have to be careful; but I always am."

Phillip expected lithium to solve all of his problems. When it did not, he became ambivalent and distressed, though he derived comfort from his opinion that there was something medically wrong with him that medications could cure. He reflected the belief held by this group that they had a biochemical imbalance, correctible by taking lithium.

In discussing the side effects of lithium, no one in the group felt that the disadvantages outweighed the benefits of the medication. Each stated that the initial discomfort of gastrointestinal distress subsided. They considered themselves fortunate not to have the visible problems associated with Prolixin.

Miscellaneous Meds

Clients expressed interest in the medications taken by other clients. Some directed this curiosity to staff, who customarily would not discuss another's medications. On several occasions clients asked one another, "What're you on?" Or, if one were visibly shaking or shifting about, "You're on Prolixin, huh." The term "Prolixin Stomp" was coined by a patient one evening during social skills group when the foot-bouncing of a fellow patient was unusually loud. At another social skills session, Ben refused his meds loudly enough for all to hear. Herb, who seldom refused his own, applauded Ben by saying, "Atta boy! I wish I had the guts to do that." On other occasions, however, Ben warned Steven that he would "get sick" if he were to stop taking meds.

Several clients (at least three) valued Cogentin merely as another means of getting high. They often took a week's doses at once, reporting to staff that they had lost or had never received their supply. At times, clients shared or "loaned" their Cogentin. Valium, an antianxiety medication, was the medication most frequently requested by clients.

Meds and Making It Crazy

A major contribution of Prolixin and lithium is the reduction of psychiatric symptoms or thoughts, feelings, and behaviors that not only distress clients but often damage their relationships with others. This particular interpretation is well documented and has been discussed in the orientation to medications. It should be noted that psychiatric personnel are not unaware of the limitations of drug therapy. May (1976:689) has stated the wisdom well:

> Drugs may be helpful in promoting restitution and restoring perception control. But, quite apart from unwanted side effects, they do not enlighten the patient about his problems, inform him how to adapt, help him to take advantage of opportunities, or accept his limitations. They do not repair self-esteem, nor do they repair the damage that he has done to his friends and family. They cannot get him a job, they cannot make mothers and mothers-in-law change their minds, they don't handle traffic violations, and as Hollister observes, they cannot teach him to play the violin if he couldn't do so before.

What I question is whether psychiatric personnel are aware of the actual and potential social and interpersonal *costs* of meds.

I suggest that although symptoms may be reduced, the dependency on medications and the visibility of side effects serve to magnify clients' deficiencies and differentness not only to themselves but to others. Clients who are told constantly in multiple ways that they need meds, probably for the rest of their lives, are also being told that they will never "get well." They cannot persuade themselves that, with perseverance and care, they will be cured. Rather, they come to see themselves caught between a nonmedicated world that is out of reach, and a medicated world that identifies them as crazy people with problems in their heads and in their lives.

Clients may embellish this construction of reality not only by accepting their medications and their disabilities as parts of a permanent crazy self but by behaving, living, and thinking like crazy people (for they have nothing to lose). With other identities and roles cut off to them, they make the best of it. In a passively defiant way, they make it crazy. At times they do this by liking their "crazies" more than the straight life that they want, but fear or reject. Refusing meds may be a desire for health, or it may reveal a wish to be crazy (Van Putten et al. 1976) if craziness provides some escape from other realities negatively perceived. Just as society and the treatment system cannot have it both ways—telling clients they need meds (i.e., you are sick) but expecting them to feel good about themselves—clients cannot have it both ways. Perhaps the only compromise they can perceive is to accept and elaborate the patient identity.

Clients are well aware that only "nuts" need to take Prolixin and lithium. Normals do not require meds. The irony is, of course, that in an effort to become more like others (i.e., not take meds), many become increasingly different. As they become further removed from non-patienthood, they develop more despair and hopelessness about themselves. This Catch-22 poses a dilemma of major proportions. The medications prescribed for these clients, combined with intensive community-based support, guidance, and advocacy represent the best that the psychiatric treatment system has to offer at present. The PACT program's success in maintaining clients in the community with little or no hospitalization is unparalleled. In addition, their clients' measures of self-esteem and satisfaction with life exceed those consistently reported by others in the community treatment business. But this is clearly not enough to resolve the problems faced by these clients on medications with regard to social and interpersonal adjustment, integration, and the opportunity to lead lives as people, not patients.

Perhaps closer examination of the medications issue will more distinctly underline the paradoxes. For our group, taking meds almost always meant developing visible side effects. The shakes, stiffness, blank expression, gait, leg jiggling, eye rolling, and facial grimacing, were physical markers to others and were badges of patienthood to themselves. On three occasions during the research, I interviewed people immediately after they had interacted, as strangers, with one of the clients. The interviewees were told that I was doing a study of communication between strangers. They were asked to describe the most prominent impressions they had of the person they had just met. In each instance, the strangers first noted what we know to be side effects. They had concluded that the person was "on something," "a little off," "looked like he was taking drugs," "shook like he was sick or scared," "acted like a zombie, all stiff."[9] Further research of this nature is necessary to confirm our hypothesis, but we can learn from these examples.

Clients knew about side effects and could spot them in others quite well. Yet they also understood in ways that "normals" (nonmed-takers) could not. Our tiny sample of uninformed normals guessed that the clients were crazy or were on marijuana or other drugs. Their predilection was to avoid this person, or to view him or her as an unfortunate, a hippie, or a mental patient who needed help. Once their attention had been caught by the side effect, they started to notice other peculiarities about the client. Fracchia et al. (1976) report that suburban homeowners do not discriminate with regard to severity or gradations of mental dysfunction when reacting to former psychiatric patients. Perhaps regardless of visible degree of differentness and dysfunction, clients may be marked, exposed, and interacted with as crazy people. In a sense, that which is intended to help clients function in the community (i.e., meds) also hurts by contributing to suspicion, isolation, and distance from nonpatients and nonmed-takers. Patients are being asked to be insane in sane places (ibid.).

Another perverse dynamic of meds is their reinforcement of ties between clients. Medications represent common ground, similar experience, and a topic for mutual commiseration. They associate and

9. Goffman (1963:41-50) presents a corroborating discussion of social information control, visibility of disability, and personal identity. He coins the term "stigma symbols," as opposed to prestige symbols, to denote personal characteristics that "are especially effective in drawing attention to a debasing identity discrepancy . . . with a subsequent reduction in our valuation of the individual" (p. 44). He also suggests that stigma symbols are usually displayed involuntarily (p. 46). Though I would argue that these side effects may in time become stigma symbols, their origin and nature are not yet sufficiently known to the public to brand the client as a psychiatric patient. Perhaps over time, if the "phenothiazine generation" becomes more visible in communities, this ignorance will be alleviated. A true problem of symbolic stigmatization may then emerge with regard to medications and side effects.

identify the most crazy with the least crazy. That is to say, clients who take the same meds often fear or presume that their problems are similar to the problems they observe and disdain in another client. At the same time, one need not be self-conscious about side effects if one remains among others who share them and who will not reject you or view you with suspicion on this basis alone. In consequence, clients may confine themselves to social and interpersonal relations with those who understand and share this special feature, with those to whom no explanations or excuses need be made.

The paradox here is that the accessible group with which one shares similarity is a group of long-term psychiatric patients. The group that one does not perceive as accessible and with whom one has little in common is the presumed normal, unmedicated group. This identity system, constructed by self and others, perpetuates the viability of the crazy identity. Those who stay within the network are not only exposed to the continual failures, problems, inertia, and frustrations of their comrades but they experience their own. It is not difficult to ascertain possible factors reinforcing the crazy life. The dismal becomes the routine; failure and distress become the norm.

Medication side effects may also contribute, however gently and subtly, to exacerbation of the social withdrawal, the relative lack of supportive, intimate relationships, and the troubled affect (usually anxiety and depression) that are seen as both symptomatic and characteristic of long-term psychiatric patients (see Hogarty et al. 1979; Sokolovsky et al. 1978; Hammer et al. 1978). I think that the following complex and as yet obscure interaction takes place between the patients' subjective experience of self and body while on meds and his or her social and interpersonal environment. Clients who experience side effects, especially of the akinetic type, are often simultaneously depressed; appearing blunted and sad, detached and disinterested, and feeling morose, hopeless, and gloomy (Van Putten and May 1978). Clients who experience akathisia look and feel restless and agitated. They find it difficult to sit still, pacing, shifting back and forth from foot to foot, bouncing their legs, feeling the need to move. (The clinical designation for these behaviors and feelings, when combined in a patient, is "agitated depression"). We know that persons who are anxious and depressed tend to isolate and to experience disruption in interpersonal relations, seeing others as angry, uncaring or unavailable for support and nurturance (Coates and Wortman 1980). I suggest that the akinesia and akathisia as experienced by the client and others with whom they interact contribute to withdrawal and isolation, depression and despair, resulting in part in the lack of social networks typical of this population. The depression and anxiety, in experience for the client and in appearance for others, serve to perpetuate separateness and lack of involvement.

The quality of interpersonal relations may also be affected by the above complex. Lack of intimacy or avoidance of it, and dependent, asymmetrical relations typify the interpersonal networks of these persons. At a fundamental level, in order to develop and maintain an intimate relationship, one has to share time and space with another. A person literally has to sit still long enough to make emotional connections, to talk, to care and to be cared for. Many of the clients cannot or will not be physically still, comfortably, long enough to permit or facilitate the kind of bonds that the rest of us create and depend on in our lives. When they do sit in one place, often there is leg bouncing and shaking that is embarrassing to them and distracting to others. This hypothesis grew in part out of observing repeated instances of clients' inability to sit through social skills groups, needing instead to move about or to rock back and forth. When I was taking Prolixin, I grew impatient in seminars and during dinner at home. I found myself leaving prematurely because I felt so restless. Persons who are pacing, bouncing, shifting, and otherwise moving around really cannot create close relations with others who can and want to be still, or who do not understand the cause of this seeming agitation. Other clients and staff will understand, but families and community members may not.

Hogarty et al. (1979) and Schooler et al. (1980) lend sturdy support to the idea that anxiety and depression are associated with taking Prolixin. Hogarty et al. suggest that the withdrawal of schizophrenic patients from busy social networks may help them to remain in the community because large amounts of emotional stimulus seem to be noxious. Whether withdrawal and relative isolation are helpful or harmful, it seems to me that this should happen by choice for the patient rather than because of the drugs we give them with the promise of improvement, not only in the location but in the quality of their living.

The meds complex of attitudes, behaviors, and consequences contributes on multiple levels to making it crazy. On one plane, clients seem to know that to maintain themselves at a level of functioning relatively free of psychotic symptoms, meds are essential. But this recognition does not sufficiently pave the way out of the crazy system. Side effects may reveal your identity and deficits to others. They make you feel uncomfortable, physically and mentally, with yourself. Knowing and being told that you need meds makes it clear that you are different, if not crazy, and probably always will be. Your family, PACT, the courts, even landlords and supervisors at sheltered workshops tell you that meds are important, tell you that you are different.

The option of rejecting these messages and implications is hypothetically open. But as we have seen and as the statistics show, eliminating the med portion of one's crazy identity and the meanings attached to meds usually contributes to more pain and damage to self and others. In this manner, clients and others contribute to the circular solution, one that is nonsensical (crazy) in its contradictory indications. Without question, taking meds contributes more benignly to this process than not taking them. But what about the persons who develop tardive dyskinesia? What are the costs of compliance for them? They are the ones who openly, uncontrollably grimace and smack, who contort their faces for all to see. This result of medication represents a powerful socially distancing and stigmatizing condition. What kind of trade-off are we asking these persons to make? It seems to me somewhat cruel to help them clarify and organize their thinking and perceptions, when part of what they will accurately perceive is others' fear, disdain, and rejection because of stigmata that are now physical.

Antipsychotic medicines have been exported along with Western medical psychiatry to many non-Western cultural settings, but there is very little data reporting the frequency and impact of their utilization. I think it safe to say that the major tranquilizers, and this includes the phenothiazines, find unparalleled use in the West. This is an important point to consider in assessing, by means of cross-cultural data, the influence of sociocultural factors on the experience and outcome of psychosis.

Tissot (1977:111) points out that the large-scale use of psychoactive drugs has helped to transform "schizophrenia from a continual-expression syndrome, which was most frequently the case, into an intermittently expressed syndrome—by this fact alone and independent of their direct pharmacological action—drugs bring about its fundamental modification." Recently reported two-year follow-up data from the International Pilot Study of Schizophrenia (WHO 1979) indicate that the prognosis for essentially comparable psychoses is much poorer in the West than in non-Western settings. It is extremely unfortunate that the WHO investigators made no attempt to control for treatment variables during the follow-up period. But we may still question what influence differences in frequency of use of psychoactive medications has on these findings. It may be that although we are reducing the social expression of psychotic symptoms, we are in some ways contributing to the personal and social disability of patients who take drugs. Perhaps some people who do not take meds experience psychotic episodes that are more florid, but they may also experience more personal and interpersonal competence, "wellness," and freedom from their sick roles than takers of medicine in the interim. I agree with Tissot that we have transformed the expression and experience of schizophrenia with these drugs. I question whether the change is in an entirely positive direction from the patients' point of view. We need to examine cross-cultural evidence very carefully in this light, designing research that will account for major treatment variables, such as prescription and ingestion of major tranquilizers, and the personal and cultural meaning of taking medications.

In a cultural and symbolic sense, meds may also represent a subtle experience of powerlessness for these persons. Persons in our society place a premium on the sanctity and privacy of internal body space. Entry into another's inside space is usually predicated upon intimacy and mutual agreement, as in sexual relations, or upon physical need in a professional relationship, again with consent, as in surgery or examinations. Laws prohibiting and punishing rape and other intrusions testify to the importance of control of one's inner space. The actual entrance of this chemical substance into the bodies of clients, I suggest, may be seen as less than a mutually intimate, strictly medical invasion of inner space. A recent and important legal action concerning the rights of voluntary psychiatric patients to refuse medications (Rennie v. Klein) was in part based on the court's decision that "a right to refuse should be recognized, based on the constitutional right of privacy" (U.S. District Court, New Jersey, Civil Action #77-2624 1979:3).

I am arguing here that these long-term intrusions into clients' inside space may represent exercises of power, legitimated by medical affiliation of the treatment system, which underscore to clients their lack of control of themselves in relation to others. Although the medications themselves become imbued with qualities and meanings, the persons and relations involved in the processes of administering and receiving them also have significance. For example, when clients are distrustful or angry with staff, they often refuse medications. It is commonplace for power struggles between patients and staff to be acted out in the medications area. Side effects and the relative lack of "cures" occurring with these drugs often exacerbate the problems, for clients may experience the need to explain to themselves *why* they are taking these medicines they find so unpleasant. Often the answers are interpersonal and social rather than medical or personal. As we have seen, the web of persuasion to take medications is very people-oriented among the clients.

As concern grows for the unintended and sometimes perverse consequences of maintenance psychopharmacology, and as empirical evidence accumulates, involvement of the legal system increases. Protection of the individual's right to make an informed choice of treatment modalities and to refuse those considered intrusive or dangerous is becoming more legitimate and widespread. Plotkin (1977:463) summarizes the philosphy underlying this activity:

> . . . "liberty" includes the freedom to decide about one's own health. Individual autonomy generally dictates when and if one will consult a physician. The role of the physician, once consulted, is to recommend various alternatives. As long as the public is not endangered, it is the individual who retains the ultimate power of selection among these alternatives.

It is clear that these clients, and most others like them in the community mental health system, not only have insufficient drug-free alternatives but they are not encouraged to explore these few options. On the contrary, many are unaware that they have choices and are constantly urged to take medicine by the most powerful and important people in their lives. Unfortunately, as the staff member pointed out, it would require more staff time and more personnel to manage community treatment with fewer drugs.

I have meant in this chapter to highlight those aspects of maintenance drug treatment for the long-term community client that are insufficiently discussed and understood. I believe that it is not now feasible to alter drastically current practices regarding these drugs with these people. We have alternatives, however, and we are obligated to explore them. First, we need to learn a great deal more about how and whether drug treatment interacts with clients' beliefs about the nature and consequences of their troubles. Once we have learned more, we can work at providing explanations about these medicines that are more comprehensible and less reinforcing of illness. In addition, we need to acknowledge the power and prevalence of side effects and to work with clients to diminish the expression of such symptoms, diluting their personal and interpersonal significance. If we can begin to take responsibility for the conflicting and confusing messages we convey via medications, perhaps the need for making it crazy can be lessened.

6

SUBSISTENCE STRATEGIES—EMPLOYMENT, UNEMPLOYMENT, AND PROFESSIONAL DISABILITY

> No other technique for the conduct of life attaches the individual so firmly to reality as laying emphasis on work; for his work gives him a secure place in a portion of reality, in the human community. . . . And yet, as a path to happiness, work is not highly prized by men. They do not strive after it as they do after other possibilities of satisfaction. The great majority of people only work under the stress of necessity, and this natural human aversion to work raises most difficult social problems.
> —Freud (1961:33)

This chapter explores the subsistence strategies of the clients—how they obtain the basic necessities of life, such as food, shelter, clothing, and money. An overview of the employment experiences of long-term psychiatric patients living in the community is given, figures for our subjects are reported, and the employment program and orientation at PACT and among clients is described. Reciprocal exploitation and exchange within the client group is outlined, including such extracurricular subsistence activities as panhandling and the selling of drugs and sexual favors.

The employment experiences of clients comprise but a portion of the picture. Because most of the group is almost perpetually unemployed, not always by choice, it is more realistic to focus on their experiences with not working. From this perspective, consideration must be given to the role of federal and local income maintenance and assistance programs in providing our subjects their means of survival. Clients exist within a network of agencies and programs designed to rehabilitate them vocationally, if possible, or, if rehabilitation should prove impossible, to aid in their maintenance of an adequate standard of living. Learning the intricacies of the system—how to qualify for what program administered by whom—is no simple task for the outsider.

In this context, the subject of work and unemployment is not a simple one. Complexity and some confusion are inherent because although the clients exist within a money economy, based on the exchange of labor, goods, and expertise for remuneration, they are usually unable or unwilling to participate conventionally in this economic system. This fact suggests the hypothesis that what the clients do exchange or provide (intentionally or unintentionally) for their wages are their disabilities, diagnoses, and deficits. Being psychiatrically disturbed enables them to receive money and goods almost as does the possession and utilization of skills enable a carpenter to earn wages. I would not suggest in any way that these persons possess the motivation and intent of the carpenter. But in recognizing the cultural reality that one does not get money for nothing, and in looking at *why* these persons get paid, it becomes evident that their *disabilities* function as do others' *abilities*, that their *incompetence* reaps for them what others' *competence* earns.

WORK, MENTAL ILLNESS, AND COMMUNITY TREATMENT

It was not by chance that the William C. Menninger Memorial Convocation Lecture at the 1972 meeting of the American Psychiatric Association was delivered by an economist on the topic of the work instinct in America (Kreps 1973). The choice of subject and speaker underscored psychiatrists' increasing involvement with and interest in their patients' lives outside of hospitals and clinics. Dr. Kreps noted that "occupational discrepancies [between expectations and realities] exist more often, and are greater, among psychiatric outpatients than among non-patients" (ibid.:182). Concern for this circumstance, and the dismal employment histories of many long-term psychiatric patients (see Turner 1977:33; Anthony et al. 1972, 1978; Black 1957), have led to an increasing incorporation of vocational programs into the overall psychosocial rehabilitation effort.

A current psychiatric attitude in this regard is expressed by Mendel and Allen (1978:187):

> In our society one of the most important aspects of self-hood is the ability to earn a living and be productive. This ability is closely tied to self-esteem for the individual. Our client population consists of individuals who can not make it in society, who can not support themselves, who resort to "going crazy" as a way of getting help. The metaphor of treatment is rescue from crisis and rehabilitation for work. . . . The advantage of the work rehabilitation model is that it allows us to take as given certain facts of society. One of these facts is that our majority-middle class culture expects every individual who is an adult to support himself and to work. Quite apart from whether this makes sense in terms of national economics or political philosophy, it is a fact of our time that the work ethic persists and each individual has to live within that ethic. [See also Simmons 1965:4, 15][1]

The treatment program based on this judgment has demonstrated itself as highly aversive to many patients (47 percent have chosen not to participate). Among those who participate, 81 percent remain in treatment, and 23 percent of these hold competitive jobs (ibid.:195). The remainder are seeking jobs, are in school, or are working in sheltered workshops.

Many other community treatment programs focus on the employment problems of their clients. For example, Fairweather et al. (1969) found that experimental patients treated in a lodge-type (group living) system in the community had significantly higher rates of full-time employment than did a control group not living in the lodge. Those who moved away from the lodge were not able to sustain the higher employment rate; however, the lodge group started and operated its own janitorial service, which accounted for

1. Etzioni (1977) and Kreps (1973) have challenged this presumption about the prevalence and propriety of the work ethic in America. Says Kreps, "Deterioration in the quality and meaning of work has contributed to the drive for a reduction in the amount of time spent on the job" (p. 180). Etzioni adds: "A significant portion of Americans aged 55 to 64 *choose* not to work. . . . They choose in effect, to trade income (and later higher pensions) for an earlier re-casting of life to make more room for leisure, study, public life or some combination thereof—indeed, to make some nonwork activity their central life interest" (p. 18).

much of the difference between the groups. It should be noted that the patient business was begun because outside, meaningful employment did not seem accessible to lodge members.

Mosher and Menn (1978), in a fascinating and innovative approach to community treatment, found no significant differences in employment between experimentals and hospitalized controls at intervals of six and twelve months. Fountain House (Beard 1978), which began as an outpatient clubhouse, now administers an employment program that has been markedly successful in gaining the cooperation of the business community in providing jobs for its members. Stein and Test (1980) report that their community-treated experimental subjects spent significantly less time unemployed and significantly more time in sheltered employment than did their hospitalized controls. There was, however, no significant difference between the two groups with regard to competitive employment (ibid.). Turner (1977) reports comparatively high rates of employment for diagnosed schizophrenic patients who were living in the community but were not involved with a specific community treatment program. These rates were nearly equal to those of the general population and were far better than any other figures reported to date.

Perhaps because employment data are relatively objective and because of the mental health system's reflection of societal values regarding work (exemplified by Mendel and Allen), many treatment programs, in addition to procuring employment for their clients, also report these figures and use them as measures of social adjustment. These studies show that 30 to 50 percent of patients work within the six-month period after discharge, but these numbers dwindle to 20 to 30 percent by one year (Minkoff 1978:24). Community treatment programs such as PACT and Fountain House, which actively focus on work, tend to declare more success while the active push for employment lasts, but, over time, a deterioration in employment rates also occurs among their clients. Whatever the direction of causation between poor employment participation and mental illness (especially chronic schizophrenia) the correlations have been consistently reported (see Turner 1977:32–33 and Turner and Gartell 1978 for reviews of many studies).

Increasing attention is being paid to the dismal employment experiences of chronic psychiatric patients, not only for therapeutic and benevolent reasons but also because of mounting distress over the enormous direct and indirect financial costs to our society of short- and long-term mental illness. Bluntly stated, this is an expensive problem. Money allocations at federal, state, and local levels are scarce and are critically scrutinized. The latest available figures placed the cost for direct and indirect care to the mentally ill at nearly $37 billion in 1974 (Levine and Willner 1976). It has also been estimated that the cost to the country in 1971 for disability due to mental illness approached $17 billion (Levine and Levine 1975:50).

THE GOLDEN RULE: HE WHO HAS THE GOLD MAKES THE RULES[2]

It would be difficult to overestimate the emphasis placed by both staff and clients at PACT on securing and maintaining employment. Clients often greeted each other not with "Hello, how are you?" but with "You working?" or "Got a job yet?" The amount of time devoted by staff to rectifying employment problems, facilitating procurement of work, and discussing work programs for and with clients, equaled or exceeded that expended for any other problem area encountered by clients. The prevailing attitude among staff was not unlike that previously expounded by Mendel and Allen. To understand this focus, the multiple meanings associated with employment among both groups must be considered.

Among the clients in the project, part of their employment orientation was built in. One of the admission criteria had been a poor recent employment history. Several clients said that they had entered the program primarily because they had been unable to obtain or retain employment and because PACT had proposed to help them in this regard. Among staff, employment was viewed as a vital component of independent living. Working was also seen as a means of utilizing or structuring time, of learning to interact with others, as a sign of a client's responsibility for self, and as an oppor-

2. From a wall poster hanging in the office of the head nurse and service chief at PACT.

tunity to enhance self-esteem. Working was considered so important that some clients and their families were asked to maintain contact on the basis of performance, attendance, and/or procurement of employment.[3]

On the whole, staff members expressed consistent values and views of the importance of work and of their frustrations with income-maintenance programs. I asked each staff member (B) several questions related to these issues, and I received the following illustrative responses:

A. What do you think are the biggest obstacles to curing people, or to people's improving in PACT?

B. I don't believe in curing. I'm going to have to take a while on this one. Probably the biggest obstacle, I think, is employment.

A. Lack of employment opportunities?

B. I just keep seeing, you know, people coming through the program and having to settle for less—other than Goodwill or MOC—I think Goodwill is probably the better "agency," but even their job placement is poor. You know, we as a staff sit around and really push employment, and when we have to settle for, you know, a volunteer placement.

A. Dishwashing, janitor, industry.

B. And try to get job placements and people just don't do it. They keep saying, that, you know, their quotas are filled, or what is it—Title 19 or 16. I think we as a staff aren't large enough, or we can't actively go out and change the, you know, the system. We have to sit back and wait for the system to change itself.

A. Do you think it's just the nature of unemployment in Madison? Or do you think there's more that could be done if you had more time?

3. Over time, emphasis on this orientation has lessened somewhat among staff. Many have refocused their treatment efforts and have sought to provide "structured work experiences" that have not necessarily involved competitive employment. Enormous amounts of time and energy had been directed toward matching jobs with clients, often with few durable results. As a consequence, values have altered. This process of change was just beginning as I concluded my research period. The enthusiasm and commitment I observed and report here regarding the types of work is somewhat outdated; however, it was the prevailing attitude at PACT when our subjects were actively involved in treatment. For a description of the current attitude and activities, see Knoedler (1978).

B. Yeah, I think if we had more time. And I think it does settle in more staff. I don't know if we need a specific person for that area. It might be helpful.

A. Do you think it's sort of a realistic part of your psychosocial program to depend so heavily on the whole job thing? Because part of what you're saying to me is you build people up and push them, and there's nothing there for them. And if so, do you think there's an alternative area you could focus on? Especially given the majority of your people are on SSI or other forms of income maintenance.

B. I think that's a problem of society, because society is so, you know, work oriented. To have a good job, then you're a good person. Although I think a lot of our clients want to work, I think it's been ingrained in them since day one. It would be nice to have an alternative. What that alternative is right now, you know, that would have to be explored.

Another staff person gave a more client-oriented view:

A. How do you think clients feel about SSI and welfare and VA health care?

B. I think it's just so ingrained into a lot of our clients that to be a worthwhile person you have to have a job, and things like that, that it is somewhat devastating when we refer someone to SSI and put them on it. I think other people—it's, you know, they could care less—it's just, you know, this is my life, and, you know, I'm going to live it this way.

A. One perception is that there's a way of ranking among the forms of financial assistance: that city welfare is absolutely the pits, and that it is really the bottom.

B. Well, I can see why. Going to that waiting room and dealing with those people there, I mean, it makes me uncomfortable to take someone there.

A. Right. Okay. And SSI is really okay, you know. It's—it's money. And it's not that stigmatized within the group. Okay. VA's in the better form, and you call it a pension, as people do. Okay. But then—when you get outside of the group—then it becomes a problem, regardless of what it is. Do you think, as a treatment system, you deal with the reality of that way—meet the support in terms of sitting down with that person and dealing with their anger about feelings about themselves, who they are, and so on?

B. No, I don't think we do.

A. Dealing with life—not in terms of work. Leisure time—that there really is no need to work, and that, you know, your day is going to be different from jobs, you know, whatever.

B. I think we touch on that, but I don't think we really follow through that much on it. And I think that's basically from our philosophy that employment is important in a person's life. I think we are changing that philosophy, but it is a hard one to overcome, because it is so ingrained in people's minds, that, you know, all persons have to work.

Of equal significance was the role and power of money. Clients who were not working, and who had little or no money, participated in contingency programs with cash as the reward for various tasks. Those who had their own money, from savings or from other sources, were often asked to turn it over to PACT for use in their own reward and maintenance system. There were various ways a client could earn the basic daily payment of $4 for food. A client who was reluctant to attend an activity, or to do his or her laundry, might be offered $1 or $2 for so doing. Or one who was having difficulty maintaining acceptable personal hygiene might receive $2 for bathing or shaving. If clients did not complete their assignments, they would receive no payment and would be left to their own devices to obtain money for food. One client, who was particularly defiant and was reluctant to accept the work offered by the program, sent the staff this note: "You already own my stomach. Why don't you give me a fucking lobotomy?" Another was irritated by being told she should return to work at a sheltered workshop that she intensely disliked. Said she, "I don't want your money. You can't push me around anymore. I'm an adult and you can't tell me what to do." On the whole, however, the clients accepted their financial dependence on the program with less uproar than one might expect. Abe pointed out that this was because "I like the staff, and I don't like the control they have because of the money, all at the same time. It makes for a lot of ambivalence among us."

PACT also paid rent for some clients, and therefore had a decisive input into the amount these clients could spend for housing. This influence was less controversial than work-contingency programs in clients' eyes, but it did tend to concentrate clients in those hotels and residences with landlords who would accept a potentially disruptive person on short notice. Many a client was spared a night on the street by this policy.

Parents were asked not to lend or give clients money while they were in the program, and clients were discouraged from lending and borrowing from each other. Although parents generally complied, clients did not. Whether freely or under pressure, many shared the little money, food, or living space they had with a fellow client.

For staff, money was viewed as both a motivation and a source of leverage. For clients, it was a commodity, often scarce, for which they were willing to follow the "golden rule." These policies, which were operative during the research period, have since changed at PACT. These changes were brought about by staff's rethinking the paradoxical impact of creating economic dependency while attempting to nurture independence, and by changes in state policies regarding behavior modification programs. Through the use of money, staff sought to enhance a client's motivation and need to comply with the treatment program. Clients had other options—such as signing out of the program or going to city welfare. Surprisingly few did this.

A dozen clients consistently believed that work was important. No matter how reluctant they were to depend on PACT for money, they wanted powerful assistance in seeking and retaining employment. The following statement by Spanky represents the feelings of those clients who were strongly oriented toward employment.

> My main problem is I just can't work. There aren't any jobs. We have 6 percent unemployment. I went to Job Service [a state employment agency] and they said they had nothing. City welfare sent me there, and they sent me back to welfare. I had this appointment to find a job, but I went a few days early and the lady said there wouldn't be anything. I'm glad I found it out then, and didn't have my hopes up all that time. I feel helpless. I just can't seem to keep a job.

Doc, commenting on my apparent lack of employment, put it a bit differently:

> You really are lazy. Why don't you have a job yet? You ought to work, because if you don't, you'll sink lower than the people on welfare. You'll get too much rest, get moody, and get depressed. You really ought to work.

Given their orientation toward employment, it is instructive to learn that neither Doc nor Spanky was able to hold a job for more than several weeks during the research period, and that both received a permanent monthly-assistance subsidy. This paradoxical acknowledgment of the import of work, both for income and for keeping oneself from becoming "moody and depressed," combined with little or no success at obtaining a job, characterized many in the group. Some were simply paying lip service to the work ethic. Others genuinely believed in the value of work, and they had negative self-images for not being gainfully employed.

The employment program at PACT was constructed around a graduated, hierarchical system that ran a gamut from volunteer work and sheltered employment, to Division of Vocational Rehabilitation (DVR), to subsidized on-the-job training (OJT), and on to competitive work. Upon admission, those clients who were perhaps grossly psychotic, or whose work skills were unknown to staff, or for whom no other job slots were immediately available, were placed in the St. Benedict Center workshop (familiarly termed St. Ben's). Twenty-two clients worked there at some point during treatment.

The Center was a working Benedictine enclave that specialized in providing facilities for retreats and meetings for various groups. Most of the work there involved janitoring, general maintenance, housekeeping, and food preparation. This setting was selected by staff as an ideal environment in which to observe and evaluate clients' work habits, to train clients in the skills necessary to execute these types of jobs, and to facilitate some involvement in productive activity during the day. In addition, the sisters and staff at St. Ben's were considered to be better-than-average providers of supportive, nonjudgmental supervision and guidance. St. Ben's had few employees who might be disturbed or disrupted by clients and PACT staff, and this relative quiet seemed conducive to providing a calm, worklike atmosphere. Furthermore, St. Ben's, located approximately five miles outside Madison, provided a practical deterrent to clients who might like to flee the work scene. Those clients who were on time were transported by staff to and from St. Ben's at designated pickup points. Those who were late had to find their own means of transportation, or they were charged for rides occasionally given by staff.

For two weeks during the research period, I worked at St. Ben's. Though instructive, the experience was strange, for none of the sisters or employees were told that I was *not* a client. After the second day of being carefully (though subtly) stared at by the St. Ben's staff, I began to feel a little suspicious and trapped. Notions of *One Flew Over the Cuckoo's Nest* stabbed occasionally, and I developed a creeping discomfort, wondering if anyone there would believe me if I confided my "real" identity. My behavior was not contrived, though I did not initiate conversation as often as I normally would, nor did I respond with customary spontaneity, partly because I was feeling or looking flat from taking Prolixin, and partly because I did not want to draw attention to myself.

On the whole, the staff were pleasant enough, but they spoke to me as if I would not understand them, that is, slowly, with simple words, and with emphasis on distinct, loud pronunciation. It was as if they expected that I were hard of hearing or retarded. They were also protective, almost maternal. When moving furniture, I was not allowed to lift moderately heavy objects; sharp utensils were carefully explained in the kitchen; and I was allowed to shovel snow outside only at the insistence of PACT staff. The sisters preferred that I work in the kitchen because I was female.

Most of the time that I worked in the kitchen, I was joined by the hired cook, several sisters, and by Kitty, another female client. For those two weeks, Kitty's and my jobs were monotonous, repetitive, and singularly unrewarding. We peeled apples—hundreds of apples. When we were not doing that, we washed dishes, we cut up carrots and celery, or, for a treat, we made seventy-five peanut butter sandwiches. The cook made friendly conversation, but it was clear to us that we would not be allowed actually to cook, and that the simple tasks we had were carefully watched. When we worked well or efficiently, the cook seemed surprised. When the sisters stopped in to check on us, we were talked about as if we were not there. In retrospect, the most important insight I gained from St. Ben's concerned my response to being treated as dull, unintelligent, or retarded—not crazy. The low expectations, kindly manner, careful supervision, modulated voice tone—all conveyed messages to this effect. My response was to slow down in accordance with this standard and to begin to feel very sorry for myself as such an unfortunate, dim-witted character beset with problems.

It should be noted that the PACT staff also perceived this deference and demeanor among the sisters and St. Ben's staff. When a client was reprimanded or disciplined by PACT personnel, friction was sometimes created between the staffs. If a client were misbehaving and refusing to work, but refusing to leave when asked, the police might be called by PACT staff. The sisters did not appreciate this method of holding a client responsible for his or her behavior. The St. Ben's staff clearly did not adopt this stance but made allowances for clients' unfortunate circumstances.

The step after St. Ben's varied for clients. Some clients ceased work for the most part after leaving St. Ben's. Some moved horizontally to sheltered workshops, known as the Madison Opportunity Center (MOC) and Goodwill Industries (GWI). MOC was ranked lower by clients and staff on the skill and competence ladder than was GWI. Some clients began on-the-job training subsidized by the State Division of Vocational Rehabilitation (DVR). One DVR counselor handled all PACT clients, meeting weekly with staff to plan and discuss employment programs for clients. A few clients found competitive jobs.

Competitive employment was the goal ideally sought, until it became clear to staff that a client could not or would not manage this type of work. This "give up" message was communicated in a number of ways. If a client had demonstrated incapacitating anxiety, disorganized thinking, or bizarre, disruptive interpersonal conduct at St. Ben's, GWI or MOC were recommended. If there were no positions available in either of these places, a volunteer job might be found for the interim period. To some, the GWI or MOC alternatives were presented as but another step in the process of getting a competitive job. To others, GWI and MOC were presented as *the* job. Those who seemed capable and willing were helped in competitive job-seeking by staff. A client who disagreed with the GWI or MOC decision might seek a job on his or her own, but without the direct help of staff. Nonetheless, staff were indirectly supportive, feeling that if the person could succeed, even in defiance, at least he or she was motivated and active.

The above evaluation and placement process posed some dilemmas for staff. On the one hand, they did not wish to engender in the client (or themselves) hopes and expectations for employment which exceeded the capacities and motivation of the client. The danger of precipitating feelings of failure, inadequacy, and frustration was apparent to them. But the desire to explore possibilities and to encourage motivation in the client spurred them to give trial to the highest feasible level of employment. The persistently reluctant, evasive, or fearful client could after a time convince all concerned that any work, competitive or otherwise, was not viable for him or her. Staff would give up after running out of resources, patience, and hope. Clients either got to this point just ahead of staff or soon followed suit.

When and if a client did secure a job, PACT staff would frequently visit him at the job or would meet with him at some time during the day. This was especially true for volunteer and OJT slots. In general, clients disliked this practice, feeling that PACT was "looking over my shoulder," or not wanting co-workers to see them with staff. Some, however, appreciated a supportive contact on the job.

Two lunch counters near the PACT house became "friends of PACT" in that they would frequently hire clients for dishwashing or other work, often on short notice or when a client was not in presentable shape for work. The owners would at times call and ask for a client to help. Staff coordinated with these employers, enforcing contingency programs and making sure that no client was abusing their good auspices.

Within the above framework, it will be useful to examine more carefully clients' attitudes, desires, and actions regarding work, utilizing three sources of information: aggregate and individual figures on clients' work placement, CAS questionnaire responses, and observation of and interviews with clients. A numerical overview of actual employment behavior serves as introduction.

Table 3 charts type and frequency of employment, and reasons for leaving work during the research period, for individual clients and for the total group. Four categories of employment are delineated: (1) *sheltered*—St. Benedict's, Goodwill, and Madison Opportunity Center; (2) *subsidized*—person's salary contributed to either by DVR or by one of two federal-local programs, the Comprehensive Employment and Training Act (CETA) or Project Mainstream;[4] (3) *competitive*—any salaried job that a client obtained in

4. See "Subsidized Jobs" (pp. 144–145) for an explanation of these programs.

TABLE 3

Employment Type: Frequency of and Reasons for Termination

Client	Sheltered			Subsidized	Competitive	Volunteer	Quit	Fired
	St. Ben's	MOC	GWI					
Steven	—	—	2	—	2x	1	2	1
Phillip	Yes	—	1x	—	1	—	1	1
Joy	Yes	—	—	—	1	3	4	—
Dorothy	—	—	2x	—	1, 1x	—	3	—
Herb	—	—	—	1xc	1x	1x	2	—
Dennis	Yes x	—	—	1xm	1, 1, 1x	—	1	1
George	—	—	—	—	—	1	1	1
Doc	Yes x	—	1x, 1	—	1, 1	3	1	2
Sam	Yes	—	—	—	1	4	1	—
Betsy	—	1x	—	—	1	—	1	—
Beth	Yes	—	—	—	—	—	1	—
Kitty	Yes x	—	—	—	1x, 1	—	2	—
Agatha	—	—	1x, 1	1xm, 1xd	1x	3	3	—
Gail	—	—	—	3xm	—	1x	—	1
Spanky	Yes x	—	1x, 1	1d	4	2	—	6
B. J.	Yes x	—	—	2d	—	—	1	1
Christie	—	—	—	—	—	2x	2	—
Rod	Yes	—	1x	—	2	—	3	—
Alice	—	—	1x	—	1	1x, 2	1	—
Walter	Yes	—	—	1d	—	4	1	1
Andy	—	—	—	—	—	1	—	—
Charlotte	—	1	—	—	—	1	1	—
Jerry	—	—	—	1d	1, 1x	—	—	2
Mabel	—	—	2x	—	—	2x	2	—
Martha	—	—	1x	—	—	1	1	—
Wally	—	—	1x	1d	—	—	1	1
Jack	Yes x	—	—	—	—	1x	1	—
Cy	Yes x	1	—	1xc	—	1	1	2
Myrtle	Yes	1x	—	1d	—	3	1	1
Robert	Yes	—	—	—	3	—	2	1
Morris	—	1x	—	—	—	—	1	1
Alf	Yes	—	1x	1xd, 1d	2	—	1	4
Tim	—	—	1x	—	—	1	—	1
Humphrey	Yes x	1	—	—	1	2	1	1
Ben	—	1x	1x	—	1	1x	2	1
Abe	—	—	—	1xd	2x	1x	2	1
Stanley	Yes x	—	1x	—	—	—	1	—
Alex	Yes x	—	1x	—	3	—	2	2
Annie	Yes x	—	2x	—	1	2	2	2
Tex	Yes	—	1x	—	2, 1x	—	1	1
Sadie	—	—	1x	—	1x	2	2	1
Harold	—	—	—	1x, 1xc	2, 1x	—	1	1
Pogo	—	1x	—	—	—	—	—	—
Totals 43	21	8	19	14	26	25	57	38

KEY: x = longer than four weeks; d = Division of Vocational Rehabilitation subsidy; c = Comprehensive Employment Training Act position; m = Project Mainstream position.

open competition with nonpatients, with no special consideration given for disability; and (4) *volunteer*—work done for no salary, or for pay only from PACT, at a variety of social agencies and service organizations such as Red Cross, Wisconsin Division on Aging, Madison Safety Council, and so forth.

As is evident from table 3, most of the work that lasted more than four weeks was sheltered. The competitive pattern showed frequent, short-lived employment. It is interesting to note that clients quit various jobs more frequently than they were fired, though this total may be biased. Clients often quit before they could be terminated. Although twenty-six clients held some type of competitive job during the research period, only twelve of these were for periods of longer than four weeks. Seventeen never had a competitive job, though everyone did volunteer work or had a sheltered job at some time.

Another means of viewing clients' employment activities is to assess at a given time how many are working or not working, and at what type of jobs. In April 1977 five held competitive jobs and five were in sheltered workshops. Thirty were not working, and one had a volunteer position. In November 1979 five held competitive jobs, while an equal number were engaged in sheltered employment. One continued in a subsidized job. Twenty-six were not working and three had part-time volunteer jobs. The five competitive jobs were held by the same persons.

From the above, it should be clear that from 71 to 78 percent of the group were fairly constantly unemployed. But these numbers tell only part of the story. An examination of clients' attitudes toward, and experiences with, the world of work is necessary to complete the analysis.

SHELTERED WORKSHOPS

Excluding St. Benedict's, twenty-six clients worked for varying lengths of time at Goodwill Industries and at the Madison Opportunity Center. Nineteen worked at the former and seven at the latter. One worked in both places. The great majority of these placements were for two months or longer, though the range ran from several days to over one year.

Both workshops were designed to cater to persons who were physically, psychologically, and/or developmentally disabled.

Goodwill Industries (GWI) is part of a national network of facilities that exists for the purpose of training, retraining, and employing persons who can not obtain or retain other work. The financial mainstay of GWI is its practice of collecting the material discards of the community, restoring such articles as furniture, clothing, and household goods, and marketing them to the public at greatly reduced prices. In a sense, GWI serves an analogous restorative function with its employees. Clients are engaged in activities that range from sorting and cleaning clothing, to repairing small appliances, to training to operate office machines. All this is done under close supervision. A client who works at GWI has a work supervisor and a counselor, and has access to social workers and other help-giving professionals. The facility also operates an after-hours recreational program for clients and provides services, such as job placement, for those who are ready for or capable of outside employment. The State DVR often subsidizes the starting salary of a client at GWI, and it may also help with rent and clothing purchases. Any client, however, who is granted "extended employment," becomes an employee of GWI, whose salary is eventually paid in total by the facility. Extended employment indicates that GWI is probably the end of the line vocationally, or that a long period of adjustment is ahead before any other work situation can be considered. A criteria known as 'competitive' is set by the GWI staff, and the clients' performance is measured against this. Salaries are based on the competitive performance a client displays at GWI. This may range from 50¢ per hour during the initial evaluation period to minimum wage during the extended period.

The Madison Opportunity Center (MOC) caters to a somewhat different population. Developmentally disabled (retarded) and severely physically handicapped persons comprise the bulk of their clientele, though some severely psychiatrically disturbed persons also work there. MOC work is less skilled than that at GWI, and the supervision is more intensive. Few if any MOC clients are on the way to employment elsewhere. Their tasks consist of placing loops on drapery rods for a local manufacturer, wrapping plastic utensils for a local restaurant, wrapping and stamping candy, or making candles. DVR subsidy is also utilized for MOC clients, though the wages there tend to be lower than at GWI and are based on a piecework quota system. Counselors and supervisors are provided as is a recreational program.

The staffs of both workshops worked closely with PACT personnel, each helping the other to implement behavior contingency programs for mutual clients. The MOC staff would, for example, call PACT daily to let them know if clients were on time for work or were there at all, and how the day had proceeded. Often, PACT staff attended group meetings regarding clients' performance at both facilities. If a client had left GWI without authorization, or had been asked to leave, PACT staff would frequently be called.

Clients' views of MOC and GWI were mixed. Half a dozen seemed to enjoy the social acquaintances, but all had negative to ambivalent feelings about the nature of the work and the setting. The CAS responses showed, at baseline, that thirteen persons were working. Eight of these were in sheltered situations, one was volunteer, and two each were subsidized and competitive.

Two questions revealed how persons felt about work in general and about their present jobs:

2. How do you feel about working?

Dislike very much	2
Dislike some	2
Like some	3
Like	2
Like very much	4

7. How do you feel about your present job?

Like very much	1
Like	2
Like some	1
Dislike some	7
Dislike very much	2

These responses revealed that, although the clients who were working were not averse to employment per se, they had markedly negative feelings about their present placement. Those in competitive and subsidized employment accounted for the positive responses in question 7, above.

One of the reasons clients disliked work at MOC and GWI was the extremely low pay. The CAS response was revealing.

9. How much do you earn an hour right now?

Less than $1	4
$1	2
Between $1-2	6
Over $4	1

All but one person, who was employed in construction work, earned less than minimum wage and under $2. Half earned $1 or under. In addition, ten did not like working full time, though most worked a six- and not an eight-hour day. All were certain, however, that they were capable of full-time work. Also, everyone thought his or her performance at work was not what it should be.

But when asked about changing their jobs, only four indicated that they wished to do so. Some of this seeming inertia may have derived from clients' concern they could not obtain other employment. Seven indicated that they would not even try to qualify for a more highly skilled job. Six, however, were certain that they would make the attempt. But, with the exception of two persons, none reported that they were seeking other employment.

These responses would seem inconsistent but for the fact that although clients disliked their work situations and performances, their anxieties, self-doubts, and perceived inadequacies regarding nonsheltered employment outweighed the negatives expressed above. Even though their work circumstances served to lower their self-esteem even further, they did not wish to risk change or possible failure.

Alice provided an example of a client who tried persistently to leave GWI, confirming to herself that she could be hired nowhere else. She had worked at GWI for nearly one year. Though she disliked her task of sorting clothes, the low wages, and the style of supervision, she could not find another job. Over the course of six months, she had applied for more than two dozen state clerical positions, for which she had qualified on the basis of her Civil Service test scores. No jobs were forthcoming. Interview after interview ended in rejection. When she expressed the desire to obtain competitive employment, Alice was discouraged from seeking it by both PACT and GWI staffs. Her only way out of GWI, she thought, was to go to school:

> I hate my job. I just hate it. It takes the mind of a seven-year-old to work there. It's boring. My supervisor is like a slave driver. I tried so many Civil Service jobs you wouldn't believe it. Sometimes two to three job interviews a week. But no one would hire me. No one. They never did tell me why. I bet I'll be stuck at Goodwill forever. . . . The people at Goodwill are against school. They told me I couldn't get a job even if I finished school. They said I'm not spontaneous enough, and that's why I don't get jobs. They told me I act too deliberate and I don't react fast enough. I don't believe them, so it doesn't matter anyway. Actually, I'd like to do nothing. I don't like to work. I'll never get a real job anyway.

Despite GWI's advice, Alice quit her job and attended technical school. Though she made excellent grades, she was unable to find employment. She entered an anxious, psychotic period. Upon recovery, she engaged in volunteer work for several hours per day.

Alice's experience illustrated the predicament of the dissatisfied or unwilling sheltered-workshop employee. Alice had no feasible alternatives, but she deplored the only available work. Ironically, despite these extremely negative feelings about working at GWI, Alice maintained an active social life with her co-workers. She became romantically involved with a string of men who also worked there. In almost schoolgirl fashion, she seemed to have a new man every week. Alice loaned money and gave food and shelter to all these men, and she was often openly exploited by them. At the same time, she repeatedly told me that they were "no good" and that she would drop any of them for "someone with a lot of money and a good job." Perhaps her behavior was best understood as an adaptive strategy, an adjustment to the seemingly unchangeable realities of her life. This adaptation found Alice participating in a work situation with persons whom she evaluated in a most derogatory fashion.

Others who worked at GWI made similar adaptations. Dorothy acknowledged that her ambivalence about GWI derived from the low status and pay. She spent many months in silent struggle—walking off the job, coming in late, causing disturbances. But each time she quit, she found herself destitute, financially and interpersonally. And so, she would return, saying, "I really hate it there. It's the status, you know. But, I guess I'd rather be poor than insane."

Perhaps the most frequent reason given by clients for disliking MOC and GWI was an abhorrence for the retarded and physically handicapped persons who also worked there. Association with these people was most difficult for clients. Many illustrated this point by repeating versions of a joke with the punch line "I may be crazy, but I'm not stupid." Alf put it this way, "I don't like to be around people who are mentally inferior. It makes me feel bad. I'm not like that." One of the doctors told Alf he was being a snob. Ben said of MOC, "I have the worst job. I'm stupid for working there. It's boring and I only make $10 a week. The people that work there are dumb. I must be, too, if I work there. No, I'm not." Wally stated simply that it was "demeaning to work at Goodwill." Doc's observations expressed feelings shared by others in the group:

> . . . working there with all those retarded people. I just couldn't take it. But Goodwill isn't as drastic as MOC. MOC is the bottom of the bucket. It makes you feel like you're retarded, too, or at least that somebody thinks you are. How do they expect me to feel when they tell me I should work there? Man, it's just too depressing, looking around at who's there and knowing you are too. I feel sorry for those people, but not enough to work with them. They can't even talk to you.

On the whole, clients saw GWI and MOC as the most pessimistic indication of their inadequacies and differentness. Being urged to work at either place could produce panic, defiance, or depression. Even Pogo, who had blossomed socially at MOC and had worked there for nearly two years, admitted, "Well, I guess work is so boring. I mean, Ben and me, we decided it was so bad we should kill ourselves to get out of it. I mean, there isn't any place else to go. But, gee. I don't want to stay at MOC forever." His friend, Ben, had had an illustrious career at MOC, having frequently been kicked out for the day because of his disruptive behavior. Soon after discharge, Ben quit MOC and seldom if ever saw any of his former co-workers.

Cy absolutely refused to accept that he was a candidate for GWI. The following exchange took place between him and Alice:

A. Hey Cy, I heard you just walked out of Goodwill and didn't come back. What's the matter with you? Don't you like it there?

C. I won't work there. I won't work there.

A. But they're just trying to evaluate you and find out what's the best job for you.

C. They won't find me a job. Look at you.

A. Well, if you'd just try it.

C. Yeah, and end up there when I'm forty-five like a damn idiot.

Several weeks later, as Cy continued to refuse GWI, he had no alternative but to go on city welfare for financial support. However, that also seemed to him to be a trap: "I just can't go to welfare because they think I should work, and I can't. I can only go to Goodwill, and I hate it there." One month later, Cy attempted to resolve his dilemmas by jumping out of the window of his fourth-floor YMCA room.

Though this final example presents a dramatic and unusual response to the sheltered workshop message, it suggests the potential impact of sheltered employment on clients' feelings about themselves and their futures. They seemed willing to acknowledge psychiatric difficulties, but they were most averse to equating these with handicap or disability. Being crazy was not as negatively valued by them as was the permanent and tangible condition of retardation or physical handicap. They did not wish to perceive themselves thus, but being sent to GWI or MOC blared this message to them. If they rejected this option, volunteer work or unemployment probably awaited, but either of these represented more dignified alternatives. In accepting GWI or MOC, they associated and identified themselves with others upon whom they looked down.

There was, it should be noted, a positive side to the sheltered workshop experience in terms of its impact on clients' self-image. It provided one situation in which they could feel more capable, competent, and productive than others. As Morris explained, "There are only a few normals here at MOC. There are a lot of handicapped people here. *We* are in the minority."

To summarize, most clients had strongly negative feelings about sheltered employment. Their reasons included low wages, the monotonous nature of the work, its stigmatizing impact, their poor performance, and their aversion to retarded and physically handicapped co-workers.[5] Three clients left GWI for competitive employment. At present, two retain these jobs. The remainder of those who were in sheltered employment quit or were terminated. They are presently not working or are working only sporadically. Only one person remains at MOC. Two of the original eight left after discharge from PACT, and the others left during treatment. Three clients returned of their own volition to GWI after discharge. In general, sheltered workshop employment decreased sharply among the group after discharge.

VOLUNTEER WORK

Volunteer jobs held an ambiguous place in the work hierarchy. For some, volunteer work indicated an inability to manage even GWI or MOC. For others, it implied a less extreme alternative, attesting to their possession of good work skills but their inability to use them because of anxiety, reluctance, or psychotic symptoms. For still others, volunteer placement represented a holding plateau—a place to spend time until another position became available, or until they were functioning well enough to find competitive work. In some instances, the DVR counselor required that clients demonstrate their motivation and stability by doing volunteer work for a period of time before he would consider counseling them. Twenty-five clients had volunteer jobs at some time during the research period. Some had as many as five different placements.

Clients' attitudes toward volunteer work, as elicited by the CAS, ran the full range:

28. In general, how do you feel about volunteer work?

Like very much	6

5. Hogarty (1971:201) suggests another reason for this negative experience: "Unfortunately, the model of vocational rehabilitation for the mentally ill remains closely tied to rehabilitation of the physically handicapped. Thus many rehabilitation counselors are unprepared to deal with the residual limitations of chronic mental illness."

Like	4
Like some	7
Dislike some	6
Dislike	8
Dislike very much	4

The volunteer placement was reported by most clients as a positive experience, but they viewed it as "pretend work" or "Mickey Mouse." Three were asked to become regular employees after several months at a job. All accepted, but they stayed only a short period of time in this status.

Staff attempted to simulate a "real" work setting, urging co-workers to place responsible expectations on clients, meeting with supervisors and clients to facilitate feedback or communication among them regarding the clients' behavior in the work setting. Many supervisors and co-workers were reluctant to do this. They preferred to avoid reprimanding clients, making allowances for their behavior because they were experiencing psychiatric problems. This was precisely the type of deference PACT staff was attempting to change. The philosophy at PACT was that if a client were held responsible for his or her misconduct and ceased to receive any kind of gain from it, the behavior could be altered and eventually eliminated. In this sense, the PACT concept of the crazy or sick role followed clients throughout the community treatment setting.

Compared to the sheltered workshop, clients viewed volunteer jobs as providing a more benign atmosphere in that the handicapped identity was not thrust upon them. But they were well aware of the contrived nature of this setting. Motivation to perform well was customarily low. Inclement weather, the offer of a drink, or almost any distraction could convince a client not to appear for work. Volunteer work was seen by some as a way to combat boredom or loneliness—two feelings often experienced by the unemployed majority of the group.

NOT WORKING

Clients who did not have any sort of job for more than several weeks or days at a time comprised the majority of the group. This was especially true after discharge, or when the intensive treatment phase had ended. During treatment, most were kept busy with St. Ben's or with volunteer work, if competitive work were not possible and if sheltered options were either unavailable or rejected. At discharge, or when intense treatment ended, twenty-seven clients were not working. Five of these did not complete the CAS questionnaire.

Of the twenty-one who did complete the CAS, more than 75 percent indicated that they were not actively seeking employment. Thirteen expressed some displeasure with unemployment. Eight reported that they enjoyed not working. These same eight persons thought they would not find work soon, and indicated that they were unable to work full time. Those thirteen who remained in each of the above questions, felt they would probably find work and were capable of full-time employment. It is important to know that each of the forty-three clients was unemployed for at least some time during treatment, so my resources for clients' attitudes about not working were not restricted to the twenty-one who answered the questionnaire. In addition, clients often expressed thoughts and feelings not entirely consistent with their behavior. I encountered not only a variety of attitudes about working and not working but also a variety of rationales as expounded by clients.

Fifteen persons in this group were uninterested in conventional employment. Their reasons ranged from the restrictions of their symptoms, to deciding that simply getting through the day imposed a sufficient task for their attention. Morris represented one of these positions in his assertion to staff: "I'm a little too mentally ill to go to work today." A variant of this stance was expressed by George, whose definition of work differed from the usual. As he put it: "I never have any intention of having a paying job again. I work harder than most people." His "work" consisted of attending religious services and classes more than thrice weekly, conducting a public ministry, "sharing the peace and beauty of God in our lives," and handing out money to children. Even though his religious orientation eventually weakened, he still did not care to pursue material gain. Sadie shared this view. She considered my questions about employment pointless. She preferred to ponder the nature of her own and others' existence, to wander about meeting and talking with people. Once, when discussing this research project, she commented, "That's the trouble with you anthropologists, all you talk about is culture. The only thing culture explains is culture." (Many a social scientist might agree.) At times, Sadie expressed a desire to become a nurse (a common theme among clients), but she did not wish to go through the necessary training to reach this goal.

Several clients expressed the view that simply maintaining themselves one day at a time occupied all available energy. Phillip provided a good example. He had worked as a beautician prior to his PACT experience. After working at St. Benedict's, he returned to beauty school, passed his state licensing test, and lasted one week at his job placement. GWI was the next step for him, though he struggled ferociously with the implications of this move. Eventually, he was terminated there, and he decided that it was more important to feel stable and comfortable with himself than to undergo the stress of working:

> I really have learned a lot. You see, when I was nineteen, I had a great job, a beautiful apartment, lots of friends and all that. But it was just building up inside of me. I was under a lot of pressure. Oh, I used to travel, and it was really nice, and then I found myself without anything. No money; no friends. I see now that life doesn't end at twenty-three. I felt that way before. I hated myself and what I was doing for so long. I still have problems, but it's not like it was. What I need to do now is learn to enjoy myself and life. It's a big accomplishment. It may not seem like much to you. But it's a full-time job.

Another attitude expressed by members of this group was a staggering lack of motivation to work. Jack vacillated between wanting to catalyze his inertia and not caring whether he accomplished anything:

> I don't have any drive. There's nothing I really feel like working for. I guess I wouldn't mind being a song writer. But I never wrote anything worthwhile. No, I'd like to be an architect. I'd like to design bizarre houses. I'll never do it, because I'd lose interest. I'd like to do something with my life, but what I don't know. I guess maybe I'll be an 85-year-old derelict on welfare. I'm wasting my life, but I really don't care. It's terrible the way I waste myself, but it just doesn't matter.

The changes of heart in this one conversation were reflective of Jack's ambivalent feelings about his own capacities. Despite his assertions, he was a good song writer. One of his songs seemed to express his wit, apathy and indirection. His desire to disappear and hide seem to me to poignantly reflect his lack of meaningful place in society. He could not find anything to do with his life, and, cynically, he did not care.

> *If I were blue*
> *I'd hide in the sky.*
> *And if I weren't true*
> *I'd hide in a lie.*
> *And if I weren't there,*
> *No one would care.*
> *'Specially not me.*

Others who were unmotivated were less cynical, stating simply, "I don't want to work. Why should I? I always get fired or end up quitting." Still more evaded my questions with promises of future occupational endeavors.

Nearly a dozen clients expressed strong desires to work, but they were so nervous and disorganized, or they behaved so strangely that, through repeated failures, they learned they could not be employed. Rod provided a pointed example:

> When I'm on the job, it gets to the point where I just can't work. Everything goes wrong. I start my dreaming, my horrible dreaming. I don't like it, and I want help being set free from it. If I am ever to hold a job I have to be set free from thoughts of spacemen, gods, superheroes, and demons.

Doc presented another aspect of the predicament:

> I used to be able to work. Oh, one thing usually just leads to another and I end up getting fired. I'd like to be able to work, but I just can't keep a job. I don't want to do something that's boring and menial. I like to have fun.

Part of the dilemma for this subgroup was their aspiration to employment requiring skills, experience, and peace of mind that they did not have. Attractive competitive employment was not accessible to them, given their deficits and poor work histories. They were unwilling to accept the menial or sheltered work that was available.

Competitive work, with very few exceptions, meant dishwashing, maintenance, or janitorial tasks. These were low-paying, monotonous, low-esteem jobs and held little lure for these already reluctant members of the work force. Their tenure in these positions was short.

Certainly another and major reason for these clients' failure to seek or to hold jobs was the fact that many did not have to do so in order to survive. They could receive financial assistance from a number of agencies and programs.

SUBSIDIZED JOBS

Five clients qualified for special employment programs designed to offer competitive experience to those who might otherwise not have the opportunity. The Comprehensive Employment Training Act (CETA) provided federal funds to be matched and administered by states, cities, and counties for employment opportunities for various types of persons. Clients who could pass the necessary tests entered a number of special programs such as Mainstream and Project Skill. As Herb explained it:

> They sometimes hear about state jobs. It's a federal program. If you're in Project Skill you can get an oral interview if you want one. You take a two-part written test, and if you pass you can go on interviews.

These programs were all consolidated under the CETA rubric, which was in turn under the aegis of the United States Department of Labor. Local sponsors were given autonomy in allocating these funds, and CETA provided caseworker job counselors for their clients.

Three clients held these positions during treatment, and two obtained them after discharge. Their placements were largely clerical positions. Though all were pleased by and proud of this accomplishment, anxiety ran high regarding their performance and the temporary nature of the jobs. Gail complained that "I'm just getting comfortable at this job, and now I have to find a new one. Mainstream can help, but I want to get one on my own. I'll feel better about myself if I do it that way." Although she was able to extend her job, she was not able to find another after its conclusion. Herb had worked primarily in a volunteer job during treatment. After discharge, he worked part-time in a fast-food restaurant, eventually securing a CETA position with the state. Securing this new job helped to precipitate a near-psychotic episode. He became paranoid, aggressive, and had some strong ideas about the imminent end of the world. This was in marked contrast to his usual easy, congenial manner. Said he months later, when he called to apologize for his behavior at our last meeting, "It's the pressure. I was starting a new job."

The purpose of the CETA programs was to aid persons in breaking an unemployed or underemployed cycle by providing a gratifying work experience. In this way, they could not only gain skills but could establish confidence and references for future employment. At present, two of the five clients who participated in CETA have obtained competitive work. Of the other three, two are not working and one has a volunteer job.

HAVING A REAL JOB

A "real job" for clients meant work that paid well (minimum wage or above) and that had been obtained by them without consideration for their "special status." Short-lived dishwashing or janitorial jobs were secured by many. Clients left these jobs as often from boredom, disinterest, or anxiety as from being fired.

Eight clients secured and retained competitive work for periods longer than three months during the research period. Two held jobs as housekeepers in hotels, and two had clerical placements. One worked at a film-processing plant, matching pictures with negatives. Another returned to his occupation as a construction worker. One client was a clerk in a small grocery, but he was fired after four months. Another worked first in maintenance and then as a delivery person for an auto parts business. With the exception of the construction worker, whose salary was ten times that of any other, all remained ambivalent about their jobs. They would express an initial sense of pride and accomplishment at having secured such work. This enthusiasm would soon wane and reports of tedium, boredom, and lack of meaning of the work would increase. It seemed that work as an ideal goal exceeded the rewards of work as an actual endeavor.

The jobs to which clients aspired were infinitely more interesting than those that were actually available to them. These ranged from nuclear engineering, to accounting, to being a stockbroker. Such fantasizing was discouraged by PACT staff. Clients learned that these hopes were unrealistic, both through the realities of everyday life and through the constraints of their own fears, symptoms, and views of themselves. As Sam said, "I was real depressed. I was thinking about dying. There's nothing I want to be. I'm thinking I'll be a maintenance man or a janitor for the rest of my life. I'll never go to college, so I can't get an interesting job."

OVERVIEW

Within this complex network of attitudes, behaviors, agencies, and experiences, it has become apparent that very few clients worked or enjoyed having a job. Many said that they valued work, but they did not make the necessary moves to obtain it. Most rejected the alternatives available to them in sheltered and volunteer work. Others expressed little or no interest in attaching themselves to this "portion of reality," as Freud put it. If Freud is correct, these clients did not hold a secure portion of community reality. They were unable to share in this, not only because of their own values and actions but because of those of others. For most of us, the aversion to work noted by Freud remains but a grumble. For these clients, it was an operative reality.

Clients demonstrated overwhelming reluctance, fear, anxiety, distaste, lack of skill and experience, and inertia regarding work. Part of this aversion stemmed from prior multiple terminations, from the wish to avoid close interaction with other persons, and from an inability to cope successfully with the actual and perceived pressures of a work setting. They substantiated for themselves and others, time and time again, that they could not or would not work. Many could probably have executed the necessary tasks in a vacuum, but they could not do so when other factors were entailed, as they always were. Absenteeism, tardiness, low productivity, and lack of motivation characterized their work performances. Some staff felt that this was deliberate, calling this behavior "sabotaging" and seeing it as a purposeful attempt to lose jobs. Whatever the interpretation, clients either did not care enough about the significance of work in the conventional setting or they could not manage even if they did care.

This means of defining and enhancing selfhood, as Mendel and Allen interpret it, is perhaps not identified by clients as such. If it is, the definition based on it must be extremely derogatory. Mikkelson (1977:83) points out that marked impairment in terms of mental status is a less potent factor for persons applying for disability payments than is the *feeling* of inadequacy and inability to work. A cycle of lack of confidence, failure, termination or quitting, and increased feelings of inadequacy is thus perpetuated. Clients are caught. If they put heavy emphasis on the social and personal significance of work, they seem destined to experience frustration, failure, and negative evaluations of themselves. If they reject the work ethic, they become alienated even further from community reality and must seek out other means of supporting themselves. This most often means becoming dependent on family and, when patience and resources run out, on an agency or institution.

The clients alone were not responsible for this gloomy circumstance. Many of the alternatives presented to them by the treatment system were markedly unattractive and were seen as humiliating and degrading. The original purpose of the sheltered workshop was therapeutic. This did not seem to have been realized for our subjects. Though I saw little overt evidence, a subtle discrimination was practiced by the community at large. Volunteer job co-workers either patronized clients, underscoring their deficits and need for special attention, or they avoided honest communication altogether. Some employers simply would not hire clients when they saw the poor work history or when they evaluated the person as a poor employment risk. Still others reluctantly offered clients a chance at menial work, firing them if another choice presented itself or if the clients' anxiety or bizarreness became apparent. A few employers worked in conjunction with PACT, thereby effectively compromising the independence from PACT and patienthood that was sought by some clients.

INCOME MAINTENANCE AND PSYCHIATRIC PATIENTHOOD

A practical question is in order. If all these people did not work, how did they support themselves? Most did not. They were involved in income maintenance programs of several sorts.

As is evident in table 4, with the exception of two persons, virtually every client received some form of financial assistance. For nearly all, this represented their economic mainstay. There were five major sources for this money: (1) various forms of federal Social Security; (2) veteran's benefits; (3) Unemployment Compensation; (4) City Welfare; and (5) family.

Social Security Payments

Three forms of Social Security were received by clients: Supplemental Security Income (SSI), Social Security Disability Insurance (SSDI), and Social Security (SS). Twenty-six received SSI, two received SSDI, and one received the Social Security accumulated by his father, who had died several years earlier.

SSI

Eight persons who received SSI did so before their entry into PACT; fourteen began during treatment; five began after discharge or change in active status. Sixteen of those who received SSI had financial guardians or payees other than themselves. Financial guardians were appointed by the court with the permission of the client. Several clients were reluctant to sign for a guardian, but they were convinced to do so by PACT staff and by their own inability to budget for a full month's period. All the financial guardians for the group were lawyers, though parents were the payees in three instances. Having a financial guardian indicated that a person was either unable or unwilling to manage his or her money. These guardians were paid for their services by the client from the income check. Most often, the duties of the financial guardian included paying the client's rent, providing a weekly or even daily allowance for food and spending, approving and providing money for necessary

TABLE 4

TYPES OF FINANCIAL ASSISTANCE TO CLIENTS

Client	SSI	VA	Welfare	SSDI	Unempl[1]	Fin. G.[2]	Family
Steven	Yes, o						
Phillip	Yes, +				Yes		
Joy							Yes
Dorothy							
Herb					Yes		
Dennis	Yes, *	Yes, *					
George				Yes*		Yes	
Doc	Yes, *						
Sam							
Betsy	Yes, +					Yes	
Beth							Yes
Kitty			Yes, x				
Agatha	Yes, +		Yes, x				
Gail			Yes, e				
Spanky	Yes, o		Yes, x				Yes
B. J.	Yes, +					Yes	
Christie	Yes, *						
Rod	Yes, +		Yes, x			Yes	
Alice				Yes, +		Yes	
Walter		Yes*					
Andy	Yes, *	Yes*				Yes	
Charlotte							
Jerry	Yes, o		Yes, x				Yes
Mabel	Yes, +					Yes	
Martha							
Wally	Yes, +				Yes	Yes	
Jack				Yes*			
Cy	Yes, +		Yes, x			Yes	
Myrtle	Yes, o		Yes, x				
Robert	Yes, +				Yes	Yes	
Morris	Yes, *					Yes	
Alf	Yes, +		Yes, x				
Tim	Yes, *					Yes	
Humphrey	Yes, *	Yes, +				Yes	
Ben	Yes, *		Yes, x				
Abe							Yes
Stanley	Yes, +		Yes, x			Yes	
Alex	Yes, +		Yes, x			Yes	
Annie	Yes, +						
Tex			Yes, x				
Sadie	Yes, o		Yes, x				Yes
Harold							
Pogo	Yes, +					Yes	
Totals	27	4	14	3	4	16	6

KEY: o = post-PACT; + = during PACT; * = pre-PACT; x = longer than four weeks;
e = emergency welfare from city.
1 = Unemployment Compensation,
2 = Financial Guardian appointed

purchases such as clothing, and accomplishing assorted budgeting tasks. At the beginning of the research period, the monthly SSI payment to persons with no other income in Wisconsin was $234. This increased to $254. All clients received the full amount.

SSI was created by Congress in 1972 and was implemented in 1974 as part of an effort to reorganize multiple existing state and federal benefit programs for the aged, blind, and disabled. It was intended as a federal cash benefit program for aged, blind, and disabled persons who had little or no other income and who needed help in meeting basic living needs, such as food, shelter, and clothing (see Blong et al. 1975; and Staff Report 1977 for a more complete explanation). The program was also intended for persons who had not worked enough to make the minimum contribution to the Social Security system.

In Wisconsin, a person who is eligible for SSI also receives Medical Assistance. In order to receive SSI under the disabled label, one must meet three criteria: (1) the physical or mental impairment must be medically determinable and medically verifiable; (2) the impairment must be expected to result in death or must have lasted or be expected to last for at least twelve months; and (3) the impairment must make the claimant unable to "engage in substantial gainful activity" (Ozawa 1977; Kochhar 1979).

SSI requires the applicant to profess his or her disability and to have such certified by a qualified physician. Under SSI regulations, a person may earn up to $200 per month and still be eligible, though benefits are reduced by fifty cents for each dollar earned in excess of $65 per month. The benefits are calculated retroactively from the time of first eligibility or when application is made, resulting often in large first payment checks. (One client received $3,000 in retroactive payments. This put him in the curious position of having to spend half of this sum quickly, for one could not have over $1,500 in assets and still receive SSI.)

For our subjects, applying for SSI required that they formally recognize their inability to work, that they demonstrate the existence of at least a year-long pattern, and that they acknowledge, as the reason for this pattern, a mental disorder to be validated by the PACT service chief or another physician. In essence, qualifying for SSI meant exposing and confronting the nature, duration and consequences of their disability, or at least presenting evidence persuasive enough to receive the money.

The practice at PACT was to apply for SSI when it became evident to staff and clients that the client could not or would not be able to survive without some form of financial assistance. Staff were generally reluctant to assist in this process until most efforts at gaining some means of self-support were exhausted. Clients were much more willing, were almost eager, to apply. In fact, at least two persons very much wanted to make application but were discouraged from doing so by staff. The service chief declined to write eligibility-substantiating reports for these persons until they made more of an effort to work. In this way, staff had some control over clients' access to SSI. Staff envisioned SSI, in part, as simply another form of dependency. At the same time, they recognized its benefits as a helpful resource to those who consistently had subsistence struggles. Thus, SSI was both a bane and a boon from staff's perspective. Their cooperation in the application process almost always signaled the end of intensive efforts to rehabilitate a client vocationally. At times, staff expressed a sense of defeat, feeling that clients had "won" a battle to retain their roles and actions as dependent, different, and inadequate persons.

The staff's perspective on income maintenance programs became clear through their answers (B) to the following questions:

A. Do you feel that patients who do not support themselves financially should be able to get welfare and SSI? Do you resent that you work for your money and that they do not? Be honest now.

B. I guess it comes down to being more than an across-the-board kind of thing, a personal thing. Basically, I think: Yeah. It should be all right for them to get some sort of financial support, be it welfare, or SSI, or veterans' benefits, or whatever. I guess the thing about that whole issue that irks me more than anything else is, I feel it's an abuse when people, like a couple of the clients, can get $700 or $800 or $900 a month to support themselves. I guess I don't mind supporting people if I don't have to support them better than I'm living, or if they get supported, you know, where they're able to have a decent place to live and enough money for food and clothes, and the basic necessities. But I guess there comes a point where I don't think being able to drive a big car, and buying a lot of new clothes, and that sort of thing, is a necessity. And, you know, there's some of the nice things, that maybe they could work five hours a week and, you know, at a drop-in kind of job, and pick up some of those things for themselves.

A. Do you think that the system, the SSI system or the VA system, contributes to people not "getting better," or working toward improving things, or developing job skills?

B. I think it can. You know. I think there are clients, and we've seen them, where they keep saying, "Why can't I get SSI," you know. "So and so gets it. I don't see why I should have to work." And I think some of them just dig into their illness in an effort to sort of, you know, prove that kind of thing. You know. I don't think all of them do that.

A. How do you think the system could be different, so that it won't work that way?

B. I really don't know. You know, I think the problem now is you try and develop a system that meets everybody's needs, and that has very broad, basic guidelines, and, I don't see where there's a lot of barriers. I guess the thing that annoys me the most is that, when we're working with clients, most of the SSI determinations are made by private psychiatrists in terms of going out, applying for SSI, and you fill out the forms showing that you're indigent, and then they send you to a couple of private shrinks for an evaluation, which is maybe an hour, or an hour-and-a-half's interview. And I think they can pick up probably that you have difficulties in there, but I sure don't know that they have the ability in that kind of an evaluation to say whether or not somebody's capable of performing work. And a lot of people, like the client we were just talking about, I think they'd obviously be able to pick up that he was unable to work at the kind of the thing he wants, for himself, which may be unrealistic in terms of his, you know, disability as such; and I don't know if there's any way to build that in, because you ask the treaters, you know, you're likely to get people who want to get paid after they've run up a large bill with clients. And so, you know, there isn't that impartiality for them to say, and it's not for us, either. I don't think we're impartial. You know, we're biased about whether we think people can do that, or whatever.

A. And you have control, too, over whether he can.

B. Yeah. Except the system is set up so that we can sometimes prevent them getting on it. But once they're on it, it's so darn difficult to take it away, and even though you go through that process, it takes sometimes six months.

A. Okay. How do you feel? Like at report I've heard, you've heard it several times now, several staff people have just really been angry and resentful that they were "suckered." What kind of effect do you think that has in terms of treatment—that kind of anger, that kind of resentment? Do you think it's justified? Do you think it's ever communicated to clients as a real double kind of message?

B. Oh, yeah. You know, I can't say that it's unjustified. I can look at staff members here who are supporting families on maybe what somebody else is receiving, you know, who is a single person, for being disabled. And yet they have a different sort of ethic, I guess, about needing to work, and supporting, and that kind of thing. And I think, you know, I think there are people who, I don't think it's a constant kind of thing, but I think there are days when they get frustrated, either with their own financial situation, or, you know, they're not making their bills, or, you know, whatever. And, let's see. Yeah. I don't think it's a constant kind of thing, but I think there are days when they can take it out on patients, in terms of they're frustrated, and then they see somebody who's drawing $700-800 a month, supporting themselves. And in addition to that, they get medical coverage, and they're eligible for food stamps, and, you know, I think they just see it as being unfair. I guess I don't know that it's so inappropriate for them to let clients know that. I think there are other people in the world. If we're going to treat clients that way, and family members, or whatever, and I, you know. If they have, as a staff member, the wherewithal to work through that with a client, perhaps—umm—or let the client deal with them back on that issue, then I think I would view it as productive.

A. Right.

B. But, I guess I don't think it's unrealistic. People in the world get crazy, you know, at other people who get welfare of some sort.

This response outlines the delicate balance between adjustment and incentive that staff attempts to strike with clients:

B. I think if we decide a client is supposed to be on SSI, I think it's our responsibility to see to it that they are satisfied with it.

A. Okay. But how can that happen when there's so many ambivalent feelings about SSI, anyway? See, part of what I'm saying is, or I've observed is, that there's a double message about SSI. It's okay. You can have this and you deserve it, but the reason that you deserve it is that you're no good. You can't hack it, and that's the price that you have to pay. It's like that statement they have to sign: I am totally and permanently disabled and unable to work. Now, that's a price. That's the cost.

B. Yeah. That all comes down to the individual basis again. But some clients have already come to the point, they believe this. And this is not going to bother them, to sign the statement that they are this. They've accepted this. They can live that way and not feel worse about themselves. Other clients see this as saying, you know, I'm a no good; and that really does knock them on their ass. How we get across to them? Maybe we can put some hope into it, that this is not a forever thing if you don't want it to be. We can say that this is to help you through this period of life that you're having trouble, but

> don't give up. If they've got enough in them to say "this makes me feel shitty," maybe they've got enough in them to say "then maybe I can try and do something to change it." And if you just leave a hope up, at the end it improves. Uh, a little ray of light up here that they can strive for. Maybe they'll never reach it, but if their quality of life is better striving for it, maybe that . . .

As will become clear, "leaving a little hope" is much easier said than done.

Clients share some of this ambivalence, but they are, on the whole, more positive about SSI. Many feel they deserve it. Some prefer it to the anxiety of constant money shortages due to sporadic employment. Still others do not wish to work at the type of jobs available to them; they see SSI as a legitimate alternative. A few feel somewhat guilty about receiving this money, but they allay these thoughts by convincing themselves that if they did not need it, someone in some bureaucracy would have denied it to them. The following examples confirm and illustrate these observations.

One month before jumping off the YMCA building, Cy applied for SSI. PACT staff felt his resistance to any type of work situation and his aversion to city welfare recommended the move. Cy was very much in favor of it, though he initially expressed some despair at his circumstances. After this period, he expressed the same mixture of resignation to, and denial of, his problems felt by many recipients: "Well, I had to fill out this form. If your medical records show you need it, you get it. Sure, I had to say I was disabled. I don't care as long as I collect. I guess I am disabled, in a way."

Phillip had more of a problem integrating SSI into his self-concept and his relations with others. But for him, it was a way out of GWI and the pressure associated with work:

> My friends hassle me about not working. I think they're jealous. But I look at it this way. If they [PACT, SSI] didn't think I deserved it, they wouldn't give it to me. So, I just take it. I figure they think I should have it, so I should. Sometimes I think that means there's something really wrong with me. I don't know. Besides, it lets me do what I need to do right now, and that's enjoy life. They [his friends] don't have to work. That's their business. But it makes me really angry when they hassle me. I don't ask them where their money comes from. I just tell them it's none of their business.

Alf, Sadie, and others became indignant when they felt that all their friends were receiving SSI while they still had to work or be on welfare. They felt they deserved SSI. Sadie was very angry with the service chief's letter to SSI: "He told them I could take care of myself, and work, and all that. It's not fair. Everybody who wants it should get SSI. What the hell else do I have to do?"

Myrtle applied for SSI, but she was turned down because she had not been disabled long enough. Though she worried that not being able to hold a job was "screwing up my life," SSI was an attractive alternative that she felt she had earned: "I think I'll go on city welfare. Then I won't have to work. I want to be a bum, a bum. No. I think I'll get SSI and just do what I want. I mean, it's for people like me, isn't it?"

Agatha, like others, wanted to get on SSI because "I have too much else to deal with right now. I don't want the responsibility of a crummy job and strange people hassling me anymore. Don't tell anyone, but I really won't mind being on SSI. I kind of like the thought."

SSI, then, was seen as a legitimate, viable subsistence strategy by many of the clients who received it. Ambivalence about its implications regarding their deficits was not discussed, but it seemed to resolve itself with the passage of time, the routinization of not working, and acceptance of the fact that, though they might in some ways have liked to work, they could not or would not. Doc (A) summed up this mixed perspective:

> A. I've always had SSI. My mother put me on it when it first came out. I don't want it. I don't want free money from the government. I'd rather work.
>
> Q. Are you looking for a job?
>
> A. No. I won't find one, and if I do, I'll get fired. Besides, I really don't want to work. I just said that because I thought that's what you're supposed to say.

Jack had a different view: "You know, the only reason they have SSI is so people will stay out of the hospital, and they won't have to deal with you anymore. That's the reason they give it out to all the crazies."

SSDI AND SOCIAL SECURITY

Two persons received SSDI or, more properly named, Old Age Survivors and Disability Insurance (OASDI). Eligibility for SSDI indicated that persons had worked enough previously to make an adequate contribution to the Social Security system. SSDI was calculated on the basis of contribution and need. Alice received $300 per month and George received $350. Both felt they deserved the money and, in unquestioning fashion, utilized it as a means to live. Alice was concerned only that she receive as much money as possible. Though she had been motivated to seek employment in the past, that was changing. She calculated that a monthly working income would have to be $800 to make it worth her while to work and give up the SSDI.

Jack felt he did not deserve his father's Social Security, but he accepted it: "Hell, I don't deserve this money, but as long as they're giving it away, I'll take it. No one else in my family needs it. They all work. Who am I kidding? I'm disabled. I've been that way since I was seventeen." The contradiction within Jack's statement, his sincere self-questioning, may mean that he was handing me a line at first, or it may reflect his genuine ambivalence and indecision about what the SSDI means.

Veteran's Benefits

Four male clients received permanent disability "pensions" (as they called them) from the Veteran's Administration for service-connected disabilities. These ranged from $173 to nearly $600 per month. Two of these persons also received SSI. The VA made two judgments regarding payments: disability and employability. Walter, for example, explained that he had a 30 percent disability rating, but a 100 percent unemployability rating. Andy was rated 100 percent in both categories and received the largest payment of all. Humphrey was receiving only SSI until someone suggested he try to get some additional help from the VA: "I went down there and told them I needed some money for the hospital, because I had this nervous condition. They put it through and I got a letter saying I'd been awarded $173 a month. I'll be getting $407 a month now with that and SSI."

Humphrey was the only one of the four who saw combat duty. That was in Vietnam, where he was a heavy equipment operator. At times he would tell war stories, but he had forgotten nearly all of what happened. As he said, "I was so freaked out I spent all day hyped up on something. I took speed every day, and then cocaine." Dennis was in the service for two weeks when he had a psychotic break. Though he was at first denied benefits, his parents applied pressure on the VA through United States senators, and Dennis was given his pension. For nearly two years he spun yarns of his combat days, entertaining some of my friends for two hours one evening with the most detailed descriptions of the Vietnamese countryside and the gore of war. Actually, he had barely unpacked in boot camp. Nonetheless, he felt he deserved his payment. "I earned it, and it's the hardest-earned money you'll ever see." Much of his time was taken up with appointments with VA counselors and advisors in his effort to utilize every possible financial benefit for which he could qualify. Though he admitted that he was "not crazy," and that "what I do is a sham, it's a con game," he felt entitled to this income.

Unemployment Compensation

Four clients had worked at competitive jobs long enough to receive state unemployment funds after termination. The amount of money varied, based on their previous wages, as did the length of time they received the stipend, based on how long they had worked. To receive this assistance, the clients had to register with the state job service and be available for work at any time. So, while unemployment compensation was viewed with some pride because it was evidence of having held a real job, it was also a source of pressure because of the time limit and work stipulation. The clients who received these funds managed to avoid most of the jobs that came their way through the job service, either by being unqualified or psychiatrically unable to do the work. This did not represent a dependable source of income and it served mainly to buy time before they were forced to seek other means of subsistence.

City Welfare

The last resort for clients with no money was city welfare. It was the bottom line for all. It had the least prestige of any form of assistance, and it was seen as a negative, aversive experience by all who received it. Most often, clients received welfare during the time that their SSI application was being processed, or for a period before applying. Being sent to welfare was, at times, a test of clients' reluctance to work. Staff reasoned that if, despite the difficulties and meagerness of welfare, a client still would not work, SSI was in order.

Abe was a long-term recipient of welfare. He had received SSI several years earlier but had lost it when he began to work. He worked at dishwashing when he felt like it, living on welfare the rest of the time. His rent at the YMCA was paid by welfare, and he managed to eat well enough. Most of his time was spent reading at the university library, or doing other things that required little or no money. In the past, he had maintained that "welfare isn't so bad when you get used to it," but he had begun considering SSI again, saying, "I had to quit that last dishwashing job. It was making me a little crazy. I think I'll reapply for SSI. I'd like to move out of the Y, bu I can't afford to do that on welfare."

Welfare had a low status among clients because it paid very little, entailed troublesome requirements, such as going on job interviews, and often meant waiting long hours to see one's caseworker in a waiting room full of destitute people. The stipend from welfare included a fixed amount for rent, 37¢ per day for incidentals, and a food allowance of $4 per day if one ate out or $1.37 per day if one cooked. Clients who had used welfare prior to their receipt of SSI had to repay this money to welfare when their first SSI check arrived. The pay-back period was calculated from the point in time that a person had applied for SSI. Since the first check was retroactive, a client would, in effect, have received double assistance for that time if there were no reimbursement policy at welfare.

Families

Five clients moved back in with their families, either during treatment or just after. PACT customarily would not work intensively with a client if he or she were living at home. Those who left treatment early to go home lost PACT input. The families then assumed financial responsibility for the client. Only one of these persons was receiving SSI.

Other Strategies

Although clients had access to financial and other resources for living, most were consistently short of cash. This was especially true during treatment and before receipt of SSI, when a client's money came primarily from PACT. Also, many in the group spent what money they had in large chunks, with little thought to the near future. An exchange system based upon reciprocity and some exploitation existed within the group, but its boundaries were not well defined or constant.

For example, thirty-nine clients smoked cigarettes. This was an expensive habit, given their incomes, and there was much "bumming smokes" among them. Staff discouraged this practice, believing that some clients were taken advantage of by others in this way, and that more aggressive members of the group played on the timidity or passivity of others. In social-skills group, role-playing provided clients an opportunity to practice refusal of persistent requests for cigarettes and money. Clients found it difficult to refuse, for the effort to do so often exceeded their motivation to keep their possessions. This behavior had its own rationale, which could best be understood in terms of the idea of giving and exchange put forth by Mauss (1967). Mauss suggested that "prestations which are in theory voluntary, disinterested, and spontaneous, are in fact obligatory and interested . . . the transaction itself is based on obligation and economic self-interest" (ibid.:1).

Some gave cigarettes because they were presented not with a request but a demand: "Hey! Give me one of those." But the majority felt obligated because they themselves had bummed before and knew they would again. Not only were they fulfilling an obligation but they were also creating one. The unwritten rule in the group was that he or she who had was expected to share. Those who did not share were excluding themselves from the system, thereby losing access to the goods they might have received. New group members who were not aware of the practices, and who made open mention of possession of money or other valued goods, rapidly learned that unless one intended to share, one kept such information to oneself.

There were various ways to sidestep the obligation. One method was to conceal or deny possession. One person customarily carried a pack with only one cigarette in it in his front pocket while a nearly full one was stashed away in his coat. He could refuse by displaying that he had only one left, because the smoker's rule precluded taking another's last cigarette. Others rolled their own smokes, not only because it was less expensive but also because it discouraged bumming. A way to obtain cigarettes without asking or incurring obligation was to smoke butts. On several occasions, a client who picked through ashtrays in front of others would be offered a cigarette in disgust or sympathy by another client or staff.

As a rule, staff would not lend cigarettes or money to a client, especially in a group situation. They did not wish to encourage dependence on others for cigarettes (or anything else). Also, whether deliberately or not, through nonparticipation they could delineate themselves as apart from the client group. As Firth (1967) points out, the significance of transactions is not simply in the exchange of goods but "in the quality of relationships which these transactions create, express, sanction, and modify." Staff also excluded themselves from this system because they were obligated to enforce contingency programs for clients which emphasized responsibility for one's own actions and budgeting of money. Thus, if one wanted to smoke, one must plan for the expense. If staff were to loan clients money, this would undermine the persuasion of the contingency. On occasion, a staff member would break this rule and buy a meal for a client who had not eaten, but this would be done covertly.

Applying Firth's principle to clients, it was clear that they interacted with peers vis-à-vis money, PACT involvement, and psychiatric problems by participating in an exchange system based upon reciprocity. Money, food, and space were also exchanged. Staff may have provided all these for the purpose of creating obligations among clients, but the exchange was asymmetrical. Clients were asked to reciprocate with behaviors and attitudes desired by staff. They had nothing else to offer in return. Among clients, there were no such contingencies, and the exchange was much more symmetrical.

Not all clients participated in the system, and those who did may not always have given and received. Clients who did not exchange with other clients were generally loners, had not made friends among other clients, and eschewed a group identity. More than half of the group was involved in triadic or more multifaceted exchange. At one level, simply being in PACT was enough to qualify. At another, prior acquaintance or companionship was required to facilitate the sharing. For example, Herb paid for Alf's food when Alf was not working and not receiving his full maintenance money from PACT. Humphrey stayed with Doc when he had no room of his own. Doc bummed cigarettes and beer from Humphrey. They both borrowed money for beer from Annie, Doc's girl friend. Alice paid for beer, food, and entertainment for many of her boyfriends, including several fellow clients. But Morris would not give a cigarette to a client unless he had known him or her before in the hospital or at work.

This system was both conscious and unconscious so its workings were sometimes deliberately utilized, sometimes reluctantly acknowledged. Doc, for instance, asked to borrow beer money from me so "that I can give them out to the guys and then they'll have to pay me back." Another time, Alex bought a six-pack of beer and brought it to a rooming-house lounge where a group of us were sitting. By the time he had fulfilled his obligations to others, one beer remained. Though he became more reluctant as his supply dwindled, the power of obligation demanded he comply. At other times, clients utilized the rules by deliberately breaking them. Wally said once, "I really like to order a pizza and sit there and not give anybody a piece."

Money was at times so scarce that some clients felt guilty for having it when others did not, so they gave it away. Others consciously invested in companionship. Steven was very upset when he had spent over $80 on Tim, who "just ate and drank it up and now he says I'm just a homosexual. I just wanted to be his friend and help him out." The accusation by Tim was his ploy to eschew the reciprocal obligation. Alice often paid for drinks to persuade her friends to go out with her despite their assertion that they had no money. She acknowledged that "they just use me for money."

There were limits to this system. Alex had borrowed and stolen so much from other clients that scarcely anyone would lend him anything. During a poker game, no one would even allow him to buy a beer from their stash in the refrigerator. Clients also knew that lending was a safer practice near the time another received his or her SSI check or his or her weekly allowance from the financial guardian. Goods were also traded. Humphrey got a sports coat for two beers, and Alex traded some uppers, "white crosses" or street pills for a meal from Cy. When Humphrey and Doc were sharing a room rented by Doc, whoever paid the rent that month was allowed to sleep in the bed. The other got the floor.

Thus, clients helped each other to survive when other resources were either unavailable or held too many unattractive contingencies. But, at times, they also undermined each other's subsistence by spending one's entire money for the month in a single week. Some amount of self-regulation occurred in this situation, for when the money of one person was spent all at once, s/he became a burden on the rest of the group for the remainder of the month. For this reason, many obtained financial guardians, who helped to decrease, if not eliminate, the extreme misuses of the exchange system.

I participated in the system, but with certain restrictions. I knew it would become a source of conflict with staff if I consistently loaned money to clients who were not working and were not following contingency programs. But I had to participate if I were to make clear to clients my nonstaff affiliation. I settled on almost always lending cigarettes and occasionally lending money. Nearly everyone paid me back. I found that any admission that I had cash was enough to invite persistent, if not demanding, requests for it. Fortunately, my income was equal to or less than that of most clients, so we were often in similar predicaments.

The important point about these networks of reciprocity, exchange, and exploitation was not only that they represented creative and adaptive survival strategies for these persons. Of greater significance were the interpersonal and sociocultural consequences of their practices. Their enmeshing system of values and behaviors not only expressed but created and perpetuated a social network among clients. Clear boundaries were delineated between themselves and others. Within these human lines, values and codes developed which excluded nonclients and included clients and their peers, such as others on SSI, others who did not work, and others in sheltered workshops. These others were also negatively different. They were not mainstream or even "regular" community members. These cultural processes must not be overlooked or underestimated in any effort to discover why it was that the clients remained "unintegrated." Even though they had been deinstitutionalized in terms of architecture (they were not housed in hospitals), they had not been so in terms of their roles, experiences, and social networks.

Three other means of subsistence in the group included panhandling, selling drugs, and infrequent prostitution. Almost all the clients had at some time approached strangers to ask for money or cigarettes. Five were notorious for this practice. Sam was an expert. I followed him around the county fair one evening, watching him collect nearly $5 in quarters. He explained that he sought out parents with children, because these people were less likely to brush him off in front of their offspring with an obscenity, choosing instead to appear generous and kind. Sadie often wandered around the University Union, asking for and receiving food because, as she put it, "it freaks people out so much that they don't know what to do and they give it to me." Morris used the same logic for cigarettes and quarters, but he would spit on those who refused him. This retribution earned him many a disorderly conduct and vagrancy charge.

Three persons sold drugs and marijuana. One was arrested for these activities and spent six months in jail. The others continued to add to their incomes in this way. They were, for the most part, entrepreneurs who bought in bulk and sold in smaller quantities. One gave away almost as much as he sold.

Two of the women and two men engaged in prostitution on occasions. This usually occurred when they were in desperate need of money or were experiencing periods of disorganization in thinking or feeling.

Clients also received money, food, and clothing covertly from their parents. Staff discouraged this whenever they became aware of it or suspected that it was occurring. Many parents gave these items because they had great difficulty seeing their children in dire circumstances, living on welfare in low-grade hotels. Clients often exaggerated their plights to gain sympathy and support from their families.

SUBSISTENCE STRATEGIES AND MAKING IT CRAZY

Certainly this system was effective at the subsistence level, but it is important now to analyze the humane, moral and cultural implications, the dynamics, and meanings for clients of the economic system that they created and within which they operated.

For a very few, conventional employment represented a positive strategy. For almost everyone, work symbolized their failures in life and underscored the painful discrepancy between expectations and realities. In response to a question on the CAS, twenty-eight of the thirty-four clients indicated that they were well below their job expectations for their age. The work that was available, both sheltered and nonsheltered, was not of the type or significance that contributed to positive self-images for the group. Annie expressed it aptly: "I wish there were some way out of this rat race. I'd like to get a job that's worth something instead of just Goodwill. I even got let off a volunteer job. Do you believe that? I just don't know if I'll ever make it. I'm too nervous or something."

Clients appeared to be enmeshed in an environment where they could not or would not see themselves as anything but negatively different, handicapped, and disabled. If they worked at GWI and MOC, they felt stigmatized and horrified to be categorized with the mentally retarded and the physically handicapped. If they did not, by their own and others' determinations, they experienced frustration and defeat in the world of work.

The alternative was to codify and to proclaim one's inadequacies to qualify for assistance programs that were perhaps the only acceptable and accessible means of receiving income. These programs could in turn be disincentives to work for fear of losing the assistance money or of having someone question the disability. As Humphrey put it, "I ain't gonna work if I don't have to. Actually, I'd rather work but not enough to lose my VA money." Without question, life was easier in some ways, was freer of responsibilities and stresses, when one had a secure and permanent source of income.[6]

6. Thoits and Hannan (1979) have recently challenged the commonplace idea that receiving a permanent source of stable income serves to decrease levels of life stress. In a study conducted among recipients of income maintenance in Seattle and Denver, they

In considering the evidence and opinions presented by researchers and clinicians, it becomes clear that there presently exists some controversy and disagreement about the benefits and possible perversity of income maintenance programs for the long-term psychiatric population. Lamb and Goertzl (1977:682) list a number of positive aspects of SSI, including (1) ability to live outside a hospital; (2) eligibility for psychotherapy and other health-care services; (3) an identity accompanied by less fear and anxiety in the welfare system; and (4) a delabeling effect. They were "impressed by the importance of SSI in providing the financial means that are so crucial in enabling persons with long-term psychiatric disabilities to remain in the community." It is difficult to argue with the first two parts of this evaluation, and there is significant consensus among clinicians and clients to this effect. I will, however, challenge the third and fourth assertions, proposing that, in fact, the opposite is true.

There is a woeful lack of data about psychiatrically disabled income-maintenance recipients in general, and in particular about the disincentives for work and other social competencies created by the system. This is so, in part because of the relative youth of the SSI system, and in part because of the relatively small proportion of federal dollars that are spent on this group compared with the aged. Nonetheless, general surveys indicate some of the broader trends.

Exact national figures measuring the current total numbers of adult persons receiving SSI due to psychiatric disability are not available. Kochhar (1979) reports, however, that in 1975 alone, 17.6 percent of the 356,892 persons awarded SSI for disability filed on the basis of psychiatric disorders other than mental retardation. In absolute numbers, Kochhar indicates that during that same year, 62,824

---

found that in no case did income maintenance have a positive impact on reported distress. In fact, several groups in the experiment responded with significantly *increasing* levels of distress. The authors explained their results with a life-events hypothesis, suggesting that the negative change in status represented simply by going onto income maintenance was as stressful as were the life events (usually negative) that necessitated this change. The sample in these projects may differ significantly from long-term psychiatric clients, in terms of negative life events already experienced by the latter group, but the data are suggestive. Further research is needed in this area, but an important possibility is that the recipients may be well aware of their negatively valued welfare status (and may share these values), and that the income per se cannot compensate for their losses in self-esteem, relationships, or jobs.

persons received SSI because of psychosis and other nonpsychotic diagnoses. This same researcher (personal communication) verifies that the proportions of SSI awards for psychiatric disability in adults, other than for mental retardation, remained fairly constant for 1976–1979. Therefore, I estimate that 372,317 adult persons are currently receiving SSI due to psychiatric disorders other than mental retardation. The estimated total federal and state costs for these persons is $64,487,800. Figures for OASDI and other programs are unobtainable.[7]

Surveying the broader scene, Sharfstein, Turner and Clark (1978) estimate that, in 1974, 1.5 million persons were chronically mentally ill, at a cost to the United States of $32 billion. This cost figure includes not only direct care but indirect expenses, such as loss of productivity of those persons not working (see Levine and Levine 1975 for formulas and reasoning used to calculate indirect costs). These numbers make clear that the broad view encompasses a significant number of people and a large amount of federal and state money.

In a recent study of the work experiences of disabled persons, Schechter (1979) examines the relationship between self-report perceived ability to work and actual labor force participation. His findings support the idea of enmeshment and interaction among the variables of perceived disability, health status, and actual employment. Schechter finds that a decline in perceived health status is likely to result in unemployment, but that improvement in perceived health status is only slightly related to becoming employed (1979:4). He concludes that successful work recovery is not dependent solely on a perceived improvement in health condition.

I think the implication is clear. Once the disabled-nonworking status is achieved, by whatever means, it is not easily shed. I suggest that economic and sociocultural realities, as well as the actual disabling condition, contribute to the maintenance of disability rather than to its alleviation or reduction. At least three complementary but discrete interactions are taking place. The first concerns experiencing one's problems as a health condition and as disabling for work. In our case, being crazy is seen as a medical condition and

7. I gratefully acknowledge the assistance of Satya Kochhar and Jennifer Warlick in obtaining the most recent SSI figures.

most clients cannot or do not work. Being in the mental health system confirms that they have a "health" problem. While in this system, they are sent to sheltered workshops with physically handicapped and developmentally disabled persons to do menial, low-paying work. Or they attempt competitive employment and customarily qualify for more menial, low-paying jobs.

The next interaction involves receiving SSI, based on this medical disability, as an alternative to conventional employment, thereby precluding the need to work. Thus, clients' perceptions of health status may be influenced and their ability and motivation to work may be undermined simply by being in the treatment system. The system conveys the messages of poor health, inability to work, and confirmed disability, connecting them with an alternative, secure form of income based on maintaining these conditions. No client need consciously manipulate these variables—few are even explicitly aware that they are operative. Once the connections are made, the system and the personal and cultural processes can carry on, often despite individual efforts to overcome them.

Other empirical data suggest that diagnosis of a medical condition and/or welfare status each contribute to poorer subjective definitions of health and to increased absenteeism from work. Prince (1978) found that the proportion of hospitalized welfare recipients reporting their health as fair to poor was 22 percent greater than among comparable hospitalized nonwelfare recipients. Haynes et al. (1978) reported that absenteeism from work due to illness increased among persons newly labeled hypertensive or reminded of existing hypertension by 71 percent more than among the general plant population in the year following hypertension screening. These dramatic increases occurred whether or not the persons adhered to treatment regimens. The implications of these studies are that labeling a medical condition or being on welfare contributes to subjective and objective declines in work-role performance and in perceptions of health, and to increases in classic sick-role behavior.

With regard to long-term psychiatric clients, more opinion and suggestion is available than data. Rethinking his earlier enthusiasm for SSI in community treatment, Lamb (Lamb and Rogawski 1978:1223) observes that "the SSI system does not counteract the pull toward regression and dependency. . . . There is little incentive to participate in a treatment program, either social or vocational."

He pinpoints the contradictions inherent in spending large sums of money and much treatment personnel energy for vocational rehabilitation, while income maintenance programs are "undermining their [clients] already weakened resolve to overcome their apprehension and try to deal with the everyday demands of life, such as self support." It is paradoxical to recognize the cultural and personal esteem associated with employment and to work therapeutically with clients to this end, while simultaneously inviting them not to need to work if only they demonstrate how disabled they are by not working.

From an economic and social perspective, Ozawa and Lindsey (1977) note that the number of mentally disabled persons receiving SSI is increasing absolutely and proportionately at a more rapid rate than the number of blind and aged, and that national unemployment rates may contribute to this process. Arguing that the very "social acceptability" of SSI may present a problem, Ozawa and Lindsey appropriately question what the impact of reliance on SSI may be for long-term prognosis. Warning of the "gentle entrapment" of persons like the PACT clients, the authors suggest the following:

> There seem to be economic incentives on the part of the mentally ill, and moral and ideological incentives on the part of the government and the community, to place and keep the mentally ill on SSI—a program perceived as benevolent, impartial, and legitimate. [p. 51]

The push and pull built into SSI, and the paradox this creates for clients, becomes vividly apparent. Clients' fragile motivation to work may be undermined by this alternative. Their not working is seen as both symptom and proof of *their* disabilities and deficits. The fact that there are few jobs for them anyway is compounded by reluctant employers, low pay, and menial tasks. A problem that is economic, social-structural, and practical is transposed into a mental health problem involving individual persons. This is accomplished by linking SSI to psychiatric disorders, as diagnosed by mental health professionals, and by the consequent cultural and interpersonal clustering of clients. The result is a cultural craziness of major proportions.

Although I am in substantial agreement with the evidence and perspectives above, I wholeheartedly disagree with Lamb's suggestion that SSI contributes to delabeling. SSI represents perhaps one of the most permanent and visible labels the clients possess. It is the culmination of the chronic client-labeling process. Once this occurs, the client becomes further removed from the realities of work and nonclienthood. Denker (1939) supports this observation, writing, ". . . it would seem that the monthly disability check eliminates the incentive to get out and fight life's struggles, and in addition, it acts as a constant reminder to the highly suggestible, mentally ill patient that he is disabled, and an invalid, and recognized as such by the outside world."

In this client sample, only two of those who received SSI or VA benefits worked. Contrary to what we might have liked to believe, these benefits were not silent or invisible. For example, clients had to reveal their source of income when applying for housing. Some were turned down because of this. They did not work, and thus they had time schedules and orientations different from those of most persons. Many had financial guardians who, in parental fashion, gave them weekly allowances. If these factors alone did not persistently remind clients and others of a disabled life and label, I am hard pressed to imagine others that would have done so more convincingly. Clients became eligible for SSI and other benefits by labeling themselves and having others agree with them or vice versa. They had to attest, under oath, on their application forms that they were disabled and to specify this disability as mental disorder.

What were the implications of being on SSI and other income-maintenance programs vis-à-vis interaction and relations with nonclients? Among the client group, some form of assistance was the norm. Outside it was not. The customary acquainting interrogatives in our culture soon focus on work or on what one does. How could a client converse with a stranger for more than a moment without revealing the disability-connected means of income? The client was caught in but another Catch 22. If he or she revealed being on SSI, others presumed differentness and, more particularly, inadequacy. If he exposed the source of his income but did not appear disabled (or even denied problems, as in Phillip's case), others became resentful, even hostile, at the life of leisure lived at the taxpayer's expense. Even some staff, who were acutely aware of clients' problems, expressed these sentiments. So one could accept the money and the concomitant losses in personal and interpersonal dignity and expectations of adequacy, or one could risk not having a secure income and probably experiencing failure, anxiety, and destitution. These were not happy alternatives, to say the very least. Clients who could not or would not manage the stresses and demands of self-support paid a price. It would be fantasizing to presume that they did not.

The safety of income-maintenance programs could and did encourage clients to perpetuate, if not to enhance, their qualifications for the money, that is, their diagnoses and disabilities. As one of many examples, Walter explained his desire to try a writing career, but he was reluctant to do so because "if I make it, then they might take away my VA money. And I can't be sure about working but I can be sure about the VA. All I have to do is keep being me and not working. So I guess I'm better off just leaving well enough alone."

The PACT staff, as a group, wrote the Veteran's Administration to object to the remuneration system. After explaining the program's success in community treatment, they wrote:

> There is a group of patients that we have been unsuccessful, however, in treating. . . . We have thought that our work with these patients is so difficult, not because of the disabilities and disorders they possess, but because of the large veteran's disability pensions that they have and are receiving. Since employment, in our estimation, is extremely important in the rehabilitation of these patients, it very seldom can become a realistic part of the treatment plan. . . . Over and over again we have heard these men talk of their unwillingness to participate in employment efforts because they do receive the money.

Defenders of SSI and other such programs point out that they are aware of potential disincentives. They suggest that recipients should be encouraged to work by the graduated fashion in which benefits decrease when supplemented with earned income. Unfortunately, this administrative reality is not recognized on the street. The operative belief among most of these clients is that if they work, they will lose all of their SSI, VA benefits, or any other form of assistance based on disability. In short, until and unless clients believe and experience that they will not lose their benefits by working, *their* reality will influence their behavior, not the actual rules at the VA or the Social Security Administration. This process will be slow, for it requires risk-taking and trust in agency or treatment personnel by a group who are characteristically (and sometimes appropriately) averse to doing either.

Thus, income maintenance may perpetuate the crazy life not only by making it attractive as a source of income but also by rewarding the continuation of inadequacy demonstrated by not working. In this sense, the system itself makes the whole situation crazy, nonsensical, and contradictory.

Studies have shown that degree of psychiatric impairment is not the most important predictor of a client's ability and desire to work (e.g., Mikkelson, 1977; Turner and Gartell, 1978; Turner, 1977). Turner (1977) found that 40 percent of his subjects had moderate pathology and were still working, reporting that "the fact of employment was associated with no greater likelihood of a lower level of symptom severity than of a higher level" (ibid.:36). What was most important was the feeling of self-confidence and the desire to work. Income-maintenance programs could undermine both these factors, first by confirming the fact of disability in awarding the benefit, and second by compromising incentives to work in providing other income.

Taking another approach, Morgan and Cheadle (1975) and Williams et al. (1980) have suggested that high or rising unemployment first serves to exclude from the work force those persons with deficits, such as outpatients. Many in our society are ready and able to work but cannot find jobs. It seems counterproductive, then, to force unwilling, unskilled persons into the already overflowing pool. Undoubtedly, income-maintenance programs grant clients some therapeutic relief from anxiety. What seems so very wrong about the system is the negative, damaging predication of disability and inadequacy.

Clients could deny or acknowledge disability, could feel they deserved benefits, and could even improve because they had a breathing period with reduced subsistence pressure. But whichever way they turned, their crazy, negative identity confronted them. They were rewarded and punished all at once. Many came to accept that they were different and inadequate because they had no other explanation for receipt of this pay. In a society where goods and labor are exchanged for remuneration, the only things they had to offer were diagnoses, defeats, and disabilities. They earned their living by being different, but negatively so. The taxpayer was their employer. As Jack surmised, the client's job was to occupy the time and interest of mental health care professionals, to maintain his or her problems, and to annoy the rest of society as little as possible. And so, along with his internal and legitimate psychiatric difficulties, the professionalization of patienthood and craziness contributed to the client's ability to make it through life as a crazy person. Our paradoxical participation in this system seems as crazy as any symptoms observed among the clients.

What would happen if there were no SSI or VA money? No doubt many clients would find themselves hospitalized or would seek to be to obtain food and shelter. Perhaps some would work. This is a question for further research (cf. Auerbach and Pattison 1976; Rivinus 1977). I believe that persons have a right to assistance in making life pleasant and less stressful. What is unacceptable is the contradiction of rewarding and negatively valuing disability all at once.

Employment, in theory, as a symbol, and in actuality has become so desired as the goal of community treatment that clinicians now speak of "vocational disability" (e.g., Meyerson 1978:134), including work performance and poor employment history as part of the symptom cluster of their long-term patients. Virtually all of the most thorough and recent psychiatrically oriented explorations of the plight of long-term psychiatric patients (GAP 1978; Talbott 1978; Lamb et al. 1978) include the employment arena not only as an obstacle to treatment but also as a serious and pervasive deficit among this population.

I think it dangerous to engage in this often subtle and unrecognized process of characterizing as a *symptom* a circumstance that is instead often social, structural, economic, political and outside the control of admittedly impaired persons. I have tried to point out that these persons often do not work because they are willingly seduced by a system that offers alternatives. To elevate a person's choice of subsistence strategy to the level of psychiatric symptom is a gross misapplication of the principles of social psychiatry. Inclusion of the sociocultural circumstances of clients in our understanding of their adaptations or maladaptations does not legitimate our consideration of these behaviors as clinical symptoms. Voices will be raised in objection to my suggestion, but I feel that it is important to look at the language being developed, at the personnel being engaged in employment-related "treatment," and at the indicators being used to measure treatment and program success. These are becoming more and more psychiatric and clinical. It is indeed appropriate and welcome to deal with the whole person as he copes with complex living. But must these dealings be increasingly in the guise of treatment that is medical, that is full of physicians and nurses, of medicine, and of the referrents of sickness?

Despite the extended criticism I have leveled at income-maintenance programs, I recognize that at present we have few reasonable alternatives. Under no circumstances do I advocate rapid reductions in these programs or changes in their availability to long-term psychiatric clients. The clients desperately need these resources to continue community life. I am suggesting that, given the paradoxes highlighted in this chapter, the obligation exists to create less noxious alternatives. For example, although these persons might not be able or willing to work full-time at rewarding, competitive jobs, they might well be responsive to job-sharing opportunities. Two persons or more could split one position, reaping the rewards of working at an interesting job and experiencing a sense of competence. This would require some adaptation by employers and coworkers, but it would represent a small price to pay. I think we would do well to expend more resources exploring and creating some alternatives to the troublesome solutions of the present.

Although clients would never criticize the income maintenance system as I have, they provide living proof of the impact of such programs in combination with the current employment scene. In some ways, their lives are less difficult and stressed. They should not be denied this welcome comfort. But very careful attention must be given to the problems of separateness and of disabled or inadequate identities with which most struggle, silently or vocally. Enough clients have voiced ambivalent views of sheltered workshops, "pretend" jobs, and income maintenance to warrant more than our cursory concern. Robert Frost, in "The Death of the Hired Hand," has characterized their problem all too well: "Nothing to look backward to with pride/And nothing to look forward to with hope."

7

NORMALS, CRAZIES, INSIDERS, AND OUTSIDERS

I have presented some of the ethnographic facts, paradoxes, and dynamics of the clients' world. These ethnographic details underscore the unique operations, frustrations, and dilemmas of this particular brand of psychiatric patienthood in a community setting. One lesson becomes clear. Clients are not the only persons caught in the web of contradiction and the Catch-22 dynamics of their own and others' making. So are we all. With few exceptions, whichever way we may turn and however we may act in attempts to be helpful, it seems that our psychiatric belief and treatment systems and our interactions as community members can contribute not only to the amelioration of patienthood but to its perpetuation.

The ensuing analysis of these factors and their interrelations, from the client's perspective, enables me to describe and systematize the client's categorization of others, relating his viewpoints to the factors of time, space, resources, information, and knowledge. Through this exercise, I hope to synthesize the previous material and to lay a foundation for its interpretation.

One of the reasons hospitalization has been eschewed as a means of psychiatric treatment is the institutional tendency to weaken, mortify, and control patients. Many writers have described and decried these degrading, humiliating, and controlling aspects of hospitalization. Goffman, for example, says the following:

> . . . total institutions disrupt or defile precisely those actions that in civil society have the role of attesting to the actor and those in his presence

> that he has command over his world—that he is a person with "adult" self-determination, autonomy, and freedom of action. [1961:43]

More recently, and from her perspective as a former patient, Chamberlain (1978) has written angrily and perceptively about the consequences of the cultural and interpersonal dynamics in hospitals and the mental health system:

> The whole experience of mental hospitalization promotes weakness and dependency. Not only are the lives of patients controlled, but patients are constantly told that such control is for their own good. . . . Patients become unable to trust their own judgement, become indecisive, overly submissive to authority, frightened of the outside world. A tremendous gulf exists between patients and staff in mental institutions. Patients are seen as sick, untrustworthy, and needing constant supervision. Staff members are seen as competent, knowledgeable natural leaders. These stereotypes are believed by large numbers of patients and staff members. Communication is difficult across this gulf. Staff members don't believe what other patients say. Patients begin to question their own perceptions of situations. . . . [Chamberlain 1978:6]

Not all patients view hospitalization so negatively (Weinstein 1979) or believe themselves to be "sick" (Townsend 1976), but Chamberlain points to what can happen when large differentials in power and competence, either actual or believed, are implicit and explicit in a treatment setting and its philosophy.

Control, command, choices, self-determination—these are aspects of competent selfhood in our society when applied to life situations and life actions. Our cultural emphasis on independence and individuality is curiously matched with an underlying emphasis on conformity. One pays for those behaviors and experiences that exceed codified and consensually understood limits with losses in such valued possessions as freedom, self-determination, and control of one's life. Community treatment has sought in part to dilute those perverse effects of hospitalization that create additional dependencies and weaknesses in persons who have already exceeded the limits in these value-action areas. But within the framework of a community treatment program, an examination of the clients' experiences of self in relation to others reveals some distressing repetitions of hospital patterns.

When I first began my work at PACT, one of the more perceptive nurses pointed out that its social system included three categories of people: clients, staff, and community volunteers. This analysis was correct insofar as it went. From the perspective of the client, it required alteration and expansion. Clients distinguished between themselves and all others, creating only two broad categories: (1) "Crazies," or clients, known psychiatric patients, or known crazy people; and (2) "Normies," or normal people, nonclients, or persons not known to be crazy. There were variations on these labels. Dennis called the two types of people "freaks" and "liberals." Some distinguished between "nuts" and "regular people." Still others disliked these colloquial terms and referred to themselves as clients or patients. Nearly all clients verbally or behaviorally recognized and acted upon the distinction between "us" and "them."[1]

Crosscutting these categories at a level that was unspoken and unconscious, though acted upon, were two others: insiders and outsiders. Insiders and outsiders exist for us all. Insiders are persons with whom we share intimacies, a high quality and a large quantity of information, time, space, and resources. Outsiders are those with whom we come into cursory or indirect contact, and with whom we share information that is poor in quality and meager in amount. We also share few resources and little time and space. I have used the categories as cumulative. That is to say, we may exchange large amounts of resources (e.g., money) with bankers, businesses, or the Internal Revenue Service, but little space, time, and intrapsychic information. All the factors combine to create the insider and outsider categories; no single dimension is determinative.

As with any artificial representation of reality, there are exceptions and minor divergences between actualities and this system. But I think it sufficiently representative and instructive in relation to reality to warrant careful examination. I have presented this analytic framework to describe the types of persons with whom clients interacted and to detail the content and dynamics of these relation-

1. The "us" and "them" distinction can be situational. Normals, particularly PACT staff and some volunteers, may become a part of the clients' "us" if a group of clients and staff are in a public place, with many unknown normal persons (Outside Normals). This is the only circumstance in which the distinction diminishes.

ships. I have combined the conscious distinction made by clients between normals and crazies with my own observation that insiders and outsiders exist within both these groups.

Combining the two classifications, four possible categories are generated: Inside Crazies, Outside Crazies, Inside Normals, and Outside Normals. I have categorized persons according to the amount and type of time, space, information, and resources shared with a client (ego). Determining symmetry or its lack in these relationships is also a factor; in other words, assessing who has control over enforcement power of the rules relating to the sharing process. I have focused on the dimension of control because of its implications for such institutionalization syndromes as dependency, incompetence, and inadequacy—all of which are community treatment targets; all of which are associated with hospitalization.

I have combined these criteria and dimensions within each category, to learn the characteristics of that category from the clients' point of view. Table 5 represents the combination of the classifications and the determinations of symmetry within each category. When clients' relationships with others are tabulated in this fashion, some consistent features become apparent: the lack of symmetry between clients and normals, the concentration of control among normals, and the presence of symmetry among crazies. Each category will be examined in detail to determine which persons in the clients' world belong in each.

INSIDE CRAZIES

An Inside Crazy is a person who not only knows that ego is crazy but who is crazy as well. Ego and the inside crazy share this information, and they share a special quality of knowledge through experience with medications, psychosis, and psychiatric treatment. The Inside Crazy does not reject or avoid ego because ego is crazy. S/He may, in fact, know and associate with ego because both ego and other are crazy. There are no formal or necessary restrictions in sharing time and space. Most of the limits that exist are negotiated relatively freely between ego and other. However, some temporal-spatial sharing is not controlled by either party. Staff decides, for example, which social-skills groups the clients may attend and

TABLE 5

CLIENTS' RELATIONS WITH OTHERS: SYMMETRICAL DIMENSION

Inside Normals		Inside Crazies	
Time:	Greater control of amount and type shared with ego.	*Time*:	Equal control of amount and type shared with ego.
Space:	Greater control of amount and type shared with ego.	*Space*:	Equal control of amount and type shared with ego.
Resources:	Greater control of amount and type shared with ego.	*Resources*:	Equal control of amount and type shared with ego.
Information:	Greater control of amount and type shared with ego.	*Information*:	Equal control of amount and type shared with ego.
Outside Normals		**Outside Crazies**	
Time:	Equal or greater control of amount and type shared with ego.	*Time*:	Equal control of amount and type shared with ego.
Space:	Greater control of amount and type shared with ego.	*Space*:	Equal control of amount and type shared with ego.
Resources:	Greater control of amount and type shared with ego.	*Resources*:	Equal control of amount and type shared with ego.
Information:	Equal or greater control of amount and type shared with ego.	*Information*:	Equal control of amount and type shared with ego.

which activities they may join, thus determining to some extent which clients are together at these times. Discharge, loss or change of job, and loss or change of living space are also somewhat out of ego's direct control and may affect the relationship with other. Ego and other have nearly equal control of and access to resources such as money, living space, employment, and medications. An Inside Crazy is or can be involved in the reciprocal exchange system described in the previous chapter.

With few exceptions, the clients in this group shared most of their time, space, and resources with Inside Crazies, both in treatment and nontreatment activities. This sharing included romantic heterosexual relationships, such as those among five client couples, living in the same apartment as with six sets of clients, living in the same hotel or rooming house, or among the multiple pairs and groups of same sex friends within the group. A dozen clients had known each other in high school and through rock band connections prior to their PACT encounter, and six clients had become acquainted during concurrent stays on various psychiatric wards. The remainder came to be friends through PACT activities, through living and working in the same places, and through various treatment-related factors. Toward the end of the fieldwork period, the PACT staff began to encourage companionship among clients.

These Inside Crazy relationships exhibited some interesting features. As a rule, client friends did not discuss emotional or psychiatric problems with one another. Often there was very little verbal communication of any subject. Practical problems such as lack of money, a job, or eviction were mentioned much more frequently. Part of this was owing to PACT encouragement to share psychiatric difficulties with the program staff. For example, one social-skills session focused on referring a friend who was hallucinating to staff instead of working on the problem within the client group. Clients seemed to follow this rule independently, probably because they believed that people experiencing the same problems and deficits could offer little objective advice. At times, clients might encourage one another to stay in the treatment program, to take medications, to follow staff advice, or to go to work. At another time, they might give the opposite counsel.

Clients who seemed to be friends, sharing much time away from treatment activities, often lost contact if one were discharged, or moved home, or left a common work or living situation. Dorothy and Alice shared an apartment at the three-quarter way house for nearly a year, but upon Dorothy's departure to live with a male friend, the relationship ceased to be active. Ben and Pogo worked together at MOC, regularly ate dinner together, and even planned a joint suicide. But when Ben left MOC and moved to his parents' home after discharge, their comradeship did not continue. Some clients who developed no outside relationships remained among PACT and Inside Crazy friends even after discharge. On occasion, a client would disappear from the scene. Usually his or her Inside

Crazy friends did not know that the person had been hospitalized, but I could ascertain the person's whereabouts from PACT staff.

A curious pattern of sharing and relating emerged. Even if time, space, and resources had been generously exchanged among Inside Crazies, the contingencies of PACT treatment, of periodic psychotic episodes, and of exits from the interpersonal system could be accepted in unquestioning fashion. Inside Crazies apparently had much in common, including their mutual appraisal of their friendship as satisfactory but ineffectual and powerless in coping with life problems. CAS responses revealed that this satisfaction indeed existed even though clients felt more distant from friends than they perceived friends to feel toward them, and even though friends did not help them when they were in need. This pattern may have been owing to the fact that Inside Crazies, like ego, were not seen to possess the material or mental resources necessary to provide mutual assistance and to engender feelings of trust and reliance. Inside Normals were the ones who possessed these resources. Inside Crazies perceived one another as satisfactory and accessible companions who occupied similar dependent and incompetent positions vis-à-vis all other types of persons. Clients' ambivalence and negative estimations of themselves were reflected in their judgments about their Inside Crazy friends.

Inside Crazies were usually fellow PACT clients. Also in this group were fellow clients at the county mental health center, and relatives or high school friends who had psychiatric difficulties. Salient characteristics were a relatively high quality and a large quantity of shared time, space, resources, and information, and an equivalency with regard to the symmetry of the exchanges. For example, Doc and Cy were Inside Crazies in relation to each other. They voluntarily shared large amounts of time, space, and resources, and each knew the same amount of information about the other. They drank together, loaned each other money and cigarettes, and shared an apartment.

OUTSIDE CRAZIES

This group comprised those that ego knew to be crazy by virtue of their being in PACT, or seeing them at the county mental health center, or in a psychiatric ward, sheltered workshop, or therapist's office. This may have been the only information, time, and space exchanged between the subjects. Simply having been in these places concurrently told each a great deal about the other. Resources were probably equal, but were not customarily exchanged, except for an occasional cigarette. Equal control of time and space existed, but these were not shared on a voluntary, purposeful, or consistent basis. Even though these persons might be in therapy groups together, or got their medications at the same times, or crossed paths when they utilized the same social services, they did so only because of system-dictated factors, not because they chose to share time, space, or information.

Outside Crazies were usually PACT clients in another research group or phase, or PACT clients with whom ego did not associate beyond group activities and coincidental meetings at the PACT house. They were also co-workers at sheltered workshops or fellow residents at the hotels or Y's. For example, Morris and Rod were Outside Crazies in relation to each other. They saw each other occasionally during PACT activities, on the street, or at the county mental health center. But they did not know where the other lived. No meals were shared and money did not pass between them. They shared special knowledge, namely, the subjective experience of psychosis and medications, being in PACT, receiving SSI, and being periodically hospitalized.

Other Outside Crazies included those half dozen clients in the research group who were loners, who preferred solitude to companionship of any kind, or who actively avoided identifying with or being seen with other clients outside the treatment setting. Another type of Outside Crazy was the person whom ego might encounter in a public situation, who, because of his behavior or appearance, could be identified as a crazy person. For example, one evening during a social-skills group, five clients and I decided to take a walk for our assignment. Along the way, we found an older man sitting on some steps that were overgrown with greenery and almost hidden from view. As we approached, we could hear that he was talking. No one was with him, and a row of cough-syrup bottles were lined up in front of him. He was addressing God in directive and familiar fashion. Steven turned to the rest of us and said, "He's crazy!" After we all shared a good laugh about the irony of Steven's remark, we walked on. This man was an Outside Crazy.

Only by virtue of their experiences, diagnoses, and PACT patienthood did Outside Crazies qualify for inclusion in the "us" part of the distinction between "us" and "them." Relative to insiders, they shared with ego a lower quality and a smaller quantity of time, space, information, and resources. Relative to Outside Normals, they shared with ego a higher quality and a larger quantity of these commodities. With regard to symmetry, Outside Crazies had equal control of what was shared with ego. Being in PACT directly influenced what could be shared. In other words, a certain amount of sharing was involuntary, but negotiation as equals usually characterized the exchange beyond this level. Having psychiatric difficulties and being in the same treatment program entailed sharing powerful intimacies over which clients could exert little control.

INSIDE NORMALS

This category included persons who were not crazy, and who were aware that ego was crazy, but who did not refuse to interact with ego. Many Inside Normals had contact with ego *because* they were presumed normals and ego was crazy. Inside Normals included PACT staff, therapists, family, community volunteers, financial guardians, supervisors and counselors at the sheltered workshops, and the DVR counselor. Inside Normals shared resources, time, space and information with ego, but in asymmetrical fashion. That is, control of and access to these factors was held by Inside Normals in nearly all instances.

For example, space was controlled by PACT staff at the PACT house and at their own residences. They did not disclose their home addresses to clients, and clients did not visit them at their homes. In fact, they contracted with clients' parents to keep clients away from their homes. But staff persons knew clients' addresses, entered their places of residence, sometimes provided rent money for the spaces, and could exercise control by admitting clients to the hospital. The DVR counselor, another Inside Normal, controlled resources, such as subsidy for sheltered workshop employment, rent, and clothing. Further, he controlled time with clients in that they could see him only by appointment. Inside Normals also had much more information about clients than vice versa.

Nonprofessional Inside Normals (normal friends) were rare in the clients' interpersonal network. Only five clients had friends who (to my knowledge) were not in some way involved in psychiatric treatment. The client group as a whole did not have insider relationships with normals who were not part of the psychiatric treatment delivery system. Many clients had difficulty understanding why I would spend time with them, or would even like them, demonstrating how unaccustomed they were to interaction with Inside Normals who were not somehow treating or advising them. This observation was confirmed when I met several friends of clients. They were strangers to me, but they quickly revealed their Mendota Mental Health Institute alumni status or their current psychiatric difficulties. It was as if they were identifying themselves to me so that I could categorize them, as if they, too, recognized the same divisions.

Four female clients engaged in periodic, short-lived sexual relationships with normal males they had met in bars. Dorothy was an exception, having developed a long-lasting romantic involvement with a man she had met at Alcoholics Anonymous. But members of that group term themselves "sick people," and Dorothy's shared problem with alcohol abuse brought them together. Myrtle married while in the PACT program, but she had met her spouse at Mendota Mental Health Institute. He had a long history of psychiatric difficulties and abuse of cough syrup. Dennis was one of the few clients who lived with and had friendships with normals, and he also married while in PACT. The marriage ended in divorce after six months. Although his friends did not have formal psychiatric problems, most were heavily involved with street drugs and maintained a counter-culture stance toward the "liberals" of the community at large.

The clients as a group had few relationships with normals other than those who were involved with them as professional or volunteer helpers. Some clients avoided these contacts, expressing frustration with and painful awareness of their inadequacies when they compared themselves with normals. Steven, for example, disliked seeing old friends from high school because he was ashamed to say that he was not working and had spent much time just trying to cope with daily living. He also indicated that he was embarrassed to be seen with other clients, even his friends, if he ran into a normal acquaintance. The contacts with normals that did occur for clients outside the help-giving system seemed to be short-lived, negative experiences that highlighted differentness.

Mixed exceptions to this were provided by various landlords, coworkers, volunteers, and employers who took special and genuinely caring interest in some clients. The asymmetry in giving help remained in these relationships, as did discrepancies in access to resources, but these interactions had decidedly fewer boundaries and limits than did the professional ones. For example, the client women's group was run by women volunteers from the community. These women would go to bars with the group, would drink with clients, would talk about their jobs, their families, their personal lives, and would take no active evaluative or directive role with the clients. The clients perceived these women as "leaders" and depended upon them for transportation, ideas, and sometimes advice, but they did not talk to them about symptoms and current clinical problems, and they exhibited a sense of managing information and personal disclosure distinct from their interactions with staff. An occasional landlord or employer would take special interest in a client, offering meals, companionship, special consideration on rent or work hours, and cooperation with PACT staff in reaching treatment goals. Edgerton (1967) described a similar, although more frequently occurring, relationship among his adult mildly retarded subjects and their benefactors.

OUTSIDE NORMALS

Outside Normals were community members who usually were not aware that ego was crazy. If they were, they exhibited neutral, negative, avoidance, and perhaps punitive responses. These persons were not among those with whom ego voluntarily shared information, time, space, and resources. In fact, Outside Normals were avoided by ego. This category included landlords, employers, police, business persons, and other community members who were not formally or informally involved in the mental health care system.

Clients interacted with Outside Normals as infrequently as possible. When they did, it was usually for a formal or goal-oriented purpose. My observation was that the same held true for Outside Normals vis-à-vis clients. Few persons other than those offering resources (such as apartments, food, or jobs) or services (such as police) had reason to interact with the clients. Except for university students, state employees, and downtown shoppers, few outside normals shared the temporal-spatial arena around the Square. When community events were held in this space, events such as the annual summer art fair and the weekly farmer's market, the client population tended to withdraw, stating that they did not like the crowds and all the new people.

A CLOSER LOOK AT THE SYSTEM

Careful scrutiny of this classification scheme reveals some interesting features. It is perhaps most important to note that, in nearly every dimension, normals, both insiders and outsiders, had more control than clients and other crazy people over those aspects of living that attest to independent, positive selfhood. Clients' resources, in particular, were subject to almost total control by normals. For example, a PACT client could not obtain SSI money without the cooperation of the PACT staff and the service chief in verifying the disability and its causes. SSI workers then controlled the disbursement of the money, determining whether and when the client would receive it. A financial guardian usually controlled the use of the money, and this control could, in turn, influence how a client utilized his time (i.e., the amount of money available for entertainment, school, and travel).

During treatment, PACT staff had almost complete control in each area. When there was exchange, it was not equivalent. Staff had access to information about clients which clients did not have in relation to staff. Clients were unable to exchange resources with staff, for they had few resources to offer. The list of inequalities was nearly endless.

Clients, and others like them, were equal in relation to each other. Most had virtually equivalent access to and control of resources, time, space, and information. Those on SSI received the same incomes. The quality, size, and location of their living spaces were similar and were shared symmetrically. Any restriction on such sharing was voluntarily negotiated. Clients entered each others' living spaces, spent time with each other almost at will, and made loans to and borrowed from each other. They did not have to make appointments to see each other, as they usually did with normals, and they could engage in activities with each other, such as drinking alcohol, smoking marijuana, and having sex, that they did not customarily engage in with normals, especially with Inside Normals. Clients could also exercise control of the information and knowledge passed between them. There were no medical records, staff meetings, and therapy sessions to be communicated. Clients could choose what information they shared with each other. They could also choose what they shared with staff, but such information, once shared with staff, was taken in a sense out of clients' control and put into a systematic communication network.

Such a system did not enable clients to prove themselves independent, competent, and adequate in the face of life tasks. Opportunities for experiencing or even testing independence were not in abundance within the confines of the system. But many clients demonstrated consistent inability or lack of desire to take responsibility for, or control of, these dimensions of their lives. Clients often viewed responsibility and decision-making as stressful, but they became more dependent, ineffective persons by attempting to alleviate this discomfort, that is, by seeking treatment as unequals in a system where the help-givers appeared adequate, independent, and in control. Inside Normals, who promoted independence and control for and among clients, were bound, because of the values and structure of the social and treatment system, to frustrate their own attempts. Within the existing system, not being hospitalized did not automatically remove the messages of weakness, powerlessness, and incompetence from clients' environments.

Most research on the difficulties encountered in reintegrating the chronic mentally disabled, during psychiatric treatment, into communities, has focused on the exclusionary role played by community members (e.g., Aviram and Segal 1973; Schwartz et al. 1974). Little attention has been paid to the role played by clients themselves in creating and perpetuating the circumstances. Instead of perhaps further demeaning clients by perceiving them as passive victims of discrimination, it is possible to accord them more dignity and autonomy by ascertaining whether they *want* to be "integrated" and whether their isolation or clustering might not represent reasonable strategies.

Given the prevalence and power of the asymmetry that clients experience in relation to normals, by interacting primarily with other clients, they may be availing themselves of more opportunities to experience autonomy, symmetry, and reciprocity than they would encounter in any other sphere. By staying within the client group, they may, consciously or unconsciously, be choosing to identify with others in terms of commonly held values, resources, and experiences. Relatively speaking, this may represent a "healthy" choice. The painful and real obstacles to interacting symmetrically with normals dictate that many clients will feel far more comfortable, as we all do, among others like themselves. Comer and Piliavin (1972; 1975) found that physically handicapped persons exhibited and experienced more discomfort with a physically normal interviewer than with a physically handicapped interviewer. The highlighting of differentness in relation to others, especially when that differentness is negatively valued, may be sufficiently stressful to clients that they are innately wise to avoid such contacts.

In no way would I justify excluding these people from our lives or communities by saying "they want it this way." I would simply suggest that we view the processes of integration as being broadly interactive, that we acknowledge the client's capacity for choice, and that we not be ethnocentric, trying instead to understand the phenomenon from the insider's perspective. Most important, we should reexamine our own roles in perpetuating the asymmetries as we seek alternative means of relating to these people.

From a different perspective, Chamberlain (1978) suggests that one reason psychiatric patients ultimately concur with normals' evaluations of themselves as "sick" or "incompetent" is that they usually are not permitted or encouraged to help one another. This was true at PACT, but, as the CAS responses revealed, clients themselves perceived their friends as not giving help when it was needed. My ethnographic data are filled with clients' remarks about one anothers' craziness and incompetence. The empirical question should be raised as to whether these attitudes can be changed. Perhaps they are inevitably responsive to the messages that are explicit and implicit in the treatment system and our culture. We know very little about friendships among clients, their social and interpersonal networks, and the impact that these have on their lives and treatment.

In an excellent and extensive review of social networks and schizophrenia, Hammer et al. (1978) report that schizophrenic subjects tend to have smaller, more asymmetrical networks than nonschizophrenics. These networks are sparse, loosely interconnected, fluctuating, and often other-mediated. Such contacts are associated with rehospitalization, poor prognosis, and changes in levels of symptomatology. These researchers argue that the "reduced cultural predictability" of schizophrenics, as reflected in their speech and communication patterns, contributes to and is a part of what we call schizophrenia. This approach, which seems promising, focuses on cultural, value, and behavioral differences rather than on pathology.

Sokolovsky et al. (1978), investigating this subject in a Manhattan SRO hotel, confirmed that schizophrenic persons, impaired minimally to severely, had smaller networks than nonpsychotic residents. Relationships among the severely impaired schizophrenics tended to be dependent, loosely interconnected, and associated with higher rates of hospitalization. Relationships among the minimally impaired were more autonomous, goal-directed, and interconnected. These researchers point to the potential supportive and preventive features of friendships among schizophrenic outpatients, but they do not suggest modes of facilitation.

The usefulness of this classification scheme hinges upon what it tells us about the social and interpersonal relationships of clients. Inside Normals and Inside Crazies are the most powerful persons in the clients' everyday world, and these two groups provide the clients with the most paradoxically negative indications about themselves. It seems that the only persons with whom clients can have symmetrical, limitless relations are other crazies. In his relations with normals, the client encounters structures, codes, and regulations. These normals not only have more control of, and responsibility for, their own lives but often of the clients' lives as well. In addition, the normals who are most important in clients' lives (Inside Normals) usually stand in this relation *because* of the clients' psychiatric problems and consequent life difficulties. Thus, although these people are help-givers, they may also serve as potent daily reminders to clients of their own deficits and differentness in comparison with normals.

The real cultural craziness here is that not only do we describe these persons as pathologically dependent but we contribute to their dependencies. Not only do we view them as unintegrated within the community but we isolate them by constantly reminding them of their incompetencies and by introducing them to peers (in treatment programs like PACT) with whom they may be more comfortable. We provide professionals to help these persons, as a society seem to prefer to pay others to deal with them and thereby undermine any motivation that community members or other clients might have to participate in the caring and treatment process. We provide these networks and services even though hospital studies have shown that a steady diet of other clients and staff is detrimental to self-esteem and to "getting well." We negatively value these persons, collectively and as individuals, for their differentness and their dependencies, but we leave them little chance to give us anything except "getting better" (which means being more like us).

RULES FOR MAKING IT CRAZY

To summarize and synthesize the foregoing data, and to clarify the clients' perspective and working dynamics, I put forth the following rules for making it crazy:

1. Have the ability to become psychotic voluntarily or experience psychosis involuntarily.

2. Assume that if you do not take care of yourself someone else will.

3. Assume or fear that you will never get better.

4. Assume that you are going to fail at almost everything except patienthood.

5. Sincerely try new things, like working, every once in a while; but when you get fired, or quit, prove to yourself and others that you really are sick and cannot manage.

6. When you get bored or lonely (or genuinely motivated), say you want to go to school or to get a job and get someone to help you try it.

7. Assume that medications probably help, but do not trust them or the motives of the people who want you to take them; or assume you have a biochemical imbalance and must take medications forever, which are supposed to make you well but never quite do.

8. Be afraid to get better because:

   (a) It has been so long that you cannot remember what it is like, and it is therefore unknown and frightening.

   (b) You might lose the security, safety, predictability, and benefits of your sick role (i.e., lowered expectations of self, and, from others, special attention and income).

   (c) You might lose your Inside Crazy friends who are like you, and lose your therapist and other Inside Normals; and you have no reason to believe that Outside Normals will like you, and you are not sure that you will like them.

9. Do not give up altogether, because then you will have to kill yourself; or perhaps Inside Normals will give up, too, and then you will be rejected. Have just enough hope to keep yourself alive and to keep them involved.

10. Do not become too compliant and cooperative with Inside Normals, especially staff, because they will think you are too dependent and will reject you. Or if you really do comply with treatment, then you will either have to get better or get psychotic (just when things are going well so that you can start all over).

11. Periodically feel guilty, worthless, anxious, miserable, depressed, and hostile about all of the above, yourself, and others.

12. Help everyone else and yourself to make it impossible to be any different.

I suggest that if one were to follow these rules, s/he would find himself or herself in much the same predicament as our subjects. But before proceeding, we should take note of those clients who broke some of the rules and managed to make it minus their craziness.

MAKING IT WITHOUT CRAZINESS

It may seem that all the evidence presented thus far has cataloged failures, both of persons and of the sociocultural system within which they operate, to alter significantly or even to terminate the comfort and agony of making it crazy. But four clients either made it out of the system, reconstructing a well self, or are on their way at present. Before examining their particular strategies, I offer criteria for making it without craziness:

1. Perceived positive changes in feelings and behavior on the part of the client; perceived separation from PACT and from Inside and Outside Crazies.
2. Subsistence provided by positively culturally sanctioned means, apart from disability and special status.
3. Negligible to zero contact with psychiatric professional Inside Normals; concurrent decrease or termination of psychoactive medication.
4. Establishment of multiple primary interpersonal and social relationships with normals.

As is evident, I have reversed most of the criteria for making it crazy.

GOING HOME

Two persons were able to return to their parents' homes with apparent success at getting better. Sarah had a three-month tenure in the PACT program before my fieldwork began. Against the strong advice of program staff, she and her parents decided that life in Madison in one of the old hotels was not for her, and she discharged herself. During three visits to Sarah at her parents' home, her mother related to me the difficulty of their discharge decision:

> Well, when she first started in PACT she was so confused. They had her living at the YMCA, and she tried everything to get out of the program. She tried to jump off the roof. She set fire to herself. Then they moved her down to the Cardinal Hotel, which is just the most awful place. I mean, she could have been seduced or anything. People down there were on drugs and everything. That was just it for us. Our daughter was not going to live in a place like that. And then I got this letter from Dr. C. charging us with the responsibility if Sarah committed suicide. He refused to handle any medications for her.

During another interview she said:

Well, you just have to go by your heart. It was a risk, and we knew it, but we just couldn't bear it; and Sarah is doing so beautifully now. Those were hard times, and we just didn't know what to do.

Sarah's version of her experience is as follows:

The people on the staff are very nice people, but at the time all I wanted was to be away from PACT. I was too confused, scared, and lonely to get much out of it. I was angry with everyone then. I just wanted to be away. At first, it felt like they were running my life, making me do activities every night. But then I felt really lonely. At first, I thought I'd be living at home and going to PACT a couple of times a week. I didn't know I'd have to live there. That was a lot of it—having to live in Madison. I was scared.

Q. If you had stayed in PACT, do you think your life would be different than it is now?

A. Life would have been different but I wouldn't have liked it. I like it better the way it is now, here.

Q. [I pressed for hindsight on the PACT experience.]

A. I was pretty doped up then from medication. I don't remember much of it. It's a part of my life I've forgotten about. Why remember it?

Currently, Sarah's lithium dosage has been drastically reduced and her visits to a local psychiatrist are quarterly instead of weekly, as they were when she first left PACT. It is evident that, with great turmoil, Sarah and her family were able to leave the promise of PACT for a different sort of treatment.

Ben also went home, but after staying in the program for the full twelve months. He also quit his job at MOC. Upon discharge from PACT, he was discouraged. When I congratulated him on the occasion, he said, "Well, I haven't accomplished anything. I don't have anything to feel proud of." Gradually, his life has changed. He has completed a semester of school and has a part-time job. Ben's process of exit from the crazy system was powerfully highlighted for me when he and I visited his brother, Steven, who was hospitalized. Steven was in seclusion when we arrived, so Ben took me on a tour of his "old stomping grounds," another ward in the hospital. His pleasure was immense at the surprise and marvel of the ward staff about his present appearance and condition. He exuded a sense of satisfaction with himself and he was not embarrassed about his past. It was as though, against that background and history, his present transition had gained momentum and new meaning.

HAVING A JOB

Tex has also left much of his patienthood behind, but with a different strategy. He was one of the few clients who had obtained the skills and experience necessary to engage in high-paying employment. A construction worker, Tex has gradually rid himself of his enemy, Prolixin, and has been working steadily for some time. Members of his union helped him to retain his membership during his difficult experiences and they paved the way for his return.

Despite these extraordinary advantages, over the four years since the research has ended Tex has continued to be involved with PACT and other help givers. He contacted me in the fall of 1979 while he was in confinement for not keeping up with child support payments to his former wife. He joked with me about manipulating the system with his disability to get the payments reduced, but I became aware of his continued enmeshment with and reliance on the legal and psychiatric system. I now doubt that Tex will ever be completely free of these supports. Still, relative to the rest of the group, he is making it.

HAVING FAITH

Jerry has succeeded in exiting the crazy system for the most part, though he keeps in touch with friends he acquired among fellow clients. His strategy in leaving was based upon his deep, nearly fanatical involvement with a religious organization. Other clients often made fun of his devout and enthusiastic faith, but he held fast to the ideals and, more importantly, to the interpersonal network of normals provided by the group. His religious involvement provided not only interpersonal support but also avenues for expending time in Bible study, in attending religious classes, and in handing out leaflets on street corners. Jerry believes that his psychotic experiences had religious significance and were intended to inform him of his need for faith and commitment to the particular church he has chosen.

Because of a special friendship, I have kept in contact with Jerry for the past five years. He held a competitive job at the University as a hospital worker for a long while, was seeing a psychiatrist monthly, and was taking minimal amounts of medication. I envisioned him making linear progress toward a life free of his past troubles.

The despair and pain I experienced when I met Jerry, quite unexpectedly, on an inpatient psychiatric unit where I was engaged in another research project, were immense. He was aggressive, suspicious, vulgar, and argumentative. He had lost a noticeable amount of weight. He had been eating very little and sleeping even less. I found that he had been selling encyclopedias door to door and living at home with his mother. This was an incredible contrast with the happy, sensitive, independent person I had come to know. He was psychotic.

Over time on the unit, his psychosis cleared and he became more like the Jerry I had known before. His psychiatrist believes that Jerry was previously misdiagnosed, and he now prescribes lithium carbonate for what seems to be a bipolar affective disorder. To date, Jerry has not been readmitted and he seems to be piecing his life back together with the help of an outpatient program run by the hospital. His active religious involvement has definitely waned, but his faith remains firm.

Meeting again under such circumstances was a wrenching experience for both of us. It was embarrassing for Jerry, instructive for me. I re-encountered my old naivete and hopefulness about these people, and I learned that really making it out of this system, this crazy way, may be an even more difficult task than I had thought.

Within this small sample, if any patterns are to be found, they would seem to revolve around having someplace else to go and having long-term involvement with Inside Normals other than psychiatric professionals. It is difficult to make more than anecdotal note of these cases, for they are so few. Furthermore, the future brought psychiatric relapses for some of the members of this group. They have indeed grown in many ways since our PACT days, but I concede an inability to predict or fully understand who will make it, how, and for how long.

PART III

INTERPRETATIONS AND CONCLUSIONS

. . . by the time people discover what is going on, they are so deeply involved that they can't back out.
—Hall 1966:5

PROLOGUE

Everything outside was coated with inches of lovely and awesome ice in the early spring of 1976. Nothing mechanical was working well; artificial heat and light that had been yesterday's taken-for-granted conveniences were today's irritatingly absent necessities. My main concerns were the welfare of my tropical fish and how difficult it had become to have hot coffee when I wanted it.

Downtown, Sam was thinking in different terms. He had a paying job for the first time in a long while. And he had moved out of the YMCA into an apartment that was the envied meeting place of his friends, Cy, Doc, and Humphrey. But that morning, none of this seemed to matter. Sam went to a store and purchased a gun. Walking into a nearby alley, he removed his gloves, lay down, and shot himself in the head.

His death bewildered, hurt, saddened, and angered all of us who knew him. We felt helpless, frightened, and unable to understand why he had taken his own life. Especially then, when things seemed to be going well for the first time in ever so long. Reflecting on this loss, on this seemingly senseless act, helped me to discover what was happening to the people I was trying to understand. Sam, I think, recognized the trap that he and others had made of his life. He saw where he was going, who he had become, who his friends were, and what they were all doing with their lives. He was surrounded with broken dreams, bleak futures, and the stagnant present of his friends. Their days were filled with marijuana and beer; and he was having a difficult time being different from them and going to work. His recent successes highlighted how far he had to go—indeed, how far from his expectations he had drifted or even run. It must have seemed to him that the only way to resolve these discrepancies was the way he chose. Perhaps he saw himself as another psychiatric patient saw herself: "a pitiful creature who could not cope with life as she found it—nor could she escape it—nor adjust herself to it" (Kaplan 1964:9).

I do not mean to suggest that death was the only way clients could extricate themselves from the crazy identity and circumstances with which they existed. Rather, I hope to communicate the potency of their predicament. In analyzing the interactions of persons with psychiatric disorder, their treatment, and the larger sociocultural context of their lives, it is too easy to avoid or to oversimplify the human, often tragic, dimension. It is seductively less unsettling to examine social structures and processes minus their personal, immeasurable impact on individual lives. And it is persuasively simplistic to stress the tragedy and to overlook the essentially bittersweet, paradoxical nature of these lives. We must remind ourselves that we are trying to understand persons who are absorbed in the creation of day-to-day living that, though negatively valued and often painful, is nonetheless rewarding.

8

REVIEWS OF RELEVANT LITERATURE

Perhaps nowhere does the complicated nature of our subject become more evident than in surveying relevant research and writing. Academic and clinical personnel from diverse disciplines have joined forces to describe, assess, plan, and implement community-based treatment for psychiatric patients. For reasons of emphasis, the focus of this review is on two areas: (1) community treatment of long-term psychiatric patients, and (2) psychiatric anthropology and ethnography of deviant or marginal persons.

Because extensive bibliographic (Bloom 1968; Driver 1972; Pearsall 1963) and analytic (Bachrach 1976, 1978; Test and Stein 1978*a* and *c;* Paul 1969; Talbott 1978; Fabrega 1972*b;* Lieban 1973) reviews already exist, such areas of inquiry as evaluation research, epidemiology, public health, medical sociology, and community psychology, which could be included in an orientation to the subject of psychiatric patienthood in a community setting, are excluded. Material is included in the discussion based on its pertinence to our specific subject, its utility in highlighting important issues, and its capacity to represent areas touched on only briefly in this book. My purpose is to place the book in its historical, theoretical, and empirical contexts.

COMMUNITY PSYCHIATRIC TREATMENT[1]

The majority of related writing in this field can be classified as follows:

1. Discussions of the development, theory, concepts, potentials, and goals of community psychiatry (Roberts 1966; Sabshin 1966; Caplan 1964, 1965; Dunham 1969; Susser 1968; Bellak 1974; Klerman 1977; Bachrach 1978).

2. Negative criticism (Denner 1974; Arnhoff 1975; Kirk and Therrien 1975; Kubie 1968; Chu and Trotter 1974; Slovenko and Luby 1974; Lamb and Goertzl 1971; *U.S. News and World Report* 1977:90-91; Bachrach 1976:15, note 5) and defense (Zusman and Lamb 1977; Langsley and Barter 1975; Lamb and Goertzl 1972; Barahal 1971; Bachrach 1976:15-22) of community psychiatry and community treatment in practice and theory.

3. Descriptive, outcome, and follow-up studies of various community treatment programs (Greenblatt and Budson 1976; Fairweather et al. 1969; Rutman and Baron 1975; Sanders, Smith, and Weinman 1967; Weinman et al. 1970; Pasamanick et al. 1967; Stein, Test, and Marx 1975; Marx, Test, and Stein 1973; Test and Stein 1978*b;* Hansell and Willis 1977; Segal and Aviram 1978).

Classifications 1 and 2 are included for orientation and background. Classification 3 provides a context within which to appreciate the PACT program. Because of the lack of work similar to my own, involving clients of other treatment programs, this review can provide only a minimal basis for comparison. Community treatment has not been evaluated as extensively from the client's point of view as it has been in relation to the goals and purposes of the providers of treatment. In a sense, therefore, this review underscores the rationale for my project.

Many persons trace the current proliferation of community treatment or de-institutionalization (see Bachrach 1976:1-14) to the national Community Mental Health Centers Act initiated by

1. The idea and practice of social psychiatry predates the development of modern community psychiatry (see Arthur 1973; Jones 1968). The latter can be perceived to have been a clinical outgrowth and partner of the former (Sabshin 1966). Indeed, the field of social psychiatry engendered some of the earliest empirical collaboration between social scientists and psychiatrists (see Leighton et al. 1957).

President Kennedy in 1973 (e.g., Yolles 1968:279, 1969:vii; Glenn 1975). The roots of the movement, however, can be traced much further (Rossi 1969; Roman 1971; Galdston 1965; Williams et al. 1978). In a fascinating and lucid account of this subject, Caplan and Caplan (1969:3) describe its origins:

> During the first half of the nineteenth century, American psychiatrists were fascinated by the idea that the physical and social environment might play the key role in determining mental health and illness. They therefore attempted to manipulate the milieux not only of their hospital wards but also of the lay community in order to provide a therapeutic rather than a pathogenic experience. This goal was akin to that of modern community psychiatry, and the methods used to achieve it were often strikingly similar.[2]

They explain further:

> Early nineteenth century practitioners, therefore, were eager to manipulate facets of both extramural and institutional life in order to encourage optimum conditions for the prevention of mental disorder, for early case finding and rapid treatment, and for averting relapses among discharged patients. They tried to reach these objectives first in programs directed toward the lay community, second in the organization of institutions, and third in the interface between these two milieux. [ibid.:10]

So, the motivation and the rationale for community treatment were present in the American psychiatric profession nearly a century ago. Owing to setbacks not unlike those experienced by current community treatment advocates, this early enthusiasm seems to have foundered. As Caplan and Caplan surmise, ". . . a major weakness of moral treatment was that it had been oversold to the public; whatever success it had was ultimately overshadowed by disappointment in its failure to perform miracles" (ibid.:88). Compare this with Glenn's (1975:30) characterization of contemporary

2. It is interesting to speculate further on the implications of this statement, and on the evidence presented throughout the book, about the role of psychoactive drugs in facilitating community treatment. To my knowledge, psychoactive medications were not widely used or even discovered at this time. But these psychiatrists envisioned and contemplated alterations of treatment modalities which today are thought of as possible only with use of psychoactive medications.

community treatment as a humanitarian movement with four phases or periods: "The first is a period of innovation or new ideas. This peaks rapidly after the initial outburst of enthusiasm, as the community mental health movement did between 1965 and 1970. The peak is followed by a period of criticism and a time of retrenchment. . . . The wave of criticism that follows the innovative humanitarian idea is brought about by overloading the system that is responsible for implementing the new trend."

Developmental parallels have existed in the process and content, values and goals of early American psychiatry *qua* moral treatment and current community treatment. More important, practitioners have manifested a persistent concern for the quality, environment, and outcome of psychiatric treatment for their patients. This concern has led to recurrent examination of the interaction of treatment modalities, settings, and philosophies with patients' actual disorders and consequent problems in living outside the psychiatric institution.

An example of this learning and discovering process predating the PACT program is recounted by Stein and Test (n.d.). They attribute development of their particular brand of community treatment to many factors, including their experiences in discharging chronic psychiatric patients who had been involved in a special inpatient program designed to break their "code of chronicity" (Ludwig 1971).[3] They write, "It became increasingly clear to us that the crucial variable in producing post-discharge success was an intensive and sustained aftercare treatment program" (ibid.:2). "Aftercare"

3. Ludwig's (1971) account of the development and dynamics of the chronic culture, or code of chronicity, is far superior to others I have read in the psychiatric and sociological literature. With the sensitivity, perceptivity, and intuition of a clinician, he has detailed how patients come to accept and to protect their roles and identities as persons eternally crazy, inadequate, and deserving of care. In addition, he has identified attitudes on the part of hsopital staff and clients' families which contributed to this process. Ludwig has defined the chronic culture as "certain schizophrenic subcultural attitudes and behaviors, which are nurtured within a mental institution, enhanced by the presence of other chronic patients, and reinforced by a complementary set of attitudes and behaviors on the part of the hospital staff as well as the professional community at large" (p. 46). The patient code consists, in essence, of a "Topsy-turvy world in which all acceptable attitudes and standards of behavior are reversed . . . there is a 180° reversal of the middle-class, work-oriented, responsibility-laden value system" (p. 53). Staff responses to this code, such as sympathy, being effectively threatened and manipulated by psychotic behavior, and fear of enforcing responsibility expectations on disabled persons (p. 15 ff.), aided in perpetuating the code.

referred to those aspects of posthospitalization treatment designed to help the patient readjust to community life in terms of living situation, employment, and social activities. The possibility of treatment without the apparent confounding effect of hospitalization was considered. If the hospital experience were complicating life for already harassed patients, why not remove that obstacle for them by eliminating inpatient admission altogether? Through a series of innovations, experimental steps, and logical extensions of treatment philosophy regarding prevention and easing of this adjustment process, the total community treatment approach was developed (ibid.:4).

This brief historic view of the purpose and development of community treatment provides a base for assessing critical response, both within the profession and from the community, and for examining the current realities of this treatment modality. Adverse criticism of community-treatment philosophy, practice, and results has come from inside and outside the mental health-care profession (cf. Bachrach 1976:23–40; Mechanic 1975). The most prevalent and forceful attacks have included charges of:

1. Increased material and psychological costs to families of patients and community members (e.g., Arnhoff 1975; Test and Stein 1980).

2. Lack of adequate supportive and psychiatric health-care services for patients living in the community (e.g., Chu and Trotter 1974; Lamb and Goertzl 1972).

3. Poor quality of life, social isolation, and financial destitution of patients living in the community, particularly chronically disturbed persons (e.g., Lamb and Goertzl 1971; Reich 1973; Reich and Siegel 1973; Zusman and Lamb 1977; Lamb 1979*b;* Aviram and Segal 1973; Talbott 1979).

4. The promising of more services and results than the system was prepared to deliver; and personnel problems within the health-care delivery system (e.g., Denner 1974; Mendel 1978; Lamb 1979*a*).

Many of the above charges have been overstated and overdramatized with a fervor that has undermined much of their validity. But each claim has been substantiated to some degree and has been acknowledged as reasonable by treatment system personnel. Perhaps most prevalent have been the fears expressed about the dangerousness and violence of psychiatric patients released into the community. Nearly all systematic, empirical work has shown the involvement of these persons in violent crime to be equal to or only slightly more than that of the general population (Zitrin et al. 1976; Rabkin 1979). In fact, some clinicians have stressed the vulnerability of such persons to becoming victims of crime (*U.S. News and World Report* 1977). Recent debate about reported large increases in the crime rate among psychiatric patients leaves unresolved questions concerning the influence on these figures of frequent hospitalization of criminals and changes in commitment laws that make dangerous behavior a criterion for involuntary hospitalization (Armstrong 1980). Public fears seem easily fueled, but legitimate concerns remain.

Community treatment practitioners and advocates have countered these claims in two ways. First, they have presented successful programs and treatment results demonstrating that not all psychiatric patients were falling between the cracks in communities, behaving bizarrely or violently or living isolated, miserable lives. Second, the psychiatric profession has increasingly moderated its claims for achievement. The attitude has become one of acknowledging limitations while working to reduce them. Recognition of the immensity and multitude of treatment tasks has led to a reduction in hopes and claims for success. This stance might be characterized by the statement that "we are doing the best we can with the tools available to us against many stubborn obstacles" (cf. Bachrach 1976:19–22).

Community treatment exists in many forms, but my concern here is with attempts to treat without using the psychiatric hospital. Home care (Polack 1978), family care (Pasamanick et al. 1967), halfway houses (Glasscote et al. 1971*a*), psychosocial rehabilitation centers (Glasscote et al. 1971*b*), residential community treatment (Mosher and Menn 1978; Fairweather et al. 1969), and treatment using community volunteers as primary help-givers (Weinman et al. 1970) have all been utilized successfully to maintain clients in a community setting. The above experiments have demonstrated the feasibility of treating persons who might have been hospitalized in a community setting. They have shown that these subjects customarily fare better than do hospitalized controls when measured in terms of social and psychiatric adjustment. These differences have tended to fade over time, however, and, in some instances, adjustment measures between community experimentals and hospital controls have not differed significantly. There has been general agreement that chronic or long-term patients, such as our subjects, have not received adequate attention from community mental health programs (Lamb and Goertzl 1977).

Test and Stein (1978*a*) have found the data to be encouraging, and they have concluded that "such treatment approaches appear to be as effective as, and often more effective than, longer term hospital treatment and have also been found to cost less." But they also have recognized the limitations of the various programs, noting that hospital readmission rates have been significant for the chronic segment of the treated population, especially over time, and that social and personal adjustment has seemed to remain low (ibid.). Tenure of stay in the community and length of employment have been increased for experimental groups during treatment programs, but sustained satisfaction with community living and enriched or adequate social interaction within the community at large have been conspicuously lacking as long-term results of these experiments.

For the professional and lay staffs, it has proved feasible to treat the severely psychiatrically disturbed patient in the community. But for the patient and his family, the readmission rates and the lack of subjective and qualitative increases in living adjustments (such as employment and interpersonal relationships) would indicate that community treatment may have liabilities. The possibility is being increasingly considered that patients may be subject to as much social control as before, but in a different setting (Chamberlain 1978). As Klerman (1977:629) asks: "The essential question here is not whether the patient in the community is 'better off' than the hospitalized patient, it is the moral issue of whether or not he is being given a choice in the matter."

CULTURAL ANTHROPOLOGY

In studying psychiatric disorder, or abnormal and different behavior, and its treatment within a cultural context, my work has been influenced and directed by conceptions that can be identified as anthropological because of their relativistic, holistic, actor-oriented nature.[4] Psychiatry and anthropology complement each other in what Kluckhohn has called man's most interesting effort, his attempt to understand himself and his behavior (cited in Dean et al. 1976:40).

From this foundation, disease, health, and illness are seen as culturally defined conditions expressing cultural codes and social circumstances as well as organic conditions. At the individual level, therefore, the experience and the consequences of being ill are connected to the cultural context. The interaction of the individual experience and the cultural code, as conveyed by institutions and by other members of one's world, represents the arena in which illness is conceptualized, defined, and lived. Being ill, or crazy, can be viewed as a way of living that is influenced or controlled by the individual's immersion in the values and behaviors of his or her variation of the larger cultural context. On one level, the cultural group, and its values and beliefs regarding disease and health, influence the illness experience and social circumstances of the ill person. The ill person, in turn, expresses not only his or her particular disease or difference, but adapts to the constraints of the prevailing behavior and belief system about illness and disease (cf. Mechanic 1972; Fabrega 1974*b*).

ANTHROPOLOGY AND PSYCHIATRY

As is often true of interdisciplinary enterprise, anthropologists and psychiatrists have engaged in more theoretical and abstract discussion than in joint empirical projects. Collaboration and trespass be-

4. It is important to mention here that the anthropological approach has been most often applied by sociologists to the study of types of deviance in general, and of mental illness in particular. A large body of such literature has accumulated, though with little recognition of the obvious methodological and theoretical debt to cultural anthropology. Winslow and Winslow (1974) have presented individual cases of deviance as alternate world views. Douglas (1970, 1972) and others have described in detail the field methods of participant observation with deviant subjects. And Becker (1963, 1964) has advocated and utilized a relativistic, nonethnocentric, subject-oriented approach to the study of deviance. Other sociologists, notably Scheff (1966) and Mechanic (1977*b*), have stressed the importance of viewing mental illness as a social product and process expressing and reflecting cultural values about normalcy, illness, and general codes of conduct. I will not review this literature but will instead integrate these concepts and theories into the interpretive framework.

tween psychiatrists and cultural anthropologists are not new,[5] and both professions have acknowledged their potential and actual mutual relevance (cf. Kluckhohn 1944; Sapir 1932, 1938; Devereux 1956; Opler 1969; Wittkower and Dubreuil 1971; Sullivan 1964). To date, however, anthropological research germane to community psychiatry in the United States has been relatively sparse. The existing studies have been decidedly lacking in ethnographic material and have been top-heavy with enthusiastic theoretical paradigms for future research (Edgerton 1971:29; Leininger 1971).

Kennedy (1973), Edgerton (1971), Favazza and Oman (1978), and Dunham (1976) have extensively analyzed and reviewed the anthropology-psychiatry interface. My purpose will be to synthesize, to suggest the impact of each discipline on the other. To psychiatry, anthropology has brought emphasis on the great diversity in human styles of adaptation to be found globally. Its lessons have been not to underestimate human plasticity or creativity, and to take as problematic the range of variation in response to similar and different human and nonhuman environmental circumstances (cf. Wallace 1970:123–163). The lessons of ethnography have spoiled presumptive generalizations about conformity, normalcy, and stability in social systems. Expectations of homogeneity and persistence have given way to realistic appraisals of diversity and the normalcy of change. Further, because such diverse and multiple variables have been found to influence all forms of human social and personal conduct, anthropologists have learned to take a holistic,

5. Historical accounts of the relationship between psychiatry and anthropology often fail to distinguish between the actual collaboration of professionals and the inherent complementarity of the two disciplines. Dubreuil and Wittkower (1974) take the latter tack, as does Kluckhohn (1944), to a certain extent, and they recognize an essential, persistent interface between the two disciplines. Most other writers (e.g., Rossi 1969; Kennedy 1973) focus on the influences of Boas, of his students Benedict and Mead, and of Kroeber and Freud, in bringing to fruition the promises of collaboration and enrichment of each discipline with the skills and materials of the other. Convergence of interest on the varieties and meanings of human behavior, thought, perception, and religious belief have and will continue to bring these two schools together. Beyond this common ground in subject matter, anthropologists and psychiatrists employ similar means to learn and understand human behavior. Both attempt to comprehend the human experience through extensive, intensive, face-to-face interaction with their subjects. Both recognize the validity of individual constructions and perceptions of reality, though anthropologists do not diagnose large deviations from the norm as being pathological. And both learn inductively from individual, clinical observation of subjects.

nonethnocentric, nonegocentric view of human behavior. Absolute concepts of normal and abnormal behavior have been displaced by compelling ethnographic evidence of wide variability in the treatment and identification of inappropriate behavior by diverse groups in a multitude of social, ecological, and geographic situations. Appropriateness of behavior has been shown to be relative, to be determined only in context, and in light of the values, traditions, circumstances, and persons involved (Edgerton 1976).

To anthropology, psychiatry has contributed the particular wisdom and tools needed for examining the interaction of individual development and personality configuration with cultural codes and conventions. Psychiatry has conveyed a view of the individual as a feeling, perceiving entity, and not simply as a bearer of culture. Psychiatrists have learned not to view individuals in a psychic vacuum, but within a social, cultural, and interpersonal system. Anthropologists have learned less well to consider individual psychological processes and stresses as aspects of broad cultural phenomena (Estroff 1978).

From within the ethnographic diversity noted above, a set of universal propositions has emerged concerning the relationship of culture to psychiatric disorder. Wittkower and Dubreuil (1973:691-692) have summarized these tenets: (1) mental illness is found in all human societies; (2) the rates of mental illness are higher in some cultures than in others; (3) some cultures seem to predispose specific psychopathological patterns; and (4) all or most cultures have devised techniques by which the mentally ill are identified, treated, rejected, or classified into particular social clusters. The third and fourth principles find application in medical-psychiatric anthropology and in transcultural psychiatry.

MEDICAL-PSYCHIATRIC ANTHROPOLOGY AND TRANSCULTURAL PSYCHIATRY

Medical anthropology is a label recently adopted for an area of inquiry that has always been a part of ethnographic research. Varieties of human thought and behavior regarding physical and mental misfortune, birth, and death have been recorded for cultures throughout the world under the topic headings of magic and belief systems, witchcraft, religion, ritual, curing, and "primitive" medicine or explanations of disease. Only during the past three decades, however, have these subjects received rigorous attention, and most of this activity has occurred within the past ten years. Even more recent has been the widespread investigation of Western, particularly American, systems of behavior and belief regarding physical and mental health, illness, and curing (Foster 1974; Olesen 1974; Torrey 1972).

Recent transcultural psychiatric studies include descriptions of the concepts and phenomenology of disease and health (Manning and Fabrega 1973), disease etiological systems (Foster 1976), illness behavior, definition, and treatment as aspects of culture (Glick 1967; Cawte 1974; Westermeyer and Wintrob 1979*a* and *b;* Scheper-Hughes 1979), and indigenous treatment of psychiatric disorder (Kennedy 1967; Kiev 1964, 1968). Conceptions of the treatments for psychiatric disorder vary widely, as do social and personal consequences for the ill individual, depending upon notions of causality, cure, and cultural significance of the malady (Kennedy 1973:1173; Waxler 1977). Kennedy (ibid.) has suggested that labels applied to deviants in non-Western cultures produce less fear and anxiety in the individual, not only because a wider range of variation in behaviors is tolerated, but because such notions of causality as sorcery and spirit possession, offer more comprehensive and efficacious curing paradigms than our own.

Utilizing the perspective of medical-psychiatric anthropology, the same naiveté and curiosity can be focused upon the intricacies and cultural connections of American psychiatry and conceptions of psychiatric disorder. Within this paradigm, disordered persons can be viewed as individuals living with "both the symptoms and consequences of disease in its physical and mental, medical and social aspects" (Von Mering 1970:272). Concepts of disease can be seen as cultural classifications of adversity reflecting the group's general attitude toward misfortune. The individual reaction of the ill person to his symptoms, and to their identification and treatment, can be seen as the particular expression of important cultural values (Lieban 1973:1047). All this is brought into sharper focus by the attempt to understand the individual's experience of being ill within a particular cultural context, that is, to perceive the act of being crazy as an anthropological subject, as one of man's many experiments in living (Von Mering 1970:278).

ANTHROPOLOGICAL ACCOUNTS OF DEVIANTS AND PERSONS WITH PSYCHIATRIC DISORDERS

Relative to the theoretical and transcultural ethnographic literature, very few anthropological studies have focused on persons in North America who have psychiatric disorders or who are seen as deviant, marginal, and negatively different. Reynolds (Reynolds and Farberow 1977) studied psychiatric aftercare facilities in California by assuming a patient identity and living in several of these homes. By immersing himself in the role and the environment he was able to learn about the boredom, aloneness, peacefulness, and comfort experienced by many discharged psychiatric patients. Much of his residential care seemed an invitation to inadequacy, for his treatment was either too impersonal or too solicitous. Friendly residential care, oriented toward enhancing feelings of personal adequacy, could, he suggested, do much to bolster and comfort the ex-patient. But a delicate balance needed to be struck, he found, between nurturing the ex-patient's security and encouraging his responsibility for himself.

Spradley's (1970, 1973) study of urban nomads and drunks was also made from the perspective of the researcher as insider. Spradley sought to discover the culture of urban nomads and to provide information and rules of conduct for operating in a like manner, and for understanding the world as they did (Spradley 1970:7). He demonstrated that the nomad's interaction with legal and correctional institutions served to perpetuate the drunken hobo culture, not only by encouraging mobility to avoid incarceration for vagrancy but by fostering the "deserved" drunk after release from jail (ibid.:5).

A group of similar studies on street drug addicts has been reported (Stephens and McBride 1976; Weppner 1973; Agar 1973). From a cultural, interactionist, and participant's point of view, Weppner has described the street addict's values, behaviors, and attitudes, concluding that

> The street addict is very ethnocentric in defending his cultural system against the culture of the "square" whom he scorns anyway. To the street addict, the square's life style is useless, and it may be part of what drove the addict to drugs in the first place. Recidivism or relapse, may not be so much a failure to adopt a new way of life as a comfortable regression to one which is known, understood, and has many positive

> reinforcement features. Essentially, the street addict is as much hooked to a way of life as to a chemical. [1973:118]

The similarities to what I have described among some long term psychiatric patients are indeed striking.

Edgerton (1967) studied ways in which mildly retarded adults living in the community coped with stigma. He reported a fascinating set of accounts and adaptive strategies. Somewhat like the adult mentally ill person, the retarded person must struggle to overcome the incorrigible proposition of his legitimated incompetence to survive. Edgerton found that benefactors, or unusually concerned and genuinely caring community members, proved invaluable in providing the ongoing support and guidance needed by these retarded adults.

Scheper-Hughes (1979) examined the social conditions that contributed to or lessened a marked tendency among rural Irish to become schizophrenic. Combining the elements of a disease theory of schizophrenia, the lively verbal play among normals, the characteristic verbal poverty and confusion among schizophrenics, and the asylum of institutionalization compared with rather dreary outside alternatives, Scheper-Hughes suggested cultural contributions to the expression and continuation of schizophrenia in this setting.

Selby's (1974) study of Zapotec deviance is relevant because of his approach and interpretation. Using an interactionist and labeling orientation to deviance, he examined the definitions and consequences of being a Zapotec deviant. Deviation from normative and expected kinship relations defined the deviant person in Selby's community. He argued that the social and cultural construction of deviant categories and labels served to protect the integrity of Zapotec social order by stigmatizing relations that would upset or threaten it (ibid.:42).

The institutional studies of Caudill (1958), Edgerton (1973), Goffman (1961), Rapoport (1960), Reynolds and Farberow (1976) and others have presented social and culturally constructed features of patienthood as it has experienced by handicapped and crazy persons in controlled environments. In each of these studies, reality has been presented as the subjects created and experienced it. The authors have identified the views and attitudes of persons labeled as negatively different and culturally unacceptable. They have provided a special kind of understanding of the different persons' world, and they have looked beyond pathologies and prescriptions directly into the strategies for living adopted by these persons. Each work has outlined the ways in which the subjects adopted, elaborated, and/or rejected their deviant identities while interacting with the culturally defined values and actions of others.

Each author who has worked in an American setting has suggested that American values and actions regarding deviance and psychiatric disorder have influenced the deviant individual in his construction of a separate reality and identity closely tied to the cultural prescriptions and beliefs regarding his particular malady. Being a deviant person in our culture carries costs vis-à-vis the larger society, for which the deviant may compensate by perpetuating, elaborating, and adopting the separate reality, despite its negative valuation. The deviance of the drunks and addicts studied by Spradley and Weppner was aided and abetted by the treatment and values of the larger culture. Goffman's subjects were humiliated and given new identities that they accepted and elaborated, becoming better patients and worse "real people." Awareness of these processes and alternate life strategies has provided important, though preliminary, insight into the paradoxes of the diseased-deviant experience in the American cultural context.

9

THE SOCIAL CONSTRUCTION OF A CRAZY REALITY

"Is Orr crazy?"
"He sure is," Doc Daneeka replied.
"Can you ground him?"
"I sure can. But first he has to ask me to. That's part of the rule."
"Then why doesn't he ask you to?"
"Because he's crazy," Doc Daneeka said. "He has to be crazy to keep flying combat missions after all those close calls he's had. Sure, I can ground Orr. But first he has to ask me to."
"That's all he has to do to be grounded?"
"That's all. Let him ask me."
"And then you can ground him?" Yossarian asked.
"No. Then I can't ground him."
"You mean there's a catch?"
"Sure there's a catch," Doc Daneeka replied. "Catch-22. Anyone who wants to get out of combat duty isn't crazy."

There was only one catch and that was Catch-22, which specified that a concern for one's safety in the face of dangers that were real and immediate was the process of a rational mind. Orr was crazy and could be grounded. All he had to do was ask; and as soon as he did, he would no longer be crazy and would have to fly more missions. Orr would be crazy to fly more missions and sane if he didn't, but if he was sane he had to fly them. If he flew them he was crazy and didn't have to; but if he didn't want to he was sane and had to.

—Heller 1962:46-47

In the preceding chapters, I have described aspects of the clients' world, including their uses of and experiences with time, space, resources, and information. Their subsistence strategies and their experiences with and attitudes toward medications have been explained. I have suggested throughout that clients, staff, and the community at large participate in the construction and perpetuation of a paradoxical, nonsensically contradictory (crazy) world within which clients receive and express somewhat contradictory indications about who they are and how they are expected to behave, think, and feel. Threading through my discussion has been a tone of nearly whimsical, often distressing, ambivalence about the discrepancy between perceived and actual reality, and perceived and actual options for clients. To clarify what is occurring in the interaction among clients, and between them and others (especially inside and outside normals), I will utilize, as an interpretive framework, a mode of conceptualizing interpersonal conduct known as symbolic interactionism. By approaching the data from this perspective, I hope to clarify the multiple meanings inherent in my interpretation of "making it crazy."

Models and theories abound about how persons become and remain psychiatrically disturbed, being regarded as crazy not only by their fellows but by themselves (cf. Siegler and Osmond 1966; Mechanic 1977*b*). These paradigms are usually dichotomized as (1) the medical, organic, and psychiatric, or (2) the social and interpersonal. Although the approaches are frequently presented or perceived as competitive and in conflict, they are, in fact, complementary (Meehl 1973). The differences between them are primarily in emphasis, in terminology, and in the weighting of widely recognized variables.

The current medical-psychiatric stance includes investigation of genetic (Heston 1970), neurochemical (Stein and Wise 1971; Wise and Stein 1973), and biochemical (Wyatt and Murphy 1976) foundations for the occurrence of the primary symptoms of mood, thought, and behavior disorders. Regarding the secondary consequences of these primary processes, the medical-psychiatric and clinical perceptions reflect a growing recognition of social, interpersonal, and cultural factors affecting the course of illness and individual prognosis (Wing 1978).

Sociological theories about the causes, meaning, and course of psychiatric disorder have usually been more extreme, emphasizing the role of sociocultural and interpersonal factors that cause, define, or label mental illness, and that stigmatize, stereotype, and further humiliate the person experiencing difficulties in living (e.g., Scheff 1966; Szasz 1960, 1976). The origins of primary symptoms or primary deviance remain problematical in these paradigms. It is unfortunate that the obvious impact of cultural values and social structures on the definitions, content, and treatment of psychic suffering has led to such polemics as to obscure the nature of social reality. It seems a truism that cultural codes influence designations of appropriate and inappropriate behavior. Theoretical argument over the presence of organic disease versus social designation and control has all but ignored the empirical fact that, regardless of what *causes* and *defines* negative differentness, persons who experience and display bizarre symptoms do exist in our society, and do live with the culturally conditioned consequences and meanings of these diseases, labels, and experiences. Simply because rules of conduct or codes for living are cultural inventions does not make them less "real" or significant in persons' lives than cancer or coronary artery disease. Law is also a cultural invention. It is very real, personally meaningful, and controlling to the jailed prisoner, to the policeman, and to those of us who must pay parking, speeding, and other legally imposed penalties.[1]

I prefer to take a moderate stance in the social-medical debate. The genetic and biochemical evidence pointing to a fundamental organic predisposition and involvement of neurochemical processes in psychiatric difficulty is convincing (Hokin 1978). But this does not diminish the importance of interpersonal, social, and cultural factors in influencing the recognition, treatment, and consequences of displaying and experiencing psychiatric problems within a given cultural context. The clients in my project had already experienced

1. The argument of disease versus label, if it were resolved by conclusive proof of disease, might have some impact. Several studies (e.g., Brand and Clairborne 1976) suggest that, in our culture, physical illness may be less stigmatizing than psychiatric illness. But even if psychiatric disorder, schizophrenia in particular, were proved to be of biochemical, genetic, or neurochemical origin, this might not drastically change responses to the mentally ill person in our society. As Kirk (1974) suggests, it may be to the actual bizarre, irritating, demanding, and unruly behavior of the psychiatrically disordered person that others respond, and not to the underlying cause of such behavior.

primary symptoms, and had been diagnosed, labeled, recognized, and treated before my contact with them began. Therefore, my focus was on their reactions, adjustments, rejections, and acceptances of their labels and/or illnesses.

Thus far I have placed emphasis on the ability of individuals in interaction with others to create and to experience social and personal reality. This idea also underlies the social-labeling paradigm of mental illness (Schur 1971:8) and the medical-psychiatric view of secondary consequences. Therefore, it is important to examine the mechanisms of this process and the theory upon which it is based. Blumer (1969) and Berger and Luckman (1967) have written most cogently on the subject of the social construction of subjective and objective realities, and I rely heavily upon their thinking in the following discussion.[2]

Several central concepts and premises are included in the symbolic interactionist approach: meaning or significance; the intersubjective nature of reality; the self as subject and object and as a product of social process; and the interpretation of events, persons, and self through interaction with others as a force for maintaining and altering reality.

MEANING

Fundamental to the interactionist paradigm is the idea that meaning is derived from and produced through interpersonal communication and exchange (Blumer 1969:2–4; Berger and Luckman 1967:30). Objects and experiences possess few absolute, inherent qualities, but are endowed with qualities and significance through persons' encounters with them. These encounters are interpreted and understood by persons on the basis of their commonsense knowledge, which has been established, confirmed, and altered through their interactions with other persons who have had similar encounters and made similar interpretations (Berger and Luckman 1967:23). In other words, meaning and significance are decided upon and learned by negotiating with others. Also, a tacit, shared sense of significance

2. Blumer, Berger, Luckman, and others who espouse this approach, acknowledge their intellectual debt to the thought and writings of George Herbert Mead.

and knowledge is essential to communication and interpretation, which in turn generates new meanings and knowledge, or maintains an initial, shared presumption. Without at least a minimum of common knowledge and shared meanings, communication becomes difficult if not impossible. This is well understood by anyone who has tried to speak with someone who does not know or use the same language. Shared knowledge and meaning at a tacit, everyday, commonsense level is not only the foundation for interaction, but is also generated, maintained, and altered by interaction.

THE INTERSUBJECTIVE NATURE OF REALITY: MEANING AND IDENTITY

The intersubjective nature of reality refers to and arises from the above process. That is to say, most of what we know to be real is what we share with others. For example, if I see on a thermometer that the temperature is 85 degrees, and I say to a friend, "It is hot," and s/he agrees, we have accomplished several things. First, we have established that we have had a common perception of the atmospheric conditions. We also have agreed that 85 degrees is hot for us both, though only I have this absolute reference point. Third, we have indicated to each other that each of us has a similar notion of what constitutes heat. Then, each of us can interpret that the other shares a portion of our reality, that is, the meaning and experience of being hot. I have confirmed my judgment that 85 degrees is hot. As Berger and Luckman would say, we have established and confirmed an intersubjective reality. I have learned that "my natural attitude toward this world corresponds to the natural attitude of others, that they also comprehend the objectifications by which this world is ordered, that they also organize around the here and now of their being in it . . . I know that I live with them in a common world" (ibid.:23).

The importance and intersubjective nature of reality can also be learned by examining what happens in its absence. When I said it was hot, if my friend had denied this or had disagreed with me, I would have had several interpretive options. I could have believed that my perceptions and judgments were faulty, or that my friend's were. Or we could have decided that we experienced the same absolute temperature differently, generating a new meaning for hot or for individual variations of it. If, however, I could find no one to agree with me, the implications and consequences would be quite different. I would be receiving consistent indications that my perceptions and meaning were not shared by others, that my experience was idiosyncratic. In essence, I would lack a portion of intersubjective reality with others. Consider, then, the person who believes herself to be Venus. If she can find no one who agrees with her, as is likely, but persists in this definition of herself, then her identity cannot be a part of intersubjective reality. She can only receive from others indications of disconfirmation and disagreement. In the face of these indications, if she continues to know herself to be Venus, in our culture she will be called crazy. She will be treated or will be subjected to persuasion to alter this private conception.

Consider, also, the act of breaching. Garfinkel (1967; see also Mehan and Wood 1975:104–105) and others have experimented with breaching, which is the persistent denial of the tacit, commonsense knowledge and reality of one person by others. A classic example was enacted by A, who required that B define each word used in conversation. It rapidly became apparent that communication was chaotic, if not impossible, and B, whose meanings were being challenged and denied, reacted with great distress. She became bewildered and frustrated, and eventually withdrew from the interaction, questioning who was right or wrong, and what was happening. In another instance, the subject's identity was breached. The experimenter refused to acknowledge, in a restaurant, that the subject was not the maitre d'. The subject had, in fact, been invited to join another experimenter for lunch at the restaurant. The experimenter's persistence in denying the subject's non-maitre d' identity, and his forceful expectation that the subject perform the maitre d's duties, led the subject to think that the experimenter was crazy. The subject also became confused and agitated, wondering at moments who, in fact, he was.

These examples illustrate the power and intersubjective nature of reality, and its pertinence to identity within our culture. This is especially true of interaction with others who are important to us, emotionally or authoritatively. As Berger and Luckman have put it: "To retain confidence that he is indeed who he thinks he is, the individual requires not only the implicit confirmation of this identity that even casual everyday contact will supply, but the explicitly and emotionally charged confirmation that his significant others bestow on him" (1967:150). Some of the consequences of these processes depend also upon the numbers of persons involved. If I do not share intersubjective reality with one person, we simply have an argument. If, however, I do not share this reality with several others, I will experience the disagreement as more serious, and they are likely to strive to enforce the validity of their shared notions by changing mine.

I have discussed the formative quality of interaction in creating meaning, and I have noted that shared meaning necessarily underlies interaction. There is, however, another quality of this shaped and shaping reality: "The product acts back on the producer" (ibid.:61). This means that persons produce meanings, realities, and significances that they experience as other than their own product; the product gains an existence independent of the producer's volition. At some point in the conscious firming and sharing of the constructed reality, "it becomes real in an even more massive way and it can no longer be changed so readily" (ibid.:59). The creation is then experienced by the creators, and sometimes at heavy cost. This explains why our psychotic Venus may find it increasingly difficult to stop being crazy, if she has convinced herself and enough significant others of her condition-identity. Her Venus-identity has become a "massive" part of intersubjective reality.

THE SELF AS SUBJECT, OBJECT, AND A PART OF INTERSUBJECTIVE REALITY

At this point, it will be useful to consider further the multiple properties of the self. Identity, or the known and knowable self, is both personal and social, or subjective and intersubjective. We experience ourselves privately and subjectively, but we also receive indications or significations from others about who we are and how we are. In reflecting on and interpreting these signals from others, the self perceives itself as both subject and object (Blumer 1969:62–63). To have a sense of ourselves as perceived and acted upon by others, and thus to include identity as a part of intersubjective reality, we must be able to separate these two selves and to receive the indications of others. Then the selves must be integrated. These two selves are seldom identical, but the dialectic between social and personal self is usually stabilized as knowledge that is personally and interpersonally acceptable and that is commonly shared. This process joins us subjectively with our world, and identity can then become a part of intersubjective reality.

Our interpretations of others' interpretations of us not only can confirm but can alter who we think we are, who others think us to be, and who they think they are. Bateson (1958:175) generalizes about this process, describing it as the reactions of individuals to the reactions of other individuals. With more specificity, Blumer (1969:21) describes the process as one of designation, noting that it does not always have the same result, because "this process of designation and interpretation is sustaining, undercutting, re-directing, and transforming the ways in which the participants are fitting together their lines of action" (ibid.:53). In essence, what occurs is a process of identification, interpretation, experiencing, knowing, and changing of self through interactions with others.

THE SOCIAL CONSTRUCTION AND PERPETUATION OF NEGATIVE DIFFERENTNESS

The above processes can also go beyond confirmation and redirection to malfunction. They can contribute to personal and interpersonal havoc instead of establishing, confirming, and altering intersubjective reality in predictable, commonsense ways. The person who disrupts the usual processes outlined above, and who has different notions of who he and others are, and of how they should behave, places not only his own self in jeopardy but the selves and intersubjective realities of others. Goffman has explicated this dynamic and the dual self idea:

> . . . the self [self as subject] is the code that makes sense out of almost all the individual's activities and provides a basis for organizing them. This self [self as object] is what can be read about the individual by interpreting the place he takes in the organization of social activity, as confirmed by his expressive behavior. The individual's failure to encode through deeds and expressive cues, a *workable* definition of himself, one which closely enmeshed others can accord him through the regard they show

> his person [self as subject, object, and a part of intersubjective reality] is to block and trip up and threaten them in almost every movement they make. The selves that have been reciprocals of his are undermined. . . . In ceasing to know the sick person, they cease to be sure of themselves. In ceasing to be sure of him and themselves, they can even cease to be sure of their ways of knowing. [1971:366]

The expression of a subjective self, which, when perceived as object to others, breaches or threatens intersubjective reality, initiates subjective self difficulties for others, unsettling even the fundamental knowledge and meanings of others. Berger and Luckman (1967:100) describe this precariousness of subjective reality, noting how dependent upon relations with others identity may be. In our culture, the self that is persistently and intensely expressed and experienced as breaching the reality of others will be called crazy, surely by these others and probably by self, if one retains any portion of intersubjective reality with others.

It must be recalled that the crazy self is simultaneously being breached by the "normal" others. Venus is experiencing a conflict between her subjective and intersubjective selves. Others cannot share her reality nor she theirs. A mutual breaching is occurring between them which is not tolerable for long. Whether the lack of intersubjective reality involves identity or a conflict in meanings, as in the temperature example, a choice must be made as to which reality can prevail, either to remain the intersubjective reality of the others or to be altered to accommodate the breacher. As Berger and Luckman (1967:108–109) explain:

> The appearance of an alternative symbolic universe poses a threat because its very existence demonstrates empirically that one's own universe is less than inevitable. . . . The confrontation of symbolic universes implies a problem of power—which of the two conflicting definitions of reality will be "made to stick" in the society. Which of the two will win, however, will depend more on the power than on the theoretical ingenuity of the respective legitimators.

By definition, the breacher is either solitary, less powerful, or is in the minority in relation to more than one other. For if he or she were not, this person could not sufficiently challenge or disconfirm intersubjective reality, as in my temperature example, and in the differing implications of disagreement with one friend or all others. The psychotic qua breacher is customarily removed from interaction with others with whom he is in conflict, or he removes himself by withdrawing completely into his private reality, by killing himself, or perhaps by attempting to regain vital portions of intersubjective reality by undergoing psychiatric treatment.

I have used the example of the psychotic to demonstrate that the intersubjective nature of reality is linked to social and personal identity. Expressing and experiencing a lack of intersubjective reality with others can negatively affect the subjective and intersubjective realities of all interacting participants. I have tried to show how meaning can be generated through these processes and, in this light, how definitions or significations of craziness can be conceptualized as a lack of intersubjective reality. The majority of the interactors have the power to determine and to enforce the validity of *their* intersubjective reality. To apply this perspective to PACT clients and their world, it is necessary to understand more about breaching, psychosis, and intersubjectively real identity.

A person who breaches the realities of others is not necessarily psychotic. The anthropologist first working among a group of persons previously uncontacted by outsiders no doubt challenges the intersubjective realities of his other subjects, and feels breached himself or herself, at least initially. What joins breaching with psychosis is the duration, intensity, and substantive nature of the conflict (or lack thereof) between intersubjective realities. Crazy people are not psychotic all the time, nor do they breach all aspects of others' realities, or have all of their own reality breached by others. But if the mutual breaching has been prolonged, and if the denial or rejection of intersubjective, shareable, knowable reality is incorporated into and inseparable from the self of the person, then the preconditions for development and maintenance of a crazy being and identity have been met. If, in addition to the elements of duration and intensity, the lack of intersubjective reality includes the culturally valued and regulated elements of identity, interpersonal conduct, forms of communication, subsistence strategies, and the means of processing (or thinking about) information from and about self and others, we have defined the full-time crazy person in our culture. Other "deviants" in our culture may share some of these attributes with the crazy person, but they do not express and experience the entire cluster, nor do they have the periodic or perpetual subjective experience of psychosis (the private possession and perception of an inner reality, which is indistinguishable by the person from the outer reality, and which is solely subjective and is in conflict with the intersubjective realities of others).

A part-time or periodically psychotic person can become a full-time crazy person in identity and being, like the PACT clients, if all the above conditions are met. As with Venus, even when the psychosis remits or decreases, and as with the psychotic, when the actual or potential breaching and lack of intersubjective reality *become* intersubjectively real, this crazy person subsumes part if not all of the person's identity. Via the same processes by which acceptable intersubjective reality and identity are created and experienced, an unacceptable reality is constructed. Following the principle of the product acting back, even if the person who experiences and expresses this lack of intersubjective reality regains the capacity and desire to share again, the previous self-other product may constrain him from so doing. Others may not be able or willing to alter their realities, and therefore the person cannot alter his, either subjectively or with relation to others (unless he is willing to become psychotic again). To share intersubjective reality with others, he must acknowledge and become the crazy person. Thus, subjectively experiencing a lack of intersubjective reality with others, and expressing this absence to them, can initiate construction of a firm reality that acts back on all the producers, especially on the breacher.

Consider, then, what may occur when a number of persons participate in the above processes as sole breachers among different groups, such as families. When removed from their families and placed in contact with each other, they may find that many of their formerly incongruent actions, meanings, experiences, and conflicts can be shared, known, and real. A basis thereby exists for producing and maintaining an intersubjective reality. The same confirming, establishing, learning, reality-creating process recurs, but within this different group. In relation to the larger group, this one remains unknowable and unreal or deviant. But intersubjective, commonsense, everyday reality is confirmed and generated within the confines of the knowers and sharers. Thus, "if deviant versions of the symbolic universe come to be shared by groups [or even by two persons], the deviant version congeals into a reality in its own right . . ." (Berger and Luckman 1967:106; see also Kaplan 1975:4). In addition to the past confirmation of craziness, therefore, that stems from earlier interaction between the person and his prior, differentness-identifying significant others, a new confirmation develops as an elaborating process among the person and his new acquaintances, who will become significant others.

I believe that these are the processes that occurred among the clients, and that occurred between the clients and normals. Even though the clients I studied did not constitute a cohesive, solid group, the relationships among them and their lack of symmetrical contact with noncrazy, related normals provided sufficient foundations for the processes to occur. They received sufficient indications and designations from the medications complex, from their subsistence experiences, from periodic psychotic experiences, and from consistent interaction with inside normals and crazies to facilitate these dynamics. Ludwig (1971) recognized that this was occurring in his hospitalized patients. What is important to recognize, in addition, is that these processes were also at work in a community setting that was chosen partly to combat them.

I found that clients shared nearly all their time, space, resources, and information with Inside Crazies and Inside Normals who interacted with the client *because* he or she was crazy (psychotic) or a crazy person. Outside Normals avoided and were avoided by clients, either because clients feared them and disliked the negative differentness highlighted in these encounters, or because they rejected, feared, or had no interest in interacting with clients. The interactional foundation and arena was not as concentrated as in a hospital, but it appears to have been as powerful, if not pervasive.

Clients confirmed, generated, and shared intersubjective reality with each other by taking medications, by having side effects, by being on SSI, by living at the Y's, and by being in PACT. But in the process of so doing, they also confirmed and consistently reestablished their lack of intersubjective reality with normals who did not take medications, who were not dependent upon income-maintenance programs, and who were more in control of their lives. By remaining among crazy persons, clients could retain the comfort and affirmation of self and meaning that had separated them from normals in the first place. At the same time, in becoming the chronic client, they were accepting the indications of normals and their experiences with normals that told them they were different, crazy people. The intersubjective reality and the agreed-upon identity clients *could* share with normals was their crazy one. Simultaneously, normals' views of them as negatively different were reinforced by their remaining among and acting like crazies. In time, through consistent interaction with other clients, the different reality became more real. Clients came to share, maintain, and perhaps generate more common meanings with their fellow crazies. If all of one's companions were getting SSI, then this became the norm. Clients came to feel that they deserved this money. If all of one's companions did not work or did experience depression, delusions, or fantasies, these became acceptable, shareable behaviors and experiences. Among normals, these conditions were not the norm, were not acceptable, and represented a lack of common experience and significance which held the seeds for miscommunication, if not for conflict and rejection. And, as I have pointed out, these paradoxical, double-edged swords existed in almost every arena for the clients in relation to normals.

These processes of amplifying and maintaining differences or deviance have been identified and discussed by Bateson (1958:171–197), Maruyama (1963), and Buckley (1967:163–207). They merit close examination.

Bateson's concept of schismogenesis refers to "a process of differentiation in the norms of individual behavior resulting from cumulative interaction between individuals" (1958:1975). The idea is one of complementary and progressive actions and reactions of persons and groups toward each other over time. The process may occur between individuals or groups. As it applies to situations like the PACT program, the complementary schismogenesis occurs between clients and normals. Bateson outlines the process as follows:

> It is possible that in a complementary schismogenesis the patterns of behavior between the two groups concerned may be such that while each group diverges farther and farther from the other, the members of each also become more and more dependent upon the complementary behavior of the other group. . . . [ibid:196]

So clients and normals mutually regard each other as different. In establishing the reality of this divergence, by complementing the expectations, beliefs, knowledge, and meanings of themselves and each other, all perpetuate and encourage the divergence. The two groups depend upon each other's existence to define themselves and their differentness. The divergence can stabilize, says Bateson, "when the forces of mutual dependence are equal to the schismogenic tendency" (ibid.:197).

In translating this idea to my project, an example might be the sheltered workshop. A client's differentness could stabilize or be maintained if he accepted it and took the sheltered job. The client was then dependent upon his or her disability status to stay at the sheltered workshop, and was also dependent upon inside normals for this position and income. If the client would not stabilize at the workshop level and rejected the job there, the schismogenesis would continue with the client's becoming unemployed and receiving some form of income maintenance. In the process, staff's and others' estimations of the client's differentness and disability would also increase.

SSI provided another example. To receive SSI, the client had to experience, enhance, or maintain his or her disability for twelve months. In complementary fashion, PACT staff had to become convinced that the person could not or would not work. Once the neutralizing level was reached and the decision was made to apply for SSI, staff leveled off their expectations, maintaining their view of the client as a disabled and dependent person. The client did not have to demonstrate the disability by failing at or rejecting work any longer, and he could stabilize at the level different enough to receive SSI. If the client broke the schismogenic stalemate, either by becoming psychotic and needing hospitalization, or by getting a job and earning over the SSI limit, the SSI stabilizer-maintainer was lost.[3] Throughout, clients were more dependent upon staff than vice versa, but the complementary stabilization of divergences did occur.

Buckley's (1967:169–172) scheme, which is incorporated into Scheff's (1966:97) labeling theory, resembles Bateson's. Deviation-amplifying feedback occurs when the different or deviant actions of

3. Clients are not customarily aware that they will receive a drastic decrease in SSI payments upon institutionalization or hospitalization, but it is a dynamic of the system within which they operate. SSI is intended to support persons outside of hospitals. Rivinus (1977) has pointed out how this rule can be used to motivate patients to be discharged.

a person are responded to in a manner perceived by that person as supporting, enhancing, or rewarding the deviance. This parallels the process, discussed earlier, of encouraging and confirming *acceptable* responses, identities, and meanings. Except in this case, unacceptability and difference is perversely rewarded through deviators' interactions with those who could reject or accept the deviance, but who somehow reward or encourage it (see also Wilkins 1965:12–13). Thus, instead of stopping or altering the differentness, as one might expect, the reverse occurs.

I have pointed out, regarding medications, that the clients' differentness in taking antipsychotic medications was rewarded subjectively by a decrease in symptoms, and was rewarded intersubjectively by the persuasions, forcefulness, approval, and prescribing of meds by inside normals and PACT staff. The deviation of experiencing and displaying probable side effects or believing that one was 'sick' because medicine was prescribed was also amplified in this manner. But if the client did not take meds, and if psychotic symptoms increased, an even worse amplification of deviance or differentness could occur. Thus medications, depending, respectively, on whether they were accepted or rejected, could maintain or amplify differentness.

Buckley's idea of the maintenance and amplification of deviance via its reward is a useful one, but it does not adequately acknowledge the deviant's role in the process. The clients are not totally passive recipients with regard to medications. They experience the primary symptoms and the lack of intersubjective reality that initiated the whole process, and they actively confirm their differentness after psychosis has passed, by not taking medications and thereby becoming bizarre again, or by taking their medications and displaying side effects, or by not taking side-effect medication with regularity and thereby having worse side effects. Granted, these are not especially inviting choices, but they are available to clients.

Maruyama's (1963:164–240) concept of morphogenesis (mutual causal deviation amplification) supplements this discussion. As he points out, in each interaction or exchange, components alter each other. As one is responding to the other, each is also changing. Further, he suggests that not only does mutual amplification of deviance occur between persons, stabilizing in the deviated pattern, but it can occur *within* a person (ibid.:240). The within-person amplification in taking meds, getting side effects, and feeling and appearing different, or not taking meds and becoming psychotic again, illustrates this process.

Labeling theory hints at these processes, but it insufficiently acknowledges their mutual causal nature, superficially considering the actions and different realities of the labeled person as active components in the process (Levitan 1975; Warren and Johnson 1972:74). As Warren and Johnson (1972:90) have observed, labeling theory is remiss in "its neglect of empirical investigation into how typifications of deviance are used by, and what their use means to, social actors on the actual occasions of their use." Four of Scheff's (1966:84–101) nine sequential hypotheses make this point more concretely:

6. Labeled deviants may be rewarded for playing the stereotyped deviant role.

7. Labeled deviants are punished when they attempt to return to conventional roles.

8. In the crisis occurring when a residual rule[4] breaker is publicly labeled, the deviant is highly suggestible, and may accept the proffered role of the insane as the only alternative.

9. Among residual rule breakers, labeling is the single most important cause of a career of residual deviance.

I agree with Scheff, and I think the discussion and evidence presented thus far suggests that propositions six and seven hold some merit. But Scheff does not point out that the deviant (the client in my project) has a part in determining what constitutes reward and punishment. Also, the rewards or gains and the punishments or costs are, in some instances, reversed by the PACT clients' values and needs in conflict with a majority of others' values and needs.

For example, considered in relation to the various categories (insiders, outsiders, normals, and crazies), most clients in my project had very little control of their resources, and in relation to normals,

4. Residual rule-breaking is defined (Scheff 1966:34) as "diverse kinds of rule-breaking for which our society provides no explicit label, and which therefore, sometimes lead to the labeling of the violator as mentally ill."

they had less control of their time, space, and information. Perhaps control over and responsibility for one's life were not valued among clients. Many clients succeeded in persuading others, for whom responsibility and control were positive qualities, to allow the clients to live in violation of these values. As always, the differentness of clients from the majority culture was underscored by this choice. But the client who *did* value responsibility and control but did not have it, because it had been either voluntarily relinquished or taken away, consequently experienced himself as being dependent and not in control, and he was given indications to this effect, such as a financial guardian. Either way, the client was bound to maintain differentness and ambivalence, for, as Goffman (1963:106) has observed: "Given that the stigmatized individual in our society acquires identity standards which he applies to himself in spite of failing to conform to them, it is inevitable that he will feel some ambivalence about his own self."

A more balanced view of the rewards and punishments scheme would recognize the capacity for reversal of rewards, stemming perhaps from ambivalence on the part of the deviant, and would note that the more important dilemma centers around the capacity to amplify differentness inherent in the rewards available to, and the values chosen by, clients. If "the system" is to blame, as Scheff implies, the criticism seems more appropriately directed to the lack of culturally valued rewards available to clients, given their problems, deficits, and sometimes divergent values for living.

Ludwig (1971) and Haley (1969) have argued persuasively that craziness or psychosis is a powerful possession that can be used not only to control others but to avoid responsibility. Among the rules I proposed earlier for making it crazy, it was suggested that others would take care of you if you did not take care of yourself. It was also noted that prolonging the capacity for craziness could qualify one for receipt of a permanent, guaranteed income. Contrary to the victimization emphasized by Scheff and others, such as Perrucci (1974), it should be recognized that clients can manipulate and maneuver as well as suffer.

For example, the ultimate power a client had was the threat to hurt self or others. Harold went through a period of late-night telephoning to staff from the lobby of the YMCA, sometimes claiming to have a rope around his neck. Legally and morally, PACT staff had to respond to the calls, even though they felt (and Harold admitted this openly to me) that Harold was seeking attention from them, was flexing his "psychiatric muscle" by getting them out of bed in the early morning hours, and was not making a serious suicide threat. This is but one instance of many, and it illustrates precisely what the staff was trying to eliminate; namely, rewards for crazy, dependent, manipulative behavior. But they were not always able to do this. Perhaps, as Ludwig (1971:61) suggests: "Because patients have a far better understanding of our social value system with its inherent limitations than we have of theirs, they can employ a repertoire of behaviors that function as push buttons to elicit the desired staff or social response, thereby ensuring the attainment of their goals."

Again, paradoxically, the clients' manipulations and exercises of power customarily gained them rewards that ultimately maintained or amplified their differentness from the larger world. A common dilemma for staff at PACT involved clients who enjoyed contact with staff to the point of inventing or enhancing problems in order to gain it. Staff worked to decrease contact and involvement with the client who was not acutely psychotic or experiencing life crises. Clients learned that they received increased staff contact if they were in trouble. If the client valued staff concern and interaction, and if he maneuvered to receive this by "sabotaging" a situation he probably could manage, the clients' differentness and dependency on staff could be amplified or maintained to achieve the goals of staff attention. The problem at PACT was not so much one of conflict between staff and clients, but of staff and clients coming to care for and to genuinely like one another. For the client, separation, discharge, and getting better often meant a loss of warmth, support, and friends. Nearly every client who was discharged expressed feelings of loss and abandonment. The staff also regretted losing contact with some clients at discharge.

Returning to Scheff, it must be noted that his eighth hypothesis is unbalanced. The hypothesis does not acknowledge that the deviant might have chosen his or her career, or at some time might have actively pursued aspects of being different. At least three clients have suggested this volition. Abe has described it as follows:

> Well, when I was in high school, I started having these depressions. And I thought about life and all those routines ahead of me. I decided I

> was either going to go to a monastery or go crazy. At first it was hard, but then I sort of lost control of it. I mean it was embarrassing at first. There was this lady in our hometown and she was crazy. Everyone sort of thought she was weird and all that. When I first went crazy, it was being like her. My parents were really upset. But now it's special. It may have been a mistake in some ways, but it's who I am.

Others have conveyed the idea that they began by "playing with things" in their heads, and that at a certain point they lost control and became "crazy." Harold illustrated a different kind of choice. He said he didn't think he was really crazy, but that "the only time I ever do think I am is when I can't believe some of the things I pull to get into the hospital. I guess I just feel like I belong, or it's more secure, or something." Some clients did not have such a full range of possibilities from which to choose, because their primary thinking or mood difficulties prevented a real conscious selection of alternatives. But even these persons adapted, through desensitization to, and even appreciation for, craziness and the benefits of such a status. Ludwig (1971:17) has described the process as follows:

> It is common to find that the first mental break for chronic schizophrenics tends to be much more frightening and shattering to them than consequent ones. . . . As time elapses he no longer regards these psychotic experiences as alien. After repeated occurrences of the continued existence of this alteration in consciousness, the scary feelings of terror associated with its presence slowly diminish as a psychological adaptation takes place. In fact, patients soon come to learn that the presence of this state is not entirely disadvantageous, for it confers on them many unanticipated benefits. Not only does it provide a convenient vehicle and readymade excuse for the expression of otherwise taboo feelings, thoughts and behaviors, but it also guarantees them a kind of special attention and concerned care that they would not receive while behaving sanely.

In understanding the reversal of rewards, the power of craziness, and the appreciation of psychosis explained above, it is important to balance a sense of deliberateness and conscious choice with knowledge of the involuntary deficits and problems experienced and possessed by clients. Some, for example, had never cooked a meal or washed their own laundry. Others had "spells" or "conditions" that overcame them in a variety of situations. Doc said it was "like being away for a while and waking up and wondering what happened while I was gone."

From a clinical and psychiatric perspective, the most recent and widely accepted wisdom adds credence to the idea of balancing the voluntary and involuntary factors, and of balancing the positive and negative subjective responses to psychosis and persistent psychiatric disorder. Debate continues regarding the neurochemical and biochemical determinants of cognitive, affective, and behavioral symptoms experienced and displayed by persons such as our subjects (Meehl 1973). Cognitive deficits, such as thinking disorganization, inappropriate verbal associations, short and unfocused attention span, and inability to control the pace and content of thoughts, have been reported by numerous researchers working with schizophrenics (see Chapman and Chapman 1973). These symptoms are thought to be related to damaged neural receptors in the nonandrenergic system in the brain (Stein and Wise 1971; Wise and Stein 1973). But learning theorists have been able to teach normal subjects to think and to process information in similar ways (e.g., Levitz and Ullman 1969). The affective or emotional flatness and withdrawal repeatedly observed among schizophrenics has been attributed both to neurological defects and to behavioral, interpersonal factors (Chapman et al. 1976). In the absence of conclusive evidence regarding the influence of factors beyond and within the control of psychiatric patients, it seems advantageous to take an open position and to listen to what our subjects had to say.

Differences in severity and amount of primary symptoms existed within the client group. It was tempting to view those with the worst and most visible difficulties as suffering from a neurological pathology, and to suspect more control and behavioral influence in those whose symptoms appeared less bizarre and debilitating. Humphrey, for example, often had difficulty completing a coherent sentence or responding in full to questions from others. At times he mumbled and, if one listened closely, the thoughts were disjointed or idiosyncratic. When Doc was warning him about the possible dangers of sniffing glue, Humphrey said that "my brain doesn't work anymore anyway." Kitty, however, had never hallucinated or been delusional. Instead, she most often seemed unhappy, frightened by the world, and unable to alter cycles of parasitic relationships with men that led to abandonment, to heavy consumption of alcohol, and to depression. Kitty was able to work competitively for longer periods than most of the group. These examples represent the extremes within the group. Most clients fell somewhere between, experiencing periodic psychotic episodes, regaining firmer contact with self and others, but experiencing subsequent feelings of depression, anxiety, and inadequacy about themselves, their life situation, and their relations with others.

Some, like Steven and George, enjoyed their "craziness." Others, such as Agatha, feared it. Christie had yet another response. Although she recognized that her thinking was "loose" (at times she would interject a phrase into a conversation which was not even tangentially related), she said, "Well, mostly I just feel hurt by people all the time. It just feels bad." I am unable to judge (as are most others) whether clients voluntarily or involuntarily experienced and exhibited such symptoms. But the fact remains that regardless of etiology and volition, all clients felt and experienced themselves as different, crazy people, in part because of primary symptoms. Some verbally denied their craziness on occasion, but none of them did so at all times. It is essential not to overlook the role of primary symptoms, which were potent to clients, and to those with whom they interacted, in laying the foundations for the processes of differentness recognition and maintenance. These differences and deficits were a part of the trap which contributes to confining clients to making it crazy, but they were not, in my opinion, the most important or determining factors. It seems to me that the most potent factors were clients' subjective experiences with and responses to symptoms, the meaning attached to these experiences by the client and others, and the degree to which the client was constrained in meeting cultural expectations for health by the symptoms and by his or her responses to them.

A recent study (Wadeson and Carpenter 1976) reports that the most prevalent subjective experiences of a schizophrenic sample group were depression, confusion, and anger. The clients with whom I worked, who spoke of their subjective responses to psychosis and primary symptoms, echoed these findings. Most expressed some despair at their life circumstances and their inability to understand or control primary symptoms. Jack, for example, explained that he had difficulty talking with others because "I get lost in the spaces between words in sentences. I can't concentrate, or I get off onto thinking about something else." Doc also expresses a thinking disorder and his consequent frustration, "I'm sitting here trying to think about how to help you with your book, and all I can think about is that if I keep throwing these pebbles into the lake, it'll fill up with rocks and all the water will be gone. You know, I haven't finished a book. I can't concentrate. I'll never be able to do anything."

Others had equally powerful symptoms, but responded differently. When Steven was high or manic, he spoke so rapidly that it was nearly impossible to understand him. As he put it: "My mind is racing at the speed of light." During these times he said he felt euphoric, infinitely powerful, and able to stop time in the abstract and in others' wristwatches. When he was not acutely psychotic, he identified some of this behavior and thinking as "crazy," but he continued to believe that he was not aging, had eternal life, and that God had spoken to him one night in jail. This delusional system did not diminish after psychotic episodes, but also it did not necessarily interfere with Steven's ability to maintain himself in daily life. These ideas did interfere with relationships beyond a superficial stage. Most others would have had a difficult time accepting Steven's vision of himself and the world, and would probably have decided that he was crazy and not an acceptable companion. Steven became very insistent that he was not aging, and he expected his friends to support this, if not to believe it.

Evaluating the impact of primary symptoms, and adaptations to them by clients, requires further research. It is necessary to distinguish between primary deficits, such as the inability to think clearly or the harboring of pervasive suspicions about others, and secondary problems, such as depression, anxiety, and the feeling of being "weird" subsequent to these experiences. I have learned that primary symptoms per se did not make it impossible to communicate with, to interact with, or even to care for clients. None of them were always raving, hostile, or incoherent. Many clients could have worked, or could have had relationships with normals, for example, if primary symptoms had represented their only deficits and differences.

But this was not the case. For clients developed fears and avoidance of others, feelings of inadequacy and incompetence, and both appreciation for and repugnance toward themselves and their psychotic processes. They did this within an interpersonal, social, and cultural context that conveyed to them that they were different from normals because they experienced these thoughts and feelings. More importantly, their difference was evaluated as a negative condition, a disease that required medical treatment to eliminate or diminish it. Those clients who accepted their illness as negative and debilitating to self and relations with others were destined to feel despair, frustration, and anger when they did not "get well." Other clients, who positively valued their differentness, further undermined the possibilities for sharing intersubjective reality with normals. Instead, they created and withdrew into an alternate universe of experience and meaning that perhaps provided supportive, positive indications to them about themselves. Few clients in my sample chose the latter alternative consistently. Instead, they straddled a middle ground between the two polar alternatives. They felt depressed and angry at self and others when deficits and disparities in expectation and actuality were clear. At times they withdrew to isolation or psychosis, where these negative messages were diminished or were irrelevant. Accepting the crazy identity and living the crazy life among other crazy persons accomplished a similar compromise.[5]

Perhaps the best way to integrate these factors is to avoid ethnocentricity in presuming that "normalcy" holds the same attraction for all, especially for those who receive internal and external indications that they are, in fact, different. As Kaplan (1964:xi) has perceived, understanding the inner world of the mentally ill requires considering that "the rewards of normalcy are probably over estimated."

To summarize, one might surmise that clients not only accept and elaborate their differentness but also hate, fear, and reject it at the same time. Goffman (1963:38) writes:

> Given the ambivalence built into the individual's attachment to his stigmatized category, it is understandable that oscillations may occur in his support of, identification with, and participation among his own group. There will be "affiliative cycles" through which he comes to accept the special opportunities for in-group participation or comes to reject them after accepting them before. There will be corresponding oscillations in belief about the nature of own group and the nature of normals.

5. The career concept of the diachronic experiences of a mental patient has been put forth primarily by Goffman (1961, 1963:32-40). The career idea relates to the sequential movement of the person from one position in a network of social relations to another

Recall Steven's frustration with his capacity to get "high" and the problems this caused him, Annie's scorn of the emotionally disturbed and her romantic involvement with Doc, and Sam's predicament. Inside and Outside Normals interacted with clients in a fashion that simultaneously established and devalued their differentness. This is the essential paradox that labeling theory misses and does not appreciate. I suggest that these dynamics are the key to understanding the processes of maintaining and amplifying differentness. Clients and others participated in the differentness enhancing and maintaining process in multiple ways, as noted throughout this book, but by the time the trap was recognized, as Hall has said, it was too late to back out. For the self and social product had gained the "more massive reality" of Berger and Luckman, and were indeed acting back on the producers.

Walter provided an example of this circumstance. He explained that there were two Walters in his parents' eyes. One was their son, for whom they had affection, hopes, and expectations in living. The other was Walter, the mental patient, who disappointed them and whom they did not understand or like. Said he: "I wish they could just see me as I am. I'm not either of those people all the time, but I can't get them to put it all together. It makes me real sad because they always remember the mental patient. They won't let me forget."

Morris experienced a similar problem. During his years of aggressive panhandling and freeloading, his reputation as a crazy person became entrenched and widespread. After his PACT experience and a definite improvement in his behavior, so many police, mer-

---

position in the same or in a different network, and the presumption that these movements are accompanied by concomitant personal adjustments (Swanson and Spitzer 1970:44). The career concept is an attractive one for this study, because it conveys not only the above progressive adjustment sequence but also the idea of a long-term dedication and involvement with a means of providing oneself with income and daily activity. To my knowledge, the particular career variant I am proposing—the occupational perspective—has not been elaborated elsewhere. I am proposing that being a chronic psychiatric client can be seen not only as "what one does in life," as one's career, but also as a means of earning a living.

My view of career also diverges from Goffman's, because he has formulated it in terms of entry into the psychiatric hospital and return to the outside social, interpersonal world (ibid.:44-45). These circumstances do not apply with precision to the clients in my study. A more accurate outpatient view alters the adjustments made by the client, regardless of hospitalization, or his "co-workers" or fellow clients, or his means of obtaining the resources necessary for living.

chants, and waitresses knew him that he was excluded from the University Union and was asked to pay for meals before being served. He had not been arrested in over a year, but his massively real, crazy, disruptive self lived on despite his clinical improvement.

There is another paradoxical twist to consider. It has been argued by Lofland (1969), Kaplan (1975), and others, that part of the persistence of differentness is due to the fusion of subjective and objective self with the deviant or the crazy identity (see also Goffman 1963:105–125). Deviance is more than an objective role; being crazy is a subjective as well as a social, observable phenomenon. I suggest that when the different person has made the acceptance (the transformation required in our culture if one experiences and expresses a consistent lack of intersubjective reality with others) and when this reality is threatened (that is, subjected to psychiatric treatment), the response may be to defend this crazy self, stubbornly remaining crazy or becoming more so. To have established oneself as a crazy person has exacted great trial and testing within self and among others. The observable conflict is between universes of meaning and intersubjective identity, not merely between disease and treatment. A person believes and is told that he is different, and then he is told that he cannot be this way any more, but must be someone else. If the different reality, values, meanings, and rewards are comfortable enough and real enough, then the expectation and demand for change cannot succeed. Paradoxically, the client who clings to the crazy identity and reality wins the battle for control of identity and definition, but loses the social war. The client who succeeds in holding on to the intersubjective reality of the differentness that he and others have created, loses in the world at large. He probably perceives security in remaining among other crazy people, who will not threaten to change, reject, or alter this self, but who will confirm and share a sense of it with him.

What has society to offer the crazy person to replace this self, this negatively different identity and reality? It seems to be precious little. Who else can mobilize the interest, concern, support, anger, frustration, and bitterness that these clients do? What other accessible characteristics, aside from psychosis and life-threatening behavior, carry such power and mystique in our culture? In short, are there any alternate roles and ways of being, any other less costly places and spaces for these people to occupy in our culture? At a more pragmatic level, what meaningful jobs are accessible or offered to clients if they leave GWI or remove themselves from SSI?

Recall Alice's attempts at employment. She hated GWI and its crazy-disabled designation, so she tried to find a "real job." None was forthcoming. She stayed at GWI, engaging in an active social life. The men with whom she voluntarily associated, once she was constrained to be there, were also disabled in some way, and they exploited her sexually and materially. Either way, whether she moved toward "normalcy" or chose to remain among those like herself, her differentness was maintained and amplified. Remember, also, that Alice was told that she "looked like a zombie," and that for this reason she would not be hired, not because she did not possess the skills. Frankly, sometimes she did look zombie-like. Part of that was owing to the side effects of medication, as was her eye-rolling. But she did not routinely take her Cogentin. Consciously or unconsciously, she was contributing to the creation of her multiple exitless mazes.

If all this seems confusing, it is. The reality is inconsistent and involuted, turning always back on itself, feeding on perversity as often as on positive maintenance or change. If it appears that I am arguing many sides of the issue, I am. There are no black and white, clearly divided factors. Almost *everything can and does work both ways.*

I have outlined the processes through which the clients, and nearly all with whom they interact, have participated in the construction of a social and perhaps personal reality and identity that ensures and perpetuates their existences as long-term psychiatric patients. I have wondered why and how so few of these persons make it minus their craziness and I have pointed to factors that may help to provide an answer. I have put forth an idea about long-term negative differentness, focusing on what happens when individuals and groups lack intersubjective reality about the culturally valued areas of identity, interpersonal conduct, forms of communication, subsistence strategies, and internal cognitive and affective processes. Most important, I have suggested the paradoxical, traplike nature of these factors and processes, emphasizing how difficult it is to alter these conceptions once they have become intersubjective and sociocultural.

The argument cannot be refuted by claiming, as Townsend (1976) has, that the clients do not believe or perceive themselves to be crazy. The point is that they are treated as if they are, that they live as if they are, and that the burden of proof that they are not crazy rests unfairly with them. The burden is unfair because we have participated in constructing these circumstances. It is unfair because we, as well as they, have perhaps underestimated how massive the social reality of their perpetual negative differentness has become. But given the nature of our culture and the nature of what we call schizophrenia, I suspect that if and when we can counteract these particular contradictions, we will create still more.

10

THE SOCIOCULTURAL CONTEXT OF ILLNESS AND CRAZINESS

> Most diseases can be separated from one's self and seen as foreign intruding entities. Schizophrenia is very poorly behaved in this respect. Colds, ulcers, flu, and cancer are things we get. Schizophrenic is something we are. It affects the things we most identify with as making us what we are.
> —Vonnegut 1976: Preface

The ambivalent, paradoxical view held by clients and others regarding the crazy self and the chronic sick role in American culture has been articulated in the past, perhaps first by Parsons (1972). In Parsons' perceptive scheme, the balance of rewards between the legitimized dependency and lowered expectations of being ill, and the motivations and obligations to return to healthy, effective task and role performance is tipped in favor of the latter. The ill person is motivated to become well, to perform his tasks, to participate in society in accordance with his role, thereby demonstrating his commitment to the values of the larger group. A tension between the legitimate exemptions of the sick person and his recognition "that to be ill is inherently undesirable" should help this person realize that he "has an obligation to try to 'get well' and to cooperate with others to this end" (ibid.:117).

Problems arise when the benefits of sickness outweigh the obligations to get well. Further difficulties are generated when the constraints and symptoms of the illness outnumber and *include* not only a lack of capacity but also a lack of desire to get well (as Parsons has defined health).

With the chronic psychiatric patient, the latter seems to be true. The symptoms of his psychosis and his or her adaptations to them often include being not only unable but unwilling to return to health or to active participation in the "normal" performance-expectation system, somewhat like the drug addicts described by Weppner (1973:33). Ludwig (1971:53) has explained it as follows: "What many therapists fail to understand about these patients is that they are in fact highly motivated but in a negative direction, to attain the nihilistic goals of security without responsibility, reward without effort, and survival without meaningful living." Pathology is fused with the lack of motivation and desire to expend effort and to take on the responsibilities of "well" persons. Implicit is the idea that it is sick or crazy not to choose recovery. There is a divergence between the patient's interpretation and use of his or her illness and the physician's estimations of how incapacitated and legitimately disabled the patient should be, given the doctor's understanding of the illness.

With Parsons's and Ludwig's interpretations in mind, the discussion can be extended. Culturally influenced ideas about the causes and cures of illness are acted out upon patients by doctors and other health professionals in our society. Their understandings of the etiology, treatment, and prognoses of disease in turn influence general cultural notions (Fabrega 1972*a*). With psychiatric disorder, there is uncertainty, disagreement, and debate in all these areas. But it is agreed that the treater's attitudes and beliefs about an illness, and about the patient's course of recovery, influence not only the actual prognosis but also the patient's conceptions of his illness (Frank 1961; Torrey 1972; Mechanic 1972:138–139). Because significant others also play a role in defining reality and in establishing meaning, the psychiatrist's and the significant others' behavior and beliefs about mental illness in general, and about the patient in particular, influence the 'sick' reality of the patient. And the patient's demonstration and experience of symptoms informs these others ahout illness (but these are probably less powerful determinants of the others' beliefs than vice versa). Though all symptoms are subjective to some degree, psychiatric malfunction has few absolute indicators, such as blood pressure or bacteria count. So a rich opportunity exists for mutual molding of behavior, expectation, and experience, factors comprising the intersubjective reality regarding the illness.

With apparently chronic psychiatric illness, the nature, cause, and prognosis of which is uncertain, the patient is destined to be caught in the unhappy position of being unable to be positively self-accepting as sick. Others have ambivalent perceptions and attitudes, because they cannot be sure why the patient is not getting well. They cannot be sure whether the patient is violating cultural values by not wanting and not trying to get well, or whether the disease itself is responsible (cf. Erickson 1957). Amid the uncertainty about psychiatric disorder, the influence of the interacting beliefs and practices of treaters, significant others, and the patient is further enhanced. I am suggesting that the consciously expressed and unconsciously believed ideas of PACT staff about craziness as a disease (ideas shared by other Inside Normals, the SSI system, and sheltered workshops), indicate to clients not only that they are sick but also that they will probably never "get well." Inside Crazies also give each other this message by repeated life failures, psychotic episodes, and not "getting better." By cooperating in applying for SSI, continually prescribing and giving medications, and suggesting GWI and MOC for employment, the staff confirms the client's belief in and acceptance of his or her disability and chronicity. At the same time, clients are sometimes gently, sometimes forcefully prodded not to accept the eternity of their craziness and to try to function as "well." A delicate balance between these indications would be difficult to achieve under any circumstances. It seems that the scales tip toward chronicity for this group.

In support of this formulation about staff influence, Petroni (1972:53) found that "the doctor-patient relationship seems to be important insofar as the patients' acceptance of the therapist as a significant other strongly influences his acceptance of the psychiatric sick role. The latter however, also seems contingent on situational influences . . . and whether or not one had had repeated episodes of psychiatric treatment." At PACT, the entire staff may be viewed as therapists, and they are without question very significant others to clients. In this position, their influence is enormous. And even though the staff is battling against perpetuation of the clients' psychiatric difficulties, trying to leave some hope, they are also indicating to clients, both subtly and overtly, that they will never get better. Part of this adjustment process is essential if the client is to have a realistic and, in some ways, less painful view of his or her life; and some of this is essential to preserve staff morale in setting attainable goals. But the contribution of the clients is also a factor. Petroni's work is supportive of my position, for he indicates that the patient's experience with repeated need for treatment (the experience of distress), is also a factor in constructing a perpetually sick, negatively different reality.

Our cultural ideas about appropriate illness behavior reflect a recognition of the lure and haven of disease as it legitimately exempts us from responsibility and expectations of performance in culturally valued tasks and roles. The person who experiences persistent though undecided-upon-illness can become caught in this tension between the harbor of disease and the obligation to get well. The disease status of psychiatric disorder in our cultural system of knowledge, belief, and behavior about illness is ambiguous. Therefore, significant others and the patient play important parts in determining each others' ideas of the cause, nature, course, and consequences of being mentally ill. Within the context of disagreement about mental illness, not wanting to and being unable to get well have been joined as symptoms of chronic psychiatric disorder. Patients interact with significant others who, consciously or unconsciously, communicate the message of chronicity. Patients also experience repeated psychotic and life-failure episodes that help them to stabilize and live within this contradictory intersubjective reality. This is what has occurred with the vast majority of the clients I have studied.

Erickson (1957:270) lends eloquent support to this formulation when he writes:

> ... the mental patient is in double jeopardy. He acquires recognition as a "sick person" only at a considerable emotional price, if at all; later he is able to withdraw from this recognition only with extreme difficulty, for he then faces the widespread conviction that legitimate mental illness cannot be completely cured anyway ... on several counts his experience with sickness may become crucial to his developing sense of direction and identity. *The danger is that patienthood may become a model for his image of the future rather than a provisional shelter in which he resets*

> *himself for a life already in progress. In some cases of lifelong difficulty, the patient's efforts to be recognized as a patient may be the first definite attempts he has ever made to establish himself in a clear cut social identity* . . . [emphasis added].

Long-term psychiatric patients are entwined in the paradoxes of constructing and living with a crazy identity and with uncertain illness in a sociocultural environment that communicates and denies, enhances and devalues who they are and how they are. This is what "making it crazy" means. This fusion of illness with identity may not be confined to psychiatric patients in our culture. It may have more to do with chronicity. For example, we say that "I *am* a diabetic" or "I *am* an epileptic" or "I *am* a leper." More transient diseases do not seem to result in the same sort of joining. We say that "I *have* a cold" or "I *have* strep throat." I am suggesting that the duration of difficulty lays the groundwork for the meshing of self and symptoms.

Perhaps the most important questions that should arise from this discussion are: "What are the relationships between sociocultural factors in illness and disease and the development of chronicity? How do sociocultural factors affect prognosis? What contributes to good outcome and what contributes to poor?" I have been suggesting rather ardently and persistently that the urban American sociocultural context is in some ways not helpful to persons attempting to cope with or to leave behind long-term psychiatric problems in living. At this juncture, it will be helpful to look for corroborating or challenging data and for theoretical orientations.

The most interesting and exciting evidence suggesting that cultural variables somehow affect prognosis in psychiatric disorders comes from the World Health Organization's (WHO) International Pilot Study of Schizophrenia (IPSS) (WHO 1973, 1975). Begun in 1966, and carried out in nine countries,[1] the research established that observers and clinicians trained to use the same scales and measures could identify persons with similar symptoms in all the settings. The sample of 1,202 patients yielded 811 persons with symptoms identified as schizophrenia, 164 with diagnoses of

1. Taiwan, Colombia, Czechoslovakia, Denmark, India, Nigeria, the Soviet Union, Great Britain, and the United States.

affective disorders, and 227 with other psychotic and nonpsychotic designations. Two years after the initial interviews, an average of 82 percent of the original participants were seen again for a follow-up study.

Marked crosscultural differences in the two-year outcome were reported. Patients in non-Western countries, particularly in India, Colombia, and Nigeria, fared much better on all course and outcome measures than did patients in the Euro-Western world, specifically in Denmark, Great Britain, the Soviet Union, Czechoslovakia, and the United States (Sartorious, Jablensky, and Shapiro 1977, 1978; WHO 1979). Murphy and Raman (1971) reported similar results comparing patients in Mauritius with those in Great Britain. In the IPSS study, Ibadan, Nigeria, reported the fewest patients with the worst outcome, while Washington, D.C., Prague, Aahrus, and London reported the most patients with the worst outcome. Even after rigorous data analysis, location proved to be the best predictor of outcome among all the measures taken.

Beyond this finding, which invites and requires much more culturally pertinent research to provide adequate explanations, was the intriguing information that the percentage of patients with poor outcome was similar among Western, developed countries and non-Western, developing countries. The large differences showed up in a greater concentration of Western patients in the intermediate and unfavorable outcome categories and the large number of non-Western patients in the very favorable group (Sartorious, Jablensky, and Shapiro 1978:105). It is tempting to see these middle-range persons as the most susceptible to cultural and social influences, and to speculate again that the measures of social impairment are picking up cultural variations in sick roles and the consequences of such roles for prognosis.

Another interesting result of the IPSS follow-up lends support to my argument and relates to prognosis for persons with acute versus insidious onset. In all the research centers, persons with acute, sudden onset had a significantly better prognosis than those with insidious onset, and these former outcomes were generally favorable. But patients with insidious or slow onset in the developing countries had a better overall outcome than the same types of patients in developed countries, especially those who had been troubled for more than six months before the first interview (ibid.: 106). In short, these results point to a "hypothetical 'factor' protecting schizophrenic patients from chronic deterioration [in the developing countries] (or, by the same logic, the presence of a 'factor' with a negative influence on course and outcome in the developed countries)" (ibid.).

Unfortunately, we lack sufficient ethnographic data on the non-Western countries in question to identify potential protective factors. We do, however, have some information about potential negative influences in at least one Western context. I have described them in this book. Clearly, much more research is needed to substantiate, alter, and sophisticate our understandings. It may well be that the poor prognosis of the slow onset cases indicates solidification of a role and career of chronic patienthood, which in turn contributes to poor outcome. Those persons with sudden, acute psychoses may not have developed an impaired identity over time and may thus have easier exit from their patienthood and the conceptions formed among their significant others.

Waxler (1977) argues that traditional societies have less of a stake in stigmatizing, isolating, and rejecting their mentally ill members than Western societies. Therefore "cure" is more often achieved. She points to the integrative and essentially sociocultural functions of the rituals and symbols surrounding primary deviance in non-Western cultures, suggesting that the treatment process itself (which may involve whole villages, if not extended families) both sanctions and reintegrates the deviating person (see also Kennedy 1967). Waxler emphasizes, as does Foster (1976), the important implications of where the illness is seen to reside (inside or outside the individual), and whose responsibility the illness is seen to be (the person's or the group's) in understanding prognosis. If the group shares responsibility and feels affected by the illness, it will mobilize to help cure the person rather than to blame or punish him. These are interesting theoretical notions that require empirical testing, but they ignore the extent to which family therapy is currently practiced in the West, and the currency of family and group theories about the etiology, exacerbation, and prolongation of psychosis (see Minuchin 1974; Lidz 1958; Vaughn and Leff 1976; Bateson et al. 1956).

The families of long-term psychiatric patients in the United

States have recently begun to organize, angrily rejecting their alleged roles in the etiology and perpetuation of their relative's problems. The keynote speaker at the first national meeting of such families said:

> We have been up against a number of unfortunate theories over the last couple of generations about mental illness—causation and treatment—that have been very devisive and difficult. . . . It must have grown out of our Calvinistic past that says whenever there's a problem somebody is to blame and he ought to be punished. When you have a mentally ill person there is a problem and families have been selected to be the culprits, to be blamed for that. We need to help providers understand what they're doing when they blame. When one blames, one is admitting helplessness and non-responsibility. What you are saying is, "I can't take responsibility. I do not know what to do." [Hatfield 1979:12-13]

She was greeted with resounding applause. Throughout the rest of the conference, it became clear how powerful the belief in a disease model of schizophrenia was among these relatives, and how squarely the locus of illness and responsibility was placed in the individual patient. I think these events and feelings underscore how mixed and often contradictory are our notions about the nature and meaning of long-term psychosis.

Sociological data is plentiful documenting the influence and association of sociocultural factors with the incidence and prevalence of psychosis (Dohrenwend 1975; Dohrenwend and Dohrenwend 1974); data is more scarce in the area of prognosis. Beck (1978) has reviewed the latter literature and has concluded that social factors such as milieu, family, group therapy, and psychosocial treatments can influence prognosis, but which factors and how remains unclear and unpredictable. Eaton (1975) has investigated the influence of social class on chronicity in schizophrenia, regarding both duration and recurrence of illness. Contrary to earlier studies, he has found no strong relationship. Kohn (1973) has questioned the consistent findings that schizophrenia is strongly associated with low socioeconomic status in the Western world. Kohn suggests that neither downward drift nor actual higher incidence sufficiently account for these relationships. He hypothesizes that the conceptions of sociocultural reality, fostered by the stressful and constricted conditions of low socioeconomic status, impair coping strategies and flexibilities, reducing the personal efficacy necessary for survival without decompensation into schizophrenia.

Still another way to assess the influence of social factors on outcome is to look at the efficacy of treatment modalities that incorporate and address sociocultural issues. Mosher and Keith (1979) reviewed psychosocial treatment programs for schizophrenics and concluded that although they are still undefined, social factors such as support systems outside the nuclear family, residential care, and rehabilitation programs provide effective treatment. Paul and Lentz (1977) have shown that long-term patients respond favorably to a highly structured social learning treatment program, even in the absence of neuroleptic drug treatment (which sometimes interfered with the learning process).

I have posed some pressing questions that I will not answer here, but I think the evidence is indisputable regarding the potential carried by interpersonal and sociocultural factors for help or harm in the lives of severely psychiatrically troubled persons, whether their illness is short-term or long-term.

In closing this chapter, I suggest that "making it crazy" represents an incorrigible proposition. An incorrigible proposition never admits to falsity, regardless of events. It is compatible with any state of affairs, even with apparent contradiction (Mehan and Wood 1975:9). Each rule for making it crazy that I have proposed, each paradox I have examined, represents an incorrigible proposition. Clients come to hold the incorrigible proposition that they are crazy people, and that they and others are unable to break through the built-in perceptual and experiential biases of this constructed reality. Nearly all of the clients have succeeded in constructing a monstrous trap, from which there seems to be no easy exit. They, in concert with their subjective and intersubjective differences, deficits, and perceptions of self and others, and we, with our well-intentioned but often contradictory, paradoxical beliefs, actions, and cures, have participated in making it crazy. Lara Jefferson (in Kaplan 1964:4) has stated the paradoxes concisely, poetically, and better than I: "Here I sit—mad as a hatter—with nothing to do but either become madder and madder—or else recover enough of my sanity to be allowed to go back to the life which drove me mad."

11

REFLECTIONS, CONCLUSIONS, AND QUESTIONS FOR FURTHER RESEARCH

It seems a long time since I plunged into this project, filled with enthusiasm and curiosity, envisioning revelations of untold mysteries. The enthusiasm and wonder remain, but the years have deepened, saddened, cleared, and clouded the visions all at once. I understand less than I had hoped, but more than I did at first. Perhaps the reader shares these sentiments. It has been my intention to convey my continuing formulations of a complex and confounding subject.

In the preceding chapters, I have described what I wanted to learn and how I thought I could learn it. An analytic, inductive approach was helpful in discovering the richness and diversity of the clients' world. The anthropological rationale and perspective allowed and encouraged me to follow the facts and to let the clients lead the way. In doing this, many paradoxes were discovered, experienced, and pondered.

One of the most interesting findings was the spatial, temporal, and interpersonal concentration of clients. They seemed to have less control of their time, space, resources, and information than did Inside and Outside Normals. But the clients had more freedom and control of these factors than they would have had in a hospital setting. Even in a community setting, where they were not strictly confined by physical barriers, they chose to interact primarily with each other. Some reasons for this companionship were not entirely voluntary, such as concentration of constraints on finances, on mobility, and on accessibility of living space. But clients usually chose solitude. For company, they preferred each other and psychiatric professionals. This may have been owing to various factors, including their perception of common differences between themselves and noncrazy people, and including their lack of relationships with normals outside the help-giving system. This friendship or symmetrical sharing of time, space, resources, and information among clients created several paradoxes, particularly in relation to medications, subsistence strategies, and interpersonal relationships.

Taking the symbolic interactionist approach, I interpreted clients' conscious and unconscious, deliberate and involuntary constructions of intersubjective reality, both among themselves and in interaction with outsiders, as contributing to their differences with the world at large. In the process of this construction and perpetuation, some clients seemed less than satisfied with their world and themselves. Few made successful moves out of this reality, for they were constrained from so doing by their perceived and actual lack of fit anywhere else. They seemed perpetually engaged in wandering multiple mazes, passing by the right exits, and pursuing dead-ends or short circuits back to the beginning.

The most important normals with whom they interacted were persons who genuinely cared for them and who wanted to help open those right doors and to deter them from making it crazy. But these normals also contributed to the end result of stabilization within the realm of negative differentness. They were unable to alter the multitude of factors contributing to the complementary schismogenesis, of which they, too, were a part.

Clients did not see themselves as regular people, nor did others. Some clients felt special, some felt awful, and some did not care to think about it. Nearly all had as many stereotypes about normals as vice versa. The ignorance, fear, and avoidance was mutual. I suggest that the clients did not have enough contact with normals to learn that they had commonalities as well as differences. Clients were not in a position to give to normals in a symmetrical fashion, so of course they felt and were dependent. Those with whom they developed the most caring, active, interpersonal relationships were staff and therapists, and such relationships had built-in asymmetries and barriers for exchange owing to professional ethics. Perhaps a rethinking of treatment in terms of these barriers and the importance of caring would be in order (Huessy n.d.).

It is clear that more research is needed regarding the possible perverse dynamics of income-maintenance programs for the disabled. Perhaps a program voluntarily tied to nonworkshop employment could be invented. Some means of providing the money with fewer negative implications must be explored. The bureaucratic time lag in applying for and receiving SSI impedes movement on and off the rolls. Also, the demonstration of yearlong inability to support oneself should be examined in light of its encouragement of disability maintenance. Bureaucratic regulations meant to dilute work disincentives in income-maintenance programs are insufficient to counteract the erroneous operative myths held by clients. Outreach and the education of clients might help, because until individuals are persuaded that they will not lose their SSI by working, the disincentives will remain.

The misidentification of the retarded and handicapped with the psychiatrically disturbed, as conveyed by the workshop system and as expressed by the general public, needs clarification and separation. PACT has made some gains with a very limited sector of the public in attempting to change the helpless image of clients, but this is not enough. It is my impression that a number of clients would have worked or at least would have obtained some training and experience if they had not considered the GWI and MOC environments to be so stigmatizing. The workshop system might consider separation of clientele. Or job-sharing might represent an exciting but unexplored option for these clients. They might not be able or willing to work at highly stressful or complicated jobs full time, but together and with some adjustments by employers and co-workers, they might be able to experience interesting jobs as rewarding and manageable.

From another perspective, there are options that community members might consider. One of the reasons that the monetary costs of long-term mental illness are so high is that professionals are being paid to care for and about persons whose psychic and material needs are great, but whose resources are few. It might cost less and help more if community members shared goods and services directly with patients. This is done on a pitifully small but meaningful scale by volunteers, but most citizens have few incentives to interact with or to help chronic patients. Instead, community members pay taxes to support the growing number of administrative and direct line personnel. I envision an experiment in which community members would receive a significant tax break in exchange for such services as cooking and serving meals for and with clients, for having clients live in their homes, or for apartment-seeking and job-seeking with clients; in other words, for engaging in helping, caring, and sharing outside the mental health system as a friend or benefactor. In this way, community members would be motivated to become involved in caring, and clients would be placed in contact with other than professional help-givers. Community members and clients could then experience the caring process as a human interchange instead of as a financial one—the citizens with their money going to federal, state, and local agencies, and the clients with SSI checks coming in the mail. The ultimate goal of this experiment would be to create situations in which community members and clients would get to know each other as people with strengths and deficits, each able to help and care for the other as different but equal. Clearly, realization of this fantasy lies in a far-distant future, but, at an experimental level, it seems worth investigating.

The medications issue also needs further thought and also has economic and political ramifications. The problems in continuing large-scale use of maintenance phenothiazines are indeed difficult. These persons could, in fact, be treated with fewer medications if more personnel were available. Role-playing and practice in controlling specific side effects with clients might be tried. Many clients do not realize how they look when having side effects, and videotaped sessions might prove helpful. In conjunction with this, talking and working directly with clients to diminish the side effects might help them to master the leg-bouncing, the flat expressions, and the stiffness that are so noticeable and uncomfortable. In outpatient discussion settings, such as Prolixin groups or among patients who meet when they get their injections, patients have talked about their feelings regarding meds, learning from and with each other. Compliance among members of such groups seems to improve, for the medication becomes linked with a socially and interpersonally rewarding experience.

We do not have enough data about how patients think and feel about medications. Clients not only need more information about their medications but they need more choice in determining dosage amounts in concert with and not in conflict with their physicians.

We also lack data regarding community perception of side effects and the possible stigma attached to the taking of psychoactive medications. Research is needed in both these neglected areas, for such information deficits impede careful evaluation of the whole medications complex.

Furthermore, it might be useful for treatment programs to recognize and adapt to the different temporal world of clients. It might diminish some of the messages that designate difference if, instead of conceptualizing time as divided between work and leisure, staff could refocus on the temporal implications of the SSI life, considering the utilization and appreciation of time from the perspective of clients. These clients seem to have little to do with their time save to reflect upon and enhance their "out-of-sync" existences. One potentially useful task would be helping each other. By this I mean that clients could orient each other to treatment programs, to new places of residence, to the job scene, and to eating places, and they could take on a meaningful role in the helping process. In this way, they could be on the giving instead of the receiving end of the spectrum—an all too infrequent experience.

Projects similar in goals and methods to mine need to be undertaken among other clients in different programs and in various community settings. Because of the lack of comparative data, and because of the special characteristics of the population I studied, generalizations from my findings are necessarily restricted. Nonetheless, we can postulate that, although community treatment is a good idea, it holds some unanticipated liabilities. Many of the interactional processes that have contributed to the negative evaluation of psychiatric hospitals seem also to be occurring in a community setting. The opportunities and resources for development and enhancement of dependency, isolation, negative self-image, and hopelessness regarding oneself have not been eliminated. In fact, the negative impact may have been enhanced by demonstrating to clients that they cannot make it, even outside the hospital.

Community treatment advocates have, in some ways, been sociologically naive. De-institutionalization has, for the most part, been simplistically effected through movement away from the architectural embrace of hospitals. But institutions, of course, are complex, extending beyond walls to the articulation of traditions and values at a societal level. In this sense, the institutions of chronic mental illness have been little affected by the escape from institutional buildings. The roles, expectations, stereotypes, and responses that accompany being a back-ward patient or a long-term community outpatient have changed little. It is as if we thought what was noxious to patients was somehow present in the actual walls of hospitals. That if we got away from the buildings it would help. Clearly the architecture has had little to do with the creation of chronicity. The people who build, inhabit, and administer the buildings, and now the programs that have taken over their functions, need our careful examination. The patient, the family, culture, and treatment beliefs need our scrutiny. The setting we must investigate is not just a physical one.

Actually, psychiatric hospitals need not be and may not have been such despicable places. Bachrach (1976) suggests that one of the functions of the psychiatric hospital is to provide asylum for the person experiencing severe difficulties in living with himself and others. I think that clients, and all of us, still need a place to rest or to be crazy if necessary. Perhaps keeping clients out of the hospital merely keeps their periodic bizarre, disorganized behavior and thinking within the view of others who might fear and reject them because of it. The psychotic or disruptive client may damage more relationships and social networks by remaining out of the hospital than by going in for a while until his behavior is less acutely discomforting to himself and others. Or, conversely, perhaps community members would learn to accept and to tolerate these episodes and persons if they were exposed to them more frequently. Perhaps community-based programs could perform an educative function, responding to public ignorance about the mentally ill. Professional involvement, to enhance public understanding and thereby reduce fear, would be necessary and would require flexible availability on the part of staff, as demonstrated by PACT.

At any rate, simply keeping clients out of the hospital is not enough to stop them and others from making it crazy. Working to alter or in some ways to diminish the simultaneous indications and condemnations of craziness and clienthood would seem to be an important additional task. Facilitating more opportunities for clients and others to see and experience each other positively, thereby reconstructing a beneficial intersubjective reality, needs further thought and experimentation. Self-help and former patient groups are increasing in number and represent a significant step toward these goals. They merit support, both financial and professional, and they deserve latitude to express constructive anger and dissatisfaction, and to suggest alternative means of caring for each other.

At present there does not appear to be a powerful subculture among clients that would constitute a barrier to constructive change. Although it possesses many of the prerequisites for the formation of a counter culture, the group is as yet too disorganized and disparate. But, if this chronic community client population continues to grow through time, the possibilities will also increase for elaboration and firming of the present negative cluster of different meanings, behaviors, and realities.

If a culprit exists in this conglomeration of injustices qua paradoxes, I think it is to be found among the vague and contradictory societal beliefs about mental illness. From the viewpoint of determining impact on prognosis, more research needs to be directed toward ascertaining the fundamental beliefs about the nature, causes, and cures of psychiatric disorder held by psychiatric professionals, patients, and their significant others. The follow-up studies of the International Pilot Study of Schizophrenia, noted earlier, have clearly indicated that some Western sociocultural factors, as yet unidentified, are associated with poor outcome of schizophrenic episodes. Anthropologists need to direct ethnomedical and ethnopsychiatric inquiry toward their own culture to learn why this may be happening. The Soteria House Project (Mosher and Menn 1978) suggests that working with a conception of psychosis different from the current one could be useful. At Soteria, psychosis is considered to be an altered state of consciousness that is not negatively valued but is to be experienced and learned from. Few medications are used, and the staff are largely nonprofessionals who approach clients with nonjudgmental friendship. Although this experiment is promising, more research is needed to begin to dismantle the factors perpetuating differentness at the fundamental belief level. Without more precise knowledge of these factors, it would be difficult to reconstruct a system that would be less paradoxical and more therapeutic.

Being a full-time crazy person is becoming an occupation among a certain population in our midst. If we as a society continue to subsidize this career, I do not think it humane or justifiable to persist in negatively perceiving those who take us up on the offer and become employed in this way. As long as we contribute to blocking their exits from this crazy system, it is ridiculously unfair to condemn and reject those who tell us and show us that they cannot leave.

Another area requiring further research and consideration concerns the ritual and symbolic components of making it crazy. Though there are many rituals and symbols of *entry* into psychiatric patienthood and the treatment system, there are few powerful correlates surrounding *exit*. The community offers no rite of passage comparable to leaving the hospital, signing multiple forms, and changing drastically one's daily routine. Without the potent ritual and symbol of hospital discharge, perhaps clients in the community are even further removed from experiencing a status passage to health. The symbols of having a job and being off medications are probably not realistic goals for these particular clients, and experimentation with the creation of such rituals and accessible symbols would be worthwhile.

The clients are not the only ones who merit consideration. So, too, do their families and the treatment staffs that care for them. The families of long-term psychiatric patients are raising angry and bitter voices, louder and louder, calling for more resources for their offspring and loved ones, and for themselves as they try to cope with the heartache, frustrations, and demands of their circumstances. Their complaints are largely legitimate and their dilemmas are real. They, too, need care and nurturance.

As community treatment loses its youthful exuberance, the problem of staff burnout (Mendel 1978, Mechanic 1978) looms large. Providing and sustaining enthusiastic, nurturant, patient, and gratified staff for these treatment programs presents one of the most serious challenges to community treatment for long-term psychiatric clients. These jobs are customarily low-paying, offer few large rewards, and are often repetitious, tedious, and frustrating. Turnover rates among staff are alarming, and so is the presence of cynical, disheartened, and pessimistic personnel on the front lines. It is indeed difficult not to become enculturated into the chronic clients' world of failure, gloom, despair, and boredom. Staff members might well benefit from sabbaticals—lateral transfers to nonpsychiatric jobs at regular intervals. More of them could be encouraged to work as staff only part-time, working at other jobs that offer them some relief. Creative solutions need to be found, for no matter how innovative a treatment design may be, it depends most heavily upon the character and spirit of the individuals who implement it.

The most important tasks revolve around acknowledging and attempting to resolve the paradoxes discussed in these pages. Undermining the process of amplifying and maintaining differentness that occurs among clients and between them and others represents the most vital of endeavors for those of us who believe that no one need make it crazy. There are alternatives. The crosscultural data indicates that within different behavior and belief systems about physical and mental illness, shamans, curers, and others can have meaningful, though different, lives and identities. It seems to me to be crazy—nonsensical, perverse, and contradictory—to persist in defining chronic problems in living and being as pathological and to value them negatively, when we are contributing to their perpetuation. As medical technology advances and as we salvage more and more lives, there will be larger numbers of persons among us with chronic problems of all types. Will we save them only to condemn them as well? We need to pursue the options and changes as ardently and persistently as we have participated in our previous and present constructions. Let us recall the words of Freud that opened this book: ". . . one of the problems that touches the fate of humanity is whether such an accommodation can be reached by means of some particular form of civilization or whether this conflict is irreconcilable."

EPILOGUE

> Madness is the most solitary of afflictions to the people who experience it, but the most social of maladies to those who observe its effects.
> [McDonald 1981:1]

INTRODUCTION

Nearly a decade has passed since I began the research on which this book is based, and almost five years have gone by since the manuscript went to press. I now write from a different locale, affiliated with a different institution, and with new people to thank for teaching me. I also write with reflection formed by experiences that have been more varied and profound than I could have anticipated when writing previously. Essentially, in the interim, the research never stopped. I have, however, changed level of focus, role, and vantage point several times, while the always incomplete process of understanding continues. Even though some social and clinical circumstances have changed, and even though I have changed, there is very little in the preceding pages that requires amendment. The advantage of several years' worth of very generous reviews and responses to this book, from varied quarters, leads me to conclude that concise additions and timely updates are in order, not major revisions.

In the next few pages, I want to accomplish two tasks. First, I intend briefly to bring the reader up to date on developments in policy and service systems, both national and local, that have had the most profound effects on the people about whom I wrote, and thousands like them. Recent research findings that provide a more precise, corroborating, or even conflicting picture will also be identified, as far as is permitted in so small a space. Second, this work has been from the beginning a chronicle of persons, settings, and ethnographer as they intertwine and influence each other. In keeping with that tradition, I intend to convey to the reader the most significant experiences and resulting shifts in perspective that I have had as an anthropologist working in the roles of administrator, clinician, researcher, and consultant.

POLICY AND SERVICE SYSTEMS

Depending on one's perspective at the start, the past several years have seen either increasing pessimism and criticism or growing realism about the social and clinical consequences and limits, both intended and unintended, of the third decade of psychiatric deinstitutionalization. Many zealous community care advocates, sobered and saddened by their own and others' failures, now face the very real possibility of losing hard fought ground, ground won initially with daring and determination. It is now commonplace to read about shortcomings, unfulfilled expectations, and downright errors made in implementing bold visions of community-based care for persons with severe mental disabilities (e.g. Mollica 1983; Feldman 1983). This is a rather startling shift in tone and direction from the research and policy literature of just a few years ago (c.f. Test and Stein 1978; Talbott 1978). The inevitable suggestion that it is time seriously to reconsider reinstitutionalization, or returning to long term public psychiatric hospital care as a treatment of choice, now come from quarters as disparate as the academic research community (Gudeman and Shore 1984), legislators (Cincinnati Enquirer 1984), hospital workers' unions, and parents of persons with chronic mental illness (Teicher quoted in Beviloqua 1984).

Ironically, amidst this circumspect sociopolitical climate, the findings from relevant research are consistent and demonstrate that comprehensive community care can be a feasible and effective alternative to inpatient psychiatric treatment for many severely disordered persons (Braun et al. 1981; Liberman and Phipps 1984). What is distressingly apparent, however, is that the existence of effective treatment technologies is by no means sufficient to create comprehensive care systems. Nor does this knowledge alleviate the poverty, social isolation, homelessness, frequent incarceration and victimization (Lamb and Grant 1982; Lamb et al. 1984), widespread unemployment, and ongoing dependence on social institutions such as income maintenance that continue to characterize the lives of persons with severe mental disabilities. Successful randomized, controlled clinical trials of innovative treatment conditions do not resolve public resource allocation or delivery of service problems, the latter currently posing perhaps the most significant obstacles to be overcome (cf. Mosher 1983). Sociocultural, political, and economic forces are expressed in current health care and social welfare policies barren of sympathetic concern, much less willing public responsibility, for the care of chronically disabled and socioeconomically marginal persons (Foley and Sharfstein 1983; Price and Smith 1983).

At the national level in terms of policy, two issues have emerged as most significant: (1) The April, 1981 initiation of Continuing Disability Investigations (CDI's) by the Social Security Administration (U.S. Senate 1983); and (2) Growing public and professional acknowledgement that substantial numbers of persons, including many with serious psychiatric symptoms and hospital histories, are homeless (Baxter and Hopper 1981, 1982; U.S. House of Representatives 1982; Hopper and Hamberg 1984).

Income Maintenance

In order to appreciate fully the magnitude of the impact of changes in the disability income maintenance system, it is important to recall the extent to which persons with mental disabilities participate in and rely on these programs. Several recent estimates indicate that nearly half of the 1.7 to 2.0 million persons with chronic mental illness in the U.S., or between 640,000 and 700,000 people, receive SSI or SSDI based on their psychiatric disability (Goldman, Gattozzi, and Taube 1981:25; HSRI 1983:40; U.S. Senate 1983:164–165). The estimated total direct cash benefits paid by SSI and SSDI to persons with chronic mental illness in 1983 is over $2.3 billion.

Currently, mental disorders are the primary disabling condition for approximately 11.7% of the 2.6 million disabled workers receiving SSDI (U.S. Senate 1983:164). Growth in the participation of disabled persons in the SSI program has been steady and pronounced (Kennedy 1982:5). In fact, the number of disabled SSI beneficiaries surpassed the number of aged beneficiaries in 1976, and has continued to increase to the present, while participation of aged persons has decreased. Of the 3.9 million people receiving SSI in September, 1983, 2.3 million were considered disabled (Table M-19 Soc. Sec. Bull 1983:29). Estimates are that 30% of SSI awards to disabled adults are accounted for by persons with mental disorders (U.S. Senate, 1983:164). Since the beginning of the SSI program, mental illness has been the most frequent cause of disability, entitling 63,000 persons in 1975 (Kochhar, 1979). If current estimates are correct, and 400,000 chronically mentally ill persons receive SSI, a growth in participation of 530% for this category of persons has occurred in the past decade.

Between January 1, 1981 and August 1982, by its own account, the SSA reviewed over 665,000 cases, terminating benefits for nearly 336,000, or over 50%. In the mentally disabled category for that period, 182,893 cases were reviewed and 86,438, or 47.2%, were terminated. Equally significant is the fact that even though a very small number (1,400) of mentally disabled persons who were terminated appealed the decision, 91% of those cases heard by Administrative Law Judges were reversed, benefits being reinstated (U.S. Senate 1983:14, 165). So, many were terminated and apparently unwilling or unable to navigate the complex appeals process, which might well have restored their financial support. The review and termination from benefits of persons with mental disabilities in five mid-western states was stopped by the order of a U.S. District Court in December, 1982. The result of a class-action suit, this ruling lead eventually to the governors of many states not covered by the decision declaring moratoria on further terminations. At the federal level, the Secretary of Health and Human Services soon declared a national cessation of reviews until more appropriate disability determination criteria could be developed.

One is hard pressed to remain objectively analytical about such a policy in view of the havoc wrecked in so many psychologically fragile and materially meager lives. I can only suggest that this represents the baldest of expressions of social and public resistance to and ambivalence about providing for dependent, disabled persons. If the SSA regulations are considered as cultural codes defining legitimate material dependence based on disability, this policy underscores how undecided-upon the nature, meaning, and consequences of mental illness remain at the cultural level. How far we seem willing to go to safeguard the status of legitimate dependency from suspected unwarranted claim bears further scrutiny than I can give here.

In view of the various incentives to apply for and receive SSI and SSDI discussed previously, and the lack of financial alternatives available to many severely mentally disordered persons, this policy represents, in my opinion, a shamefully unjust and socially irresponsible posture towards many who scarcely deserve it. Despite the numerous quandries posed by SSI that were pointed out in Chapter 6, and despite the various reservations I have outlined regarding its effects on the identities and sociocultural worlds of the clients, the fact that these reviews and terminations took place when national unemployment among *nondisabled* persons was at record high levels, and funds for community services were being reduced, emphasizes again how very carefully we must guard against creating dependencies that we are unprepared or unwilling to support. Failing that, the least obligation we have is to provide tolerably humane alternatives for subsistence.

When I moved from Madison in the summer of 1982, I was not aware that any of the clients included in this book had been reviewed or terminated, and I hope that is accurate, not ignorant.

Homelessness

In their stunning and poignant ethnography, Baxter and Hopper (1981) brought to public and professional attention the extent and forms of homelessness among an estimated 40,000 people in New York City alone. Since that time, the extent and causes of homelessness among persons with chronic mental illness have been widely and often dramatically reported in both the popular press and in scholarly journals. National estimates of homelessness range from 250,000 to over 2,000,000 people, varying by definition, method of counting, and who conducts the count. As many as half to as few as 20% are thought to be seriously mentally ill, formerly hospitalized, in need of inpatient psychiatric care, and/or suffering from substance abuse (Hopper and Hamberg 1984). As researchers and administrators squabble over definitions, numbers, responsibility, and cause, shelters and soup kitchens, often formerly hidden among charitable services in many communities, daily grow in number, in clientele, and in need for financial support.

It is undeniable that the closings and reductions in residents of public psychiatric hospitals are related in complex fashion to homelessness among persons with severe mental disorders. Yet, a host of equally important factors such as lack of money, disability benefit termination, reductions in the amount of low cost housing in urban areas, rent increases, difficulties in interpersonal relationships, competition with other dependent poor persons, and intolerable physical conditions of residences, contribute to their being undomiciled temporarily, situationally, or over a longer span of time (Caton and Goldstein 1984, Roth and Bean 1984). Pondering whether and how psychiatric deinstitutionalization *caused* homelessness among persons with chronic mental illness seems a potentially dangerous irrelevance, because this conceptualization of the problem invites consideration of reinstitutionalization as a solution. Homelessness epitomizes the lack of positive social and personal space available to and habitable by impoverished, disabled persons in our society. Psychiatric hospitals merely represent another form of disgraced and devalued space, only slightly warmer and safer than some streets or shelters. To be sure, we have closed far too many formal institutional doors and opened far too few that are informal and noninstitutional. But, returning people to the hospital will once again punish the victims of complicated social processes, leaving the latter unattended to and at work to do damage in other times, in other ways.

As the reader will recall, the PACT clients often experienced both loss and lack of a place to stay or shelter, but they were assisted in avoiding street life by virtue of participating in a comprehensive treatment program. Such programs are not only seldom available, but are often strenuously avoided by younger persons who desperately resist being engulfed by a mental patient role (Segal, Baumohl, and Johnson 1977). Yet again, they are forced to choose between the equally unacceptable options of being labeled crazy or living without assistance in undomiciled destitution. Such nonchoices constitute, I believe, yet another paradoxical, quasi-degrading/quasi-care-taking response to individuals who seem to suffer at times as much from our attention as our lack of it.

Homelessness among the clients and others like them in Madison had not reached proportions comparable to those in larger urban centers by 1982. Still, during this period the University purchased the only intermediate care residence in the downtown area, displacing hundreds of disabled people. Another nearby facility for mentally retarded persons was sold for conversion to condominiums, requiring court intervention to accomplish re-location of the residents. These changes left the YMCA as the major source of inexpensive housing for men in the central city area. Before my departure as director of services to residents, the building had been allowed to deteriorate to such an extent that a major capitol investment would be required to maintain the residence. Many board members openly advocated demolition of the building, arguing that reconstructing a fitness center only was the wisest financial strategy. Despite opposition from several board members, the residence staff, and some facile gestures on the part of the city welfare department, it is inevitable that the residence will soon close.

During 1981, a committee to shelter the homeless formed among concerned mental health and social service agency personnel. We were able to raise funds to provide vouchers for short stays in already available space, but were obstructed by the city in our efforts to reclaim, after a fire, the SRO hotel frequently used as housing by PACT clients. (See Map, p. 51, no. 8.) That area of the city overlooks a lake, and after expensive condominiums had been built nearby, a shelter or SRO hotel did not fit within development plans. In spite of the hotel owner's strong interest in running a shelter and SRO hotel, her active work on the shelter committee, and her receipt of formal training and a degree in human services, block grant money controlled by the city was not forthcoming. She was eventually forced to sell the building to a private developer in order to contend with mortgage payments.

Research Findings

The following is intended as a guide to recent, pertinent research, since I cannot adequately review and comment here. These studies provide important additional information about the clinical, social, cultural, and cross-cultural circumstances of persons with severe mental disabilities. None contradicts or directly challenges the findings of my research, but contribute welcome detail, analysis, and overview, from both quantitative and qualitative perspectives, on the persons and topics presented previously. (Studies referred to elsewhere in the epilogue are not repeated here.)

Deinstitutionalization and the Epidemiology of Chronic Mental Illness

These studies represent relatively large scale, empirical analyses and descriptions of severely mentally disabled populations in the U.S., along with information about their patterns of use of inpatient and outpatient mental health services.

Bachrach, L. L.
1983 (ed.) DeInstitutionalization. *New Directions for Mental Health Services,* No. 17. San Francisco: Jossey-Bass.

Baker, F. and Intagliata, J.
1984 The New York State Community Support System: A Profile of Clients. *Hospital and Community Psychiatry* 35(1):39–44.

Goldman, H. H., Adams, N. H. and Taube, C. A.
1983 DeInstitutionalization: The Data DeMythologized. *Hospital and Community Psychiatry* 34(2):129–134.

Goldman, H. H. and Manderscheid, R. W.
1984 Epidemiology of Chronic Mental Disorder. Paper presented at the National Conference on the Chronic Mental Patient II, Kansas City, Missouri, August, 1984.

Kiesler, C. A.
1982 Public and Professional Myths about Mental Hospitalization: An Empirical Reassessment of Policy Related Beliefs. *American Psychologist* 37(12):1323–1339.

Schoonover, S. C. and Bassuk, E. L.
1983 DeInstitutionalization and the Private General Hospital Unit. *Hospital and Community Psychiatry* 34(2):135–139.

Tessler, R. C. and Goldman H. H.
1982 *The Chronically Mentally Ill: Assessing Community Support Programs.* Cambridge, Mass: Ballinger Press.

Treatment Efficacy, Outcome, and Follow-Up Studies

Research in this area indicates that even the more effective treatment techniques for the chronically mentally ill population often do not ameliorate marked long term social and clinical disability, especially among persons diagnosed as schizophrenic. The Chestnut Lodge studies are especially important because they indicate that even among upper middle class persons, schizophrenics fare much poorer over time than those with affective disorders.

Budson, R. D. and Barofsky, I.
1984 (eds.) *The Chronic Schizophrenic Patient in the Community: Principles of Treatment.* N.Y.: Spectrum Publications.

Caton, C. L. M.
1982 Effect of Length of Inpatient Treatment for Chronic Schizophrenia. *American Journal of Psychiatry* 139(7):856–861.

Gudeman, J. E., Shore, M. F., and Dickey, B.
1983 Day hospitalization and an inn instead of inpatient care for psychiatric patients. *New England Journal of Medicine* 308:749–753.

Linn, M. W., Klett, J., and Caffey, E. M.
1982 Relapse of Psychiatric Patients in Foster Care. *American Journal of Psychiatry* 139(6):778–783.

McGlashan, T.
1984a The Chestnut Lodge Follow-up Study. I. Follow-up Methodology and Study Sample. *Archives of General Psychiatry* 41:573–585.
1984b The Chestnut Lodge Follow-up Study. II. Long-term Outcome of Schizophrenia and the Affective Disorders. *Archives of General Psychiatry* 41:586–601.

Meyerson, A. T. and Herman, G. S.
1983 What's New in Aftercare? A Review of Recent Literature. *Hospital and Community Psychiatry* 34(4):333–342.

Okin, R. L., Dolsick, J. A., and Pearsall, D. T.
1983 Patient's Perspectives on Community Alternatives to Hospitalization: A Follow-Up Study. *American Journal of Psychiatry* 140(11):1460–1464.

Social Support and Social Networks

Researchers and clinicians have devoted increasing attention to describing, assessing, and even altering the social relations of persons with severe mental disabilities. However fraught with conceptual and methodological difficulties, this area of research holds much promise, especially for anthropological investigation. Findings are relatively consistent across studies and methods, portraying patterns of social relations that are small in scope and number of contacts, densely connected to either relatives or other clients, and often either chaotic and stressful or distant and lacking emotional intimacy.

Schizophrenia Bulletin, Volume 7, No. 1, 1981. This issue is devoted entirely to the subject of Stress, Social Support, and Schizophrenia, and contains the following important contributions:

Hammer, M.
Social Supports, Social Networks, and Schizophrenia. pp. 45–57.

Beels, C. C.
Social Support and Schizophrenia. pp. 58–72.

Garrison, V. and Podell, J.
"Community Support Systems Assessment" for Use in Clinical Interviews. pp. 101–108.

Sokolovsky, J. and Cohen, C. I.
Toward a Resolution of Methodological Dilemmas in Network Mapping. pp. 109–116.

Westermeyer, J. and Pattison, E. M.
Social Networks and Mental Illness in a Peasant Society. pp. 125–134.

Pattison, E. M. and Pattison, M. L.
Analysis of a Schizophrenic Psychosocial Network. pp. 135–143.

Hammer, M.
1984 Social networks and the long term patient. In Budson, R. D. and Barofsky, Eds. *The Chronic Schizophrenic Patient in the Community*. N.Y.: Spectrum Publications.

Beels, C. C. et al.
1984 Measurement of Social Support in Schizophrenia. *Schizophrenia Bulletin* 10(3):399–411.

Greenblatt, M. et al.
1982 Social Networks and Mental Health: An Overview. *American Journal of Psychiatry* 139(8):977–984.

Lehman, A. F. et al.
1982 Chronic Mental Patients: The Quality of Life Issue. *American Journal of Psychiatry* 139(10):1271–1276.

Medications, Side Effects, and Drug Treatment Refusal

There are no major advances in drug treatment of schizophrenia to report. Several studies indicate that tardive dyskinesia is increasing in prevalence, and is associated with depot fluphenazine like many of the clients were given. Efforts are being increased to understand the etiology and possible reversal, if not prevention, of tardive dyskinesia. Concern over refusal of medication continues with relatively spare documentation of the short- or long-term effects of patient refusal, now often protected by law.

Glazer, W. M. et al.
1984 Tardive Dyskinesia: A Discontinuation Study. *Archives of General Psychiatry* 41:623–627.

Geller, J. L.
1982 State Hospital Patients and Their Medication—Do They Know What They Take? *American Journal of Psychiatry* 139(5):611–615.

Kane, J. M. and Smith, J. M.
1982 Tardive Dyskinesia: Prevalence and Risk Factors, 1959 to 1979. *Archives of General Psychiatry* 39:473–481.

Mukherjie, S. et al.
1982 Tardive Dyskinesia in Psychiatric Outpatients: A Study of Prevalence and Association with Demographic, Clinical, and Drug History Variables. *Archives of General Psychiatry* 39:466–469.

Marder, S. R. et al
1984 A Study of Medication Refusal by Involuntary Psychiatric Patients. *Hospital and Community Psychiatry* 35(7):724–726.

Mitchell, J. E. and Popkin, M. K.
1982 Antipsychotic Drug Therapy and Sexual Dysfunction in Men. *American Journal of Psychiatry* 139(5):633–637.

Brooks, A. D.
1980 The constitutional right to refuse antipsychotic medications. *Bulletin of the American Academy of Psychiatry and Law* 8:179 ff.

Anthropological Studies of Chronically Mentally Ill Persons in Western and Non-Western Settings

Far too few investigations by anthropologists have been undertaken and published. Those that have appeared in the past five years have been both valuable and reasonably well received by the mental health research community. Additional research in Western and non-Western settings would contribute badly needed and rich information about varieties of sociocultural responses to persons with chronic mental disorders, along with differing views of prognosis.

Amarasingham, L. R.
1984 "This Will Clear Your Mind." The Use of Metaphors for Medication in Psychiatric Settings. *Culture, Medicine and Psychiatry* 8(1):49–70.

Scheper-Hughes, N.
1981 Dilemmas in DeInstitutionalization: A View from Inner City Boston. *Journal of Operational Psychiatry* 12(2):90–99.

Westermeyer, J. and Wintrob, R.
1979 Folk Criteria for the Diagnosis of Mental Illness in Rural Laos. *American Journal of Psychiatry* 136:755–761.

Westermeyer, J.
1980 Mental Illness in a peasant society: Social outcomes. *American Journal of Psychiatry* 137:1390–1394.

Westermeyer, J.
1979 Folk Concepts of Mental Disorder Among the Lao. *Culture, Medicine, and Psychiatry* 3:301–317.

CHANGING ROLES AND NEW PERSPECTIVES

I was aware when I left the field after this initial research project, that I had learned about only one of many facets of a very complicated sociocultural system. So, first, I spent three years learning about clinical and research aspects of psychiatry as a postdoctoral fellow in an academic psychiatry department. I was fascinated with the clinical world, and found that sphere of meaning and action related to but different from the anthropological. The most striking difference was the implicit permission to judge, assess, label, and act among the clinicians. They had ready-made categories and explanations for the people and events that I had worked so hard to understand without those preconceived notions and without intervening. I was struck then by the awesome responsibility that accompanies making such assessments and acting on these judgements.

I left the University after the fellowship ended with the goals of experiencing that responsibility in order to know more deeply the clinical world, and to try out a more cultural approach and response to persons with chronic mental illness. For the next year and a half, I supervised a staff of seven mental health workers, carried my own share of clients as a therapist, and had administrative responsibility for both mental health services in a 150 bed residence and a drop in center program for current and former psychiatric patients attempting community life. I also tried to integrate clinical and cultural information and perspectives, approaching our treatment programs as relativistically as possible. This was extraordinarily difficult work. I learned to make snide remarks about clients in staff meetings, to get angry with them, and to think of them as sick. I found myself protecting other staff members from the demands of clients, and protecting myself from worrying too much about residents and club members who disappeared or got into serious trouble. All this staffness I experienced was reversible, but compelling at the time. On the other hand, the amount of paper work and time spent in meetings discussing organizational issues was so substantial that I found actual contact with clients to be a relief and rare pleasure. It reminded me of why I was there and why the "system" had to be changed.

I nearly always felt overwhelmed by the responsibility, and our consistent inability to do or give enough significantly to change a client's life for the better. At moments or in a crisis, what we did changed short term outcomes, but it was extremely difficult to overcome not symptoms, but obstacles inherent in the "system" of rules, agencies, politics, and funding sources. We seldom seemed to satisfy the community by curing mental illness (or at least protecting its members from annoyance), and they seldom seemed willing to give us the resources we needed to carry out our work.

Two events that occurred during this period had quite profound effects on my understanding. The first entailed the eviction of a resident who, hours later, jumped off a four story building. I had made the decision that he had to go, and had refused to readmit him to the residence, despite his protestations and requests from his family. The police notified me that he had jumped, and had told them on regaining consciousness of his eviction. Needless to say, I felt profoundly guilty, unable to justify the consequences of having followed house rules. I realized then I had lost a sense of other that I had had previously, and had begun to protect and serve the system. Everyone on the staff worked very diligently to relieve me of responsibility—and to a certain extent they were correct in so doing. But, the point for me was that this young man had made choices and decisions based on rules and needs other than ours. He was powerless, in his world, to be understood and cared for. He was willing to go much further than I had imagined to express his despair and anger at not being heard or taken care of. He has recovered from his injuries by now. I still feel defeated. After that time, I supported very few evictions, much to the displeasure of my supervisor, and no doubt would have been asked to leave my post had I not decided it was time to return to academic life.

Much more positive, but equally influential was a political action that resulted in over four hundred mental health clients, agency staff members, and clients' relatives protesting proposed budget cuts on the steps of the state capitol. Several clients gave bold and poignant speeches, pleading for services and resources that they needed for daily survival. Many of us—clients, staff, advocates, and relatives—worked for weeks to organize the rally. The exhilaration of hearing those individuals demand services, demand attention, and politicize rather than pathologize their needs was immense.

Probably for many other reasons, the budget was not cut. But it hardly mattered after that ritual of legitimation, and after those clients risked humiliation by publicly staking a claim to decent lives, openly describing their symptoms and histories. That experience confirmed for me that sociopolitical action is as necessary to progress for these people as caring, understanding, and innovative treatment programs. Clients and their relatives are organized now in virtually every state, and at the national level, for advocacy, mutual support, and self help. They represent perhaps the most promising development of the decade.

More recently, my level of focus has changed yet again as I have reviewed research and program proposals at NIMH for the Community Support Program, and worked as a consultant to a large state mental health system. The view from the federal and state level is quite different from that on the street. I now ponder policies that effect thousands of people and millions of dollars. The shape and flow of systems of care are often far removed from a social skills group or a walk by the lake with one of the clients. One has to think about societal level priorities, and how to manipulate the self interests of professional groups, senators, legislators, agency directors, and county officials. This new phase of the project of understanding is incomplete. But I am quite certain that the most important tasks remain reconciling our societal irresponsibility and ambivalence, expressed in policy or in a program, about the clients and others like them.

This is especially important because persons with long-term and severe mental disorders represent but one group in our society who depend upon the public will to provide for them in order to live decent lives. If I have learned anything since first entering the field, it is that sociocultural values and processes dwarf professional responses to persons who are disabled. At present, one has to wonder whether those values and processes will result in health and social policies and systems of care that provide adequately for those who are dependent.

In order to conclude, I wish to acknowledge the benefit I have had over these years of learning from the experiences, anguish, enthusiasm, skill, and wisdom of many clients and their relatives, clinicians, administrators, and colleagues. Members of the Off the Square Club and the residents of the YMCA in Madison, Wisconsin, all of whom apparently survived my program directorship, contributed enormously to my sense of commitment and to my knowledge. I am equally indebted to those hardy and caring souls who were my staff in those programs—those shared, ardent missions. Both members and staff helped me to learn about the limits of ideology and academic abstractions, but also to persist with enthusiasm, always just beyond those limits. Without the gentle and wise mentorship of Marilyn Chapman, Linda Keys, and Jerry Rousseau, I would have made many more clinical and administrative errors than I did. Kim, Neil, Debbie, Lynn, Pat, Sally, and Bill, each in her or his own way, struggled with me and their own difficult lives in such a way as to illuminate the unknown, to illustrate a new perspective, and encourage a different level of knowing. I owe a great deal to Harriet Shetler, Mona Wasow, and Beverly Young, whose energies and agonies as parents of persons with mental illness have inspired, saddened, intimated, and educated me.

More recently, in yet another place, and at another level of the mental health system, I have luckily found new comrades in battle, and teachers of the complexities of policy, politics, program, and principle. Pam Hyde and Marti Knisley have tried valiantly, if somewhat unsuccessfully, to point out the differences between research and reality, between the really impossible and the only-maybe-impossible. And finally, to my dear and always jovial, provocative, and encouraging colleagues in the Department of Social Medicine, I owe special thanks for the rich and warm academic home we inhabit.

REFERENCES

Baxter, E. and Hopper, K.

1981 Private Lives/Public Spaces: Homeless Adults on the Streets of New York City. N.Y.: Community Service Society.

1982 The new mendicancy: Homeless in New York City. *American Journal of Orthopsychiatry* 52:393–408.

Beviloqua, J. J.

1984 Chronic Mental Illness: A Problem in Politics. Paper presented at the National Conference on the Chronic Mental Patient II. Kansas City, Missouri. August 1984.

Braun, P., Kochansky, G., Shapiro, R. et al.

1981 Overview: Deinstitutionalization of Psychiatric Patients, a Critical Review of Outcome Studies. *American Journal of Psychiatry* 138(6):736–749.

Caton, C. L. M. and Goldstein, J.

1984 Housing Change of Chronic Schizophrenic Patients: A Consequence of the Revolving Door. *Social Science and Medicine* 19(7):759–764.

Cincinnati Enquirer
1984 "Group to Review Deinstitutionalization." November 21, 1984, p. 2c.

Feldman, S.
1983 Out of the Hospital, Onto the Streets: The Overselling of Benevolence. *The Hastings Center Report,* 13(3):5–7.

Foley, H. A. and Sharfstein, S. S.
1983 *Madness and Government: Who Cares for the Mentally Ill.* Washington, D.C.: American Psychiatric Press.

Goldman, H., Gattozzi, A., and Taube, C. A.
1981 Defining and Counting the Chronically Mentally Ill. *Hospital and Community Psychiatry* 32(1):21–27.

Gudeman, J. E. and Shore, M. F.
1984 Beyond De-Institutionalization: A New Class of Facilities for the Mentally Ill. *New England Journal of Medicine* 311(13):832–836.

Hopper, K. and Hamberg, J.
1984 The Making of America's Homeless: From Skid Row to New Poor, 1945–1984. Working Papers in Social Policy. N.Y.: Community Service Society.

HSRI (Human Services Research Institute)
1983 Estimating the Size of the Non-Institutionalized Adult Chronically Mentally Ill Population in State and Sub-state Areas. Prepared for NIMH, Contract No. 278-79-0036.

Kennedy, L.
1982 SSI: Trends and Changes, 1974–1980. *Social Security Bulletin* 45(7):3–12.

Lamb, H. R. and Grant, R. W.
1982 The Mentally Ill in an Urban County Jail. *Archives of General Psychiatry* 39:17–22.

Lamb, H. R. et al.
1984 Psychiatric Needs in Local Jails: Emergency Issues. *American Journal of Psychiatry* 141(6):774–777.

Liberman, R. P. and Phipps, C. C.
1984 Innovative Treatment and Rehabilitation Techniques for the Chronically Mentally Ill. Paper presented at the National Conference on the Chronic Mental Patient II, Kansas City, Missouri, August, 1984.

McDonald, M.
1981 *Mystical Bedlam.* London: Cambridge University Press.

Mollica, R. F.
1983 From Asylum to Community: The Threatened Disintegration of Public Psychiatry. *The New England Journal of Medicine* 308(7):367–373.

Mosher, L.
1983 Alternatives to Psychiatric Hospitalization: Why has Research Failed to be Translated into Practice? *New England Journal of Medicine,* 309(25):1579–1580.

Price, R. H. and Smith, S. S.
1983 Two Decades of Reform in the Mental Health System (1963–1983) In, E. Seidman, ed. *Handbook of Social Intervention.* Beverly Hills, CA: Sage Publications, pp. 408–436.

Roth, D. and Bean, J.
1984 Homelessness in Ohio: A study of People in Need. Office of Program Evaluation and Research, Ohio Department of Mental Health, Columbus, Ohio. 21 pages.

Segal, S., Baumohl, J., and Johnson, E.
1977 Falling Through the Cracks: Mental Disorder and Social Margin in a Young Vagrant Population. *Social Problems,* 24:387–400.

U.S. House of Representatives
1982 Homelessness in America. Hearings before the Subcommittee on Housing and Community Development, December 15, 1982. Serial No. 97-100. Washington: U.S. Government Printing Office.

U.S. Senate, Special Committee on Aging
1983 Social Security Reviews of the Mentally Disabled. Hearings held April 7 and 8, 1983. Senate Hearing Number 98-170. Washington, D.C.: U.S. Government Printing Office.

Appendix*

COMMUNITY ADAPTATION SCHEDULE

The following survey has questions which describe the community in which you live, and your life within it. Answer all questions about YOURSELF as things are NOW.

Please answer the questions on the answer sheet provided. Please do not write in the survey booklet. Beneath each question you will find answers that range from 1 to 6. For each question, choose the number of the answer that best fits you and write this number in the appropriate space for that question on the answer sheet. Answer every question.

Answers are not meant to be right or wrong and will vary from person to person. Your replies will be kept strictly confidential. If you have questions about how to answer, please ask.

*Adapted from Sheldon R. Roen and Alan J. Burnes. Copyright © 1968 by Human Sciences Press, a division of Behavioral Publications, Inc., 72 Fifth Avenue, New York, New York.

1. WORK COMMUNITY

A. EMPLOYMENT

1. How much time did you put in at work this week?

1	2	3	4	5	6
One to two days	About ½ time	3-4 days	Full time	Slightly more than full time	Much more than full time

2. How do you feel about working?

1	2	3	4	5	6
Dislike very much	Dislike	Dislike some	Like some	Like	Like very much

3. If you had time, would you put in additional work hours for more pay?

1	2	3	4	5	6
Definitely	Very likely	Likely	Unlikely	Very likely	Definitely not

4. How long have you been unemployed during the past month?

1	2	3	4	5	6
Entire time	Less than 3 weeks	About 2 weeks	About a week	Couple of days	Not at all

5. Do you think you could find a job as good as or better than your present one within four to six weeks, if necessary?

1	2	3	4	5	6
Definitely not	Very unlikely	Unlikely	Likely	Very likely	Definitely

6. How would you rate your performance in your work?

1	2	3	4	5	6
Very superior	Superior	Above average	Below average	Poor	Very poor

7. How do you feel about your present job?

1	2	3	4	5	6
Like very much	Like	Like some	Dislike some	Dislike	Dislike very much

8. Are your present duties ones that make best use of your skills?

1	2	3	4	5	6
Never	Very seldom	Seldom	Some-times	Often	Always

9. How much do you earn an hour right now?

1	2	3	4	5	6
Less than $1	$1	Between $1-$2	Between $2-$3	Between $3-$4	Over $4

10. How does what you earn match what you spend?

1	2	3	4	5	6
Much higher	Moder-ately higher	Slightly higher	Slightly lower	Moder-ately lower	Much lower

11. Do you feel that you can (or will) earn more in this job or one like it?

1	2	3	4	5	6
Definitely not	Very unlikely	Unlikely	Likely	Very likely	Definitely

12. How does your present income compare with your previous income?

1	2	3	4	5	6
Much less	Less	About the same	Somewhat more	More	Much more

13. As far as you know, how do your co-worker's wages compare with yours?

1	2	3	4	5	6
Much less	Less	About the same	Somewhat more	More	Much more

14. How often have you had trouble with money in the past month?

1	2	3	4	5	6
Never	Very seldom	Seldom	Often	Very often	Daily

15. How do you feel about changing your job?

1	2	3	4	5	6
Very happy where I am	Don't want to	Would mind	Wouldn't mind	Want to	Want to very much

16. Do you feel that you will try to qualify for a more highly skilled job?

1	2	3	4	5	6
Definitely not	Very unlikely	Unlikely	Likely	Very likely	Definitely

17. How many of your co-workers do you consider friends?

1	2	3	4	5	6
Five or more	Four	Three	Two	One	None

18. Are you as satisfied with your job as other people seem to be with theirs?

1	2	3	4	5	6
Much less	Less	About the same	Somewhat more	More	Much more

19. How much time did you spend looking for full-time work this month?

1	2	3	4	5	6
None	Hardly any	Very little	Some	Much	Very much

20. How do you feel about working full time?

1	2	3	4	5	6
Like very much	Like	Like some	Dislike some	Dislike	Dislike very much

21. Do you think you could work full time?

1	2	3	4	5	6
Definitely not	Very unlikely	Unlikely	Likely	Very likely	Definitely

B. UNEMPLOYMENT. Answer this section if you have been out of work at all during the past four weeks.

22. Over the past four weeks how often have you tried to find work?

1	2	3	4	5	6
Haven't tried	Hardly at all	Less than a day a week	About a day a week	Most weekdays	Every workday

23. How do you feel about NOT working?

1	2	3	4	5	6
Like very much	Like	Like some	Dislike some	Dislike	Dislike very much

24. Do you think you will find work soon?

1	2	3	4	5	6
Definitely	Very likely	Likely	Unlikely	Very likely	Definitely not

25. Has anyone helped you try to find work?

1	2	3	4	5	6
No one	Friends	Employment agency	Job program (Manpower, Mainstream, etc.)	PACT	Others

26. Do you think you are able to work full time?

1	2	3	4	5	6
Definitely not	Very unlikely	Unlikely	Likely	Very likely	Definitely

C. VOLUNTEER WORK

27. Over the past few months, have you done volunteer work?

1	2	3	4	5	6
None	Hardly any	Little	Some	Much	Very much

28. In general, how do you feel about doing volunteer work?

1	2	3	4	5	6
Like very much	Like	Like some	Dislike some	Dislike	Dislike very much

29. In general, would you do volunteer work if it were asked of you?

1	2	3	4	5	6
Definitely not	Very unlikely	Unlikely	Likely	Very likely	Definitely

D. GENERAL LIVING CIRCUMSTANCES

30. How much nonworking time do you spend at your own apartment?

1	2	3	4	5	6
All	Almost all	Most	Some	Very little	Hardly any

31. How do you feel about where you live right now?

1	2	3	4	5	6
Very dissatisfied	Dissatis-fied	Somewhat dissatisfied	Somewhat satisfied	Satisfied	Very satisfied

32. Do you think your home living circumstances need improvement?

1	2	3	4	5	6
Very much	Much	Some	Little	Hardly at all	Not at all

E. GENERAL SOCIAL LIFE

33. How would you rate your social life this month?

1	2	3	4	5	6
Very inactive	Inactive	Somewhat inactive	Somewhat active	Active	Very active

34. How do you feel about your social life right now?

1	2	3	4	5	6
Very dissatisfied	Dissatis- fied	Somewhat dissatisfied	Somewhat satisfied	Satisfied	Very satisfied

35. In general, how do you feel about participating in clubs or groups?

1	2	3	4	5	6
Like very much	Like	Like somewhat	Dislike somewhat	Dislike	Dislike very much

36. In general, do you think your social acquaintances are dependable?

1	2	3	4	5	6
Never	Very rarely	Rarely	Some- times	Usually	Always

37. On the whole, how would you describe the people you know in the town or city where you live?

1	2	3	4	5	6
Very unfriendly	Un- friendly	Somewhat unfriendly	Somewhat friendly	Friendly	Very friendly

F. FRIENDS

38. How many personal friends do you have at the present time?

1	2	3	4	5	6
None	One	Two	Three	Four	Four or more

39. How do you feel toward them?

1	2	3	4	5	6
Very close	Close	Somewhat close	Somewhat distant	Distant	Very distant

40. How do you think they feel toward you?

1	2	3	4	5	6
Very distant	Distant	Somewhat distant	Somewhat close	Close	Very close

41. Do your friends give you help when you need it?

1	2	3	4	5	6
Very often	Often	Some-times	Seldom	Hardly ever	Never

42. What are your feelings toward the friend with whom you spend the most time?

1	2	3	4	5	6
Dislike very much	Dislike	Dislike some	Like some	Like	Like very much

43. Do you have as much contact with personal friends as you want?

1	2	3	4	5	6
Always	Usually	Some-times	Seldom	Very rarely	Never

44. How much time do you spend with your friends right now?

1	2	3	4	5	6
None	Hardly any	One or two hours per month	Few hours per week	Many hours per week	At least an hour a day

45. In general, how often when you go out do you go out with friends?

1	2	3	4	5	6
Never	Hardly ever	Seldom	Some-times	Often	Very often

46. In general, what has your social life been like?

1	2	3	4	5	6
Very active	Active	Somewhat active	Somewhat inactive	Inactive	Very inactive

47. How often do you see or talk with your friends?

1	2	3	4	5	6
Daily	More than once a week	A few times a month	About once a month	Seldom	Never

48. In general, how do you feel about your friendships?

1	2	3	4	5	6
Very dissatisfied	Dissatis-fied	Somewhat dissatisfied	Somewhat satisfied	Satisfied	Very satisfied

49. In general, do you think your friends consider you a good friend?

1	2	3	4	5	6
Definitely not	Very unlikely	Unlikely	Likely	Very likely	Definitely

G. PEOPLE AT WORK

50. How do you find the social relationships at work?

1	2	3	4	5	6
Very unsatisfy-ing	Unsatisfy-ing	Somewhat unsatisfy-ing	Somewhat satisfying	Satisfying	Very satisfying

51. How many of your co-workers do you consider friends?

1	2	3	4	5	6
None	One	Two	Three	Four	Five or more

52. In general, how do you feel toward your co-workers?

1	2	3	4	5	6
Dislike very much	Dislike	Dislike some	Like some	Like	Like very much

53. Do you think you will get to know some of them better?

1	2	3	4	5	6
Definitely	Very likely	Likely	Unlikely	Very unlikely	Definitely not

H. NEIGHBORS

54. How often do you visit with your neighbors for a half hour or more?

1	2	3	4	5	6
Never	Hardly ever	Seldom	Some-times	Often	Very often

55. How would you rate their interest in your experiences?

1	2	3	4	5	6
Very much	Much	Some	Little	Hardly any	None

56. In general, how do you feel about your neighbors?

1	2	3	4	5	6
Dislike very much	Dislike	Dislike some	Like some	Like	Like very much

57. Could you count on a neighbor for help if you needed it?

1	2	3	4	5	6
Definitely not	Very unlikely	Unlikely	Likely	Very likely	Definitely

58. Do you think neighbors should go out of their way to help one another?

1	2	3	4	5	6
Always	Very much	Much	Some	Hardly at all	Not at all

59. How do you feel toward your neighbors?

1	2	3	4	5	6
Very unfriendly	Un-friendly	Somewhat unfriendly	Somewhat friendly	Friendly	Very friendly

60. How many neighbors do you consider as personal friends?

1	2	3	4	5	6
None	Almost none	Very few	Few	Many	A great many

61. In general, how do people in your neighborhood act toward one another?

1	2	3	4	5	6
Very unfriendly	Un-friendly	Somewhat unfriendly	Somewhat friendly	Friendly	Very friendly

Thanks a lot for answering these questions. Your answers will not be shown to anyone at PACT.

PART II

A. HOUSEWORK

62. What is your feeling about housework?

1	2	3	4	5	6
Dislike very much	Dislike	Dislike some	Like some	Like	Like very much

63. How are you managing the housework?

1	2	3	4	5	6
Very well	Well	Fairly well	Not well	Poorly	Very poorly

64. How much of your housework is done by others?

1	2	3	4	5	6
Almost all	Most	Some	Little	Hardly any	None

65. If you had to, could you do all the housework yourself?

1	2	3	4	5	6
Definitely not	Very unlikely	Unlikely	Likely	Very likely	Definitely

66. In general, how do you feel you manage your housework in comparison to how others manage theirs?

1	2	3	4	5	6
Much better	Better	Somewhat better	Less well	Poorly	Very poorly

B. WORK HISTORY

67. At what age did you start working either part time or full time?

1	2	3	4	5	6
Didn't	Over 25	25-21	20-17	16-14	Below 14

68. For how many different employers have you worked?

1	2	3	4	5	6
Over seven	Six or seven	Four or five	Two or three	One	None

69. With regard to work, are you where you thought you would be at your age?

1	2	3	4	5	6
Very much below	Below	Somewhat below	Somewhat above	Above	Very much above

C. PARENTS

70. How often do you discuss important matters or do things with your parent(s)?

1	2	3	4	5	6
Never	Hardly ever	Seldom	Some-times	Often	Very often

71. How do you feel about getting together with your parent(s)?

1	2	3	4	5	6
Like very much	Like	Like some	Dislike some	Dislike	Dislike very much

72. How do you feel toward your parent(s)?

1	2	3	4	5	6
Very distant	Distant	Somewhat distant	Somewhat close	Close	Very close

73. How much time do you spend with your parent(s)?

1	2	3	4	5	6
None	Hardly any	Little	Some	Much	Very much

74. How do you feel about your parent(s)?

1	2	3	4	5	6
Dislike very much	Dislike	Dislike some	Like some	Like	Like very much

75. How easy is it for you to express personal emotional feelings to your parent(s)?

1	2	3	4	5	6
Very easy	Easy	Fairly easy	Fairly difficult	Difficult	Very difficult

76. Do you think your parent(s) are satisfied with you?

1	2	3	4	5	6
Not at all	Hardly at all	Some	Much	Very much	Com-pletely

77. How often in the last month have you had serious arguments with either or both parents?

1	2	3	4	5	6
Very often	Often	Some-times	Seldom	Hardly ever	Never

78. How much interest do your parents have in your daily experiences?

1	2	3	4	5	6
None	Hardly any	Little	Some	Much	Very much

79. In general, how much do you agree with your parent(s)?

1	2	3	4	5	6
Not at all	Hardly at all	Some	Much	Very much	Completely

80. In general, can you count on your parent(s) for help?

1	2	3	4	5	6
Always	Very much	Much	Some	Hardly at all	Not at all

81. How does your relationship with your parent(s) compare with other families you know?

1	2	3	4	5	6
Much worse	Worse	Somewhat worse	Somewhat better	Better	Much better

D. OTHER RELATIVES (This includes brothers, sisters, aunts, uncles, cousins and in-laws)

82. How many relatives have you had some personal contact with in the last month, even if it was only by letter?

1	2	3	4	5	6
None	One or two	Three or four	Four to six	Seven to ten	Over ten

83. How many of these relatives do you feel close to?

1	2	3	4	5	6
Over eight	Seven or eight	Five or six	Three or four	One or two	None

84. How often do you see or talk to these relatives?

1	2	3	4	5	6
Never	Hardly ever	Seldom	Sometimes	Often	Very often

85. Have these other relatives who do not live in your home been of help to you?

1	2	3	4	5	6
Very much	Much	Some	Little	Hardly at all	Not at all

86. How do you feel about these relatives helping you?

1	2	3	4	5	6
Dislike very much	Dislike	Dislike some	Like some	Like	Like very much

87. How many of your relatives live within one-half hour drive?

1	2	3	4	5	6
Over eight	Seven or eight	Five or six	Three or four	One or two	None

88. How many times have you talked with relatives over the past month?

1	2	3	4	5	6
None	One or two	Three or four	Five or six	Seven or eight	Over eight

E. DATING

89. How often do you date at present?

1	2	3	4	5	6
Never	Seldom	About once a month	A few times a month	Weekly	More than once a week

90. How do you feel about being with the opposite sex?

1	2	3	4	5	6
Dislike very much	Dislike	Dislike some	Like some	Like	Like very much

91. Would you date more if you had the opportunity?

1	2	3	4	5	6
Definitely	Very likely	Likely	Unlikely	Very unlikely	Definitely not

92. How often do you think about getting married these days?

1	2	3	4	5	6
Never	Hardly ever	Seldom	Some-times	Often	Very often

93. How do you feel about getting married?

1	2	3	4	5	6
Like very much	Like	Like some	Dislike some	Dislike	Dislike very much

94. Do you think you will eventually get married?

1	2	3	4	5	6
Definitely not	Very unlikely	Unlikely	Likely	Very likely	Definitely

F. RECREATION

95. How often do you go out to the movies, theater, or sporting events?

1	2	3	4	5	6
Very often	Often	Somewhat often	Rarely	Very rarely	Never

96. How do you feel about these activities?

1	2	3	4	5	6
Dislike very much	Dislike	Dislike some	Like some	Like	Like very much

97. Do you think you would do these things more often if you had the chance?

1	2	3	4	5	6
Definitely not	Very unlikely	Unlikely	Likely	Very likely	Definitely

98. About how many hours *per day* do you spend doing such things as reading and watching T.V.?

1	2	3	4	5	6
Over three	Three	Two	One	Less than one	None

99. In general, would you rather spend your recreation time alone or with others?

1	2	3	4	5	6
Always alone	Mostly alone	More often alone	More often with others	Mostly with others	Always with others

100. If you had the chance, do you think you would spend more time doing sports like bowling, tennis, golf, or swimming?

1	2	3	4	5	6
Definitely not	Very unlikely	Unlikely	Likely	Very likely	Definitely

G. RELIGION

101. How often do you go to religious services?

1	2	3	4	5	6
Never	Seldom	Few times a year	Once or twice a month	About once a week	More than once a week

102. How much satisfaction do you get from religion?

1	2	3	4	5	6
None	Hardly any	Little	Some	Much	Very much

103. Do you consider yourself a religious person?

1	2	3	4	5	6
Com-pletely	Very much	Much	Some	Hardly at all	Not at all

104. How much time *per week* beyond religious services do you spend on activities related to religion such as family observance of ritual, affiliated clubs and groups, etc.?

1	2	3	4	5	6
None	Hardly any	Very little	Fairly much	Much	Very much

105. Considering that you have or will have a child, would you want religion to become a major part of his or her life?

1	2	3	4	5	6
Definitely not	Very unlikely	Unlikely	Likely	Very likely	Definitely

H. ORGANIZATIONS AND GROUPS. This includes groups outside of PACT that you belong to because you choose to.

106. How many different organizations or clubs do you belong to?

1	2	3	4	5	6
Over four	Four	Three	Two	One	None

107. How do you feel about participating in groups?

1	2	3	4	5	6
Dislike very much	Dislike	Dislike some	Like some	Like	Like very much

108. How often do you attend group functions?

1	2	3	4	5	6
More than once a week	About once a week	More than once a week	About once a month	Seldom	Never

109. How much satisfaction do you get from group activities?

1	2	3	4	5	6
None	Hardly any	Little	Some	Much	Very much

110. In general, what do you think about people belonging to organizations?

1	2	3	4	5	6
Of no importance	Unimportant	Somewhat unimportant	Somewhat important	Important	Very important

I. COMMUNICATIONS

111. How often do you read a newspaper or news magazines?

1	2	3	4	5	6
Never	Seldom	Less than once a week	Once a week	Daily	More than daily

112. How much importance do you attach to keeping up with current events?

1	2	3	4	5	6
None	Hardly any	Little	Some	Much	Very much

113. How many of the following do you use in learning of events in the community, nation, and world? Radio, TV, newspaper, meetings, magazines.

1	2	3	4	5	6
None	One	Two	Three	Four	Five

114. About how much time would you say you spend on current events (TV and radio news and programs, discussions, public meetings, newspapers, etc.)?

1	2	3	4	5	6
None	A few hours per month	About an hour per week	2-3 hours per week	4-5 hours per week	Over 5 hours per week

115. Are you usually *bored* by or *disinterested* in information about financial matters or news?

1	2	3	4	5	6
Very much	Much	Somewhat	Little	Very little	Not at all

116. Would you be in favor of using radio, TV, and newspapers more for information and less for entertainment?

1	2	3	4	5	6
Definitely	Very likely	Likely	Unlikely	Very unlikely	Definitely not

J. EDUCATION

117. Over the past year how often did you listen to or attend educational lectures or discussions?

1	2	3	4	5	6
Never	Hardly ever	Seldom	Some-times	Often	Very often

118. Do you think you will ever further your formal education?

1	2	3	4	5	6
Definitely not	Very unlikely	Unlikely	Likely	Very likely	Definitely

119. How much reading do you do to learn or get information (other than recreation only)?

1	2	3	4	5	6
None	Hardly any	Little	Some	Much	Very much

120. In general, how does your education compare with that of your friends?

1	2	3	4	5	6
Much better	Better	Somewhat better	Somewhat worse	Worse	Much worse

121. How much formal education do you have?

1	2	3	4	5	6
Didn't complete elemen-tary school	Didn't complete high school	High school graduate	Some non-college study be-yond high school	Some college	College

K. MOVING

122. How would you feel about moving from your present address?

1	2	3	4	5	6
Like very much	Like	Like some	Dislike some	Dislike	Dislike very much

123. Do you think you will move over the next few months?

1	2	3	4	5	6
Definitely not	Very unlikely	Unlikely	Possible	Very likely	Definitely

124. If you had to move, would you move to a different community?

1	2	3	4	5	6
Definitely	Very likely	Likely	Unlikely	Very unlikely	Definitely not

L. CIVIC COMMUNITY

125. In general, how interested are you in politics?

1	2	3	4	5	6
Not at all	Hardly at all	Little	Some	Much	Very much

126. How much time do you spend keeping up with local political issues?

1	2	3	4	5	6
Very much	Much	Some	Little	Hardly any	None

127. How often have you sought information or help from police and fire department services?

1	2	3	4	5	6
Never	Almost never	Seldom	Some-times	Often	Very often

128. How do you feel about the police?

1	2	3	4	5	6
Dislike very much	Dislike	Dislike some	Like some	Like	Like very much

129. How would you feel about being selected for jury duty?

1	2	3	4	5	6
Like very much	Like	Like some	Dislike some	Dislike	Dislike very much

M. FINANCES

130. How much money do you save per month?

1	2	3	4	5	6
Very much	Much	Some	Little	Hardly any	None

131. How do you feel about your savings program?

1	2	3	4	5	6
Very dissatisfied	Dissatis-fied	Somewhat dissatisfied	Somewhat satisfied	Satisfied	Very satisfied

132. Do you think you show good money habits or make good money sense?

1	2	3	4	5	6
Definitely not	Very rarely	Rarely	Somewhat	Usually	Definitely

133. Would you say you have had money problems lately?

1	2	3	4	5	6
Never	Very seldom	Seldom	Often	Very often	Always

134. How have you planned for your old age?

1	2	3	4	5	6
Very well	Well	Fairly well	Not well	Poorly	Very poorly

135. How do you feel about YOUR system for paying bills that are mailed to you?

1	2	3	4	5	6
Very dissatisfied	Dissatis-fied	Somewhat dissatisfied	Somewhat satisfied	Satisfied	Very satisfied

136. How would you compare your income with that of your friends? (Mine is:)

1	2	3	4	5	6
Much worse	Worse	Somewhat worse	Somewhat better	Better	Much better

137. Do you think you have your debts under control?

1	2	3	4	5	6
Definitely not	Poorly	Somewhat poorly	Well	Very well	Definitely

N. SHOPPING

138. In general, how do you feel about shopping?

1	2	3	4	5	6
Dislike very much	Dislike	Dislike some	Like some	Like	Like very much

139. Do you think looking for bargains is generally worthwhile?

1	2	3	4	5	6
Definitely not	Very rarely	Rarely	Some-times	Usually	Definitely

140. Do you find it gives you a "lift" to buy something special?

1	2	3	4	5	6
Never	Hardly ever	Seldom	Sometimes	Often	Very often

141. How many charge accounts do you have?

1	2	3	4	5	6
None	One	Two	Three	Four	Over four

O. TRANSPORTATION

142. How often do you drive a car?

1	2	3	4	5	6
Never	Hardly ever	Seldom	Sometimes	Often	Very often

143. Do you plan to take any special overnight trips this month?

1	2	3	4	5	6
Definitely not	Very unlikely	Unlikely	Likely	Very likely	Definitely

144. How often do you use any form of transportation (other than walking)?

1	2	3	4	5	6
Daily	Almost daily	More than once a week	About once a week	A few times a month	Seldom

145. Do you feel that transportation is a problem for you?

1	2	3	4	5	6
Very often	Often	Sometimes	Seldom	Hardly ever	Never

146. Do you take leisure trips on weekends and holidays?

1	2	3	4	5	6
Very often	Often	Sometimes	Seldom	Hardly ever	Never

147. In general, would you rather spend your recreation time alone or with others?

1	2	3	4	5	6
Always with others	Mostly with others	More often with others	More often alone	Mostly alone	Always alone

P. HOUSING

148. Do you feel that your living circumstances in the place where you live need improvement?

1	2	3	4	5	6
Very much	Much	Some	Little	Hardly at all	Not at all

149. How much rent do you pay each month?

1	2	3	4	5	6
Less than $50	$50-$75	$76-$100	$101-$125	$126-$150	Over $150

150. How do you feel about owning a house, whether or not you own one now?

1	2	3	4	5	6
Like very much	Like	Like some	Dislike some	Dislike	Dislike very much

151. Would you be willing to spend more of your money in making the place you live more comfortable or attractive?

1	2	3	4	5	6
Definitely not	Very unlikely	Unlikely	Likely	Very likely	Definitely

152. How do you feel about staying at your present address?

1	2	3	4	5	6
Dislike very much	Dislike	Dislike some	Like some	Like	Like very much

Q. PROFESSIONAL COMMUNITY. This section is about helping agencies such as City Welfare, Dane County Social Services, Veterans Service, Dane County Mental Health, and PACT.

153. From how many social agencies have you or your family sought help?

1	2	3	4	5	6
None	One	Two	Three	Four	Over four

154. How do you feel about such social agencies?

1	2	3	4	5	6
Like very much	Like	Like some	Dislike some	Dislike	Dislike very much

155. What amount of contact for reasons of personal or family difficulty have you had with the agency that has serviced you most?

1	2	3	4	5	6
None	1-2 sessions	3-5 sessions	6-10 sessions	11-20 sessions	Over 20 sessions

156. Would you be in favor of efforts to expand these services?

1	2	3	4	5	6
Definitely not	Very unlikely	Unlikely	Likely	Very likely	Definitely

Thank you for answering these questions. Your answers will help to make things better for the people who may be in PACT or similar programs in the future.

Becker, H. S.
1963. *Outsiders: Studies in the sociology of deviance.* New York: Free Press.

Becker, H. S., ed.
1964. *The other side: Perspectives on deviance.* New York: Free Press.

Bellak, L., ed.
1974. *Concise handbook of community psychiatry and community mental health.* New York: Grune and Stratton.

Bentz, W. K., and J. W. Edgerton.
1971. The consequences of labeling a person as mentally ill. *Social Psychiatry* 6(1):29-33.

Berger, P. L., and T. Luckman.
1967. *The social construction of reality.* Garden City, N.J.: Anchor Books.

Black, B. J.
1957. The workaday world: Some problems in return of mental patients to the community. *In* M. Greenblatt et al., eds., *The patient and the mental hospital.* Glencoe, Ill.: Free Press. Pp. 577-584.

Blackwell, B.
1972. The drug defaulter. *Clinical Pharmacology and Therapeutics* 13(6):841-848.
1973. Drug therapy: Patient compliance. *New England Journal of Medicine* 289(5):249-252.

Blong, A. W. et al., eds.
1975. *Supplemental security income advocates' handbook.* New York: National Law and Social Policy Center on Social Welfare Policy and Law.

Bloom, B. L.
1968. An annotated bibliography: 1955-1968. *In* L. M. Roberts et al., eds., *Comprehensive mental health: The challenge of evaluation.* Madison: University of Wisconsin Press, pp. 291-332.

Blumer, H.
1969. *Symbolic interactionism: Perspective and method.* Englewood Cliffs, N.J.: Prentice-Hall, Inc.

Bockoven, J. S.
1957. Some relationships between cultural attitudes toward individuality and care of the mentally ill: A historical study. *In* M. Greenblatt et al., eds., *The patient and the mental hospital.* Glencoe, Ill.: Free Press. Pp. 517-526.

Bohannon, P.
1973. Rethinking culture: A project for current anthropologists. *Current Anthropology* 14(4):357-372.

Braginsky, B. M., and D. D. Braginsky.
1973. Schizophrenic patients in a psychiatric interview: An experimental study of their effectiveness at manipulation. *In* R. Price and B. Denner, eds. *The making of a mental patient*. New York: Holt, Rinehart, and Winston, pp. 253-261.

Braginsky, B. M., M. Grosse, and K. Ring.
1973. Controlling outcomes through impression management: An experimental study of the manipulative tactics of mental patients. *In* R. Price and B. Denner, eds. *The making of a mental patient*. New York: Holt, Rinehart, and Winston, pp. 242-252.

Brand, R. C. and W. L. Clairborn.
1976. Two studies of comparative stigma: Employer attitudes and practices toward rehabilitated convicts, mental and tuberculosis patients. *Community Mental Health Journal* 12(2):168-175.

Broadhead, R. S.
1978. "Qualitative analysis in evaluation research: Problems and promises of an interactionist approach." Paper presented at the 1978 meetings of the American Sociological Association, San Francisco.

Brooks, A. D.
1974. *Law, psychiatry and the mental health system*. Boston: Little, Brown, and Co.

Buckley, W.
1967. *Sociology and modern systems theory*. Englewood Cliffs, N.J.: Prentice-Hall, Inc.

Burnes, A. J., and S. R. Roen.
1967. Social roles and adaptation to the community. *Community Mental Health Journal* 3(2):153-158.

Cade, F. J.
1949. Lithium salts in the treatment of psychotic excitement. *Medical Journal of Australia* 36:349-352.

Caplan, G.
1964. *Principles of preventive psychiatry*. New York: Basic Books.
1965. Community psychiatry: Introduction and overview. *In* S. E. Goldston, ed., *Concepts of community psychiatry*. Public Health Services Publication, no. 1319:3-18.

Caplan, R. B., and G. Caplan.
1969. *Psychiatry and the community in nineteenth century America: The recurring concern with the environment in the prevention and treatment of mental illness*. New York: Basic Books.

Carpenter, W., J. Strauss, and J. Bartko.
1974. Use of signs and symptoms for the identification of schizophrenic patients. *Schizophrenia Bulletin* (Winter):35-49.

Carpenter, W., T. H. McGlashan, and J. Strauss.
1977. The treatment of acute schizophrenia without drugs. *American Journal of Psychiatry* 134:14-20.

Cartwright, A.
1974. Prescribing and the relationship between patients and doctors. *In* R. Cooperstone, ed., *Social aspects of the medical use of psychotropic drugs.* Ontario: Addiction Research Foundation, pp. 63-73.

Caudill, W.
1958. *The psychiatric hospital as a small society.* Cambridge, Mass.: Harvard University Press.
1973. Psychiatry and anthropology: The individual and his nexus. *In* L. Nader and T. Maretzki, eds., *Cultural illness and health.* Anthropological Studies, volume 9. Washington, D.C.: American Anthropological Association, pp. 67-77.

Cawte, J.
1974. *Medicine is the law: Studies in the psychiatric anthropology of Australian tribal societies.* Honolulu: University of Hawaii Press.

Chamberlain, J.
1978. *On our own: Patient controlled alternatives to the mental health system.* New York: McGraw-Hill.

Chambers, D. L.
1978. The role of the Constitution and statutes in encouraging reliance on alternatives to involuntary hospitalization. *In* L. Stein and M. A. Test, eds., *Alternatives to the mental hospital.* New York: Plenum Publishers.

Chandler, S.
1978. Antipsychotic drugs in sheltered care. *In* S. Segal and U. Aviram, *The mentally ill in community-based sheltered care and social integration.* New York: John Wiley and Sons, pp. 232-251.

Chapman, L. J., and J. P. Chapman.
1973. *Disordered thought in schizophrenia.* New York: Appleton, Century, Crofts.

Chapman, L. J., et al.
1976. Scales for physical and social anhedonia. *Journal of Abnormal Psychology* 85:374-382.

Chouinard, G., et al.
1979. Factors related to tardive dyskinesia. *American Journal of Psychiatry* 136(1):79-83.

Chu, F., and S. Trotter.
1974. *The madness establishment: Ralph Nader's study group report on the National Institute of Mental Health*. New York: Grossman Publishers.

Coates, D., and C. Wortman.
1980. Depression maintenance and interpersonal control. *In Advances in environmental psychology*, vol. II. A. Baum, Y. Epstein, and J. Singer, eds. New York: Lawrence Erlbaum, Inc., chap. 7.

Comer, R. J., and J. A. Piliavin.
1972. The effects of physical deviance upon face-to-face interaction: The other side. *Journal of Personality and Social Psychology* 23,1:33-39.
1975. As others see us: Attitudes of physically handicapped and normals toward own and other groups. *Rehabilitation Literature* 36,7:206-221.

Cumming, J. H.
1968. Some criteria for evaluation. *In* L. M. Roberts et al., eds., *Comprehensive mental health: The challenge of evaluation*. Madison: University of Wisconsin Press, pp. 29-40.

Davis, J. M.
1975. Overview: Maintenance therapy in psychiatry: I: Schizophrenia. *American Journal of Psychiatry* 132:1237-1245.
1976. Recent developments in the treatment of schizophrenia. *Psychiatric Annals* 6(1):71-111.

Dawson, J.
1964. Urbanization and mental health in a West African community. *In* A. Kiev. ed., *Magic, faith, and healing: Studies in primitive psychiatry today*. New York: Free Press, pp. 305-342.

Denker, P.
1939. The prognosis of insured neurotics. *New York State Journal of Medicine* 39:238-247.

Denner, B.
1974. The insanity of community mental health: The myth of the machine. *International Journal of Mental Health* 3(2-3):104-126.

Devereux, G.
1956. Normal and abnormal: The key problem of psychiatric anthropology. *In Some uses of anthropology: Theoretical and applied*. Washington, D.C.: Anthropological Society of Washington, pp. 23-48.

De Vos, G.
1974. Cross-cultural studies of mental disorder: An anthropological perspective. *In* G. Kaplan, ed., *American handbook of psychiatry*, vol. II, 2d ed. New York: Basic Books, pp. 551-567.

Dohrenwend, B. P.
1975. Sociocultural and social-psychological factors in the genesis of

mental disorders. *Journal of Health and Social Behavior* 16(4):365-392.

Dohrenwend, B. P., and B. S. Dohrenwend.
1974. Social and cultural influences on psychopathology. *In Annual Review of Psychology* 25:417-451.

Douglas, J. D., ed.
1970. *Observations of deviance.* New York: Random House.
1972. *Research on deviance.* New York: Random House.

Douglas, J. D.
1977. Existential sociology. *In* J. Douglas and J. Johnson, eds., *Existential sociology*, Cambridge: Cambridge University Press, pp. 3-74.

Douglas, J. D. and J. Johnson, eds.
1977. *Existential sociology.* Cambridge: Cambridge University Press.

Driver, E. D., ed.
1972. *The sociology and anthropology of mental illness: A reference guide.* Amherst: University of Massachusetts Press.

Dubreuil, G., and E. D. Wittkower.
1974. Psychiatric anthropology, transcultural psychiatry: The past. *Transcultural Psychiatric Research Review* 11:7-11.

Dunham, H. W.
1969. Community psychiatry: The newest therapeutic bandwagon. *In* A. J. Bindman and A. D. Spiegel, eds., *Perspectives in community mental health.* Chicago: Aldine, pp. 54-69.
1976. Society, culture, and mental disorder. *Archives of General Psychiatry* 33:147-156.

Eaton, W. W.
1975. Social class and chronicity of schizophrenia. *Journal of Chronic Diseases* 28:191-198.

Edgerton, R. B.
1967. *The cloak of competence: Stigma in the lives of the mentally retarded.* Berkeley: University of California Press.
1969*a*. Conceptions of psychosis in four East African societies. *American Anthropologist* 68:408-425.
1969*b*. On the "Recognition" of mental illness. *In* S. C. Plog and R. B. Edgerton, eds., *Changing perspectives in mental illness.* New York: Holt, Rinehart, and Winston, pp. 49-72.
1971. Anthropology, psychiatry, and man's nature. *In* I. Galdston, ed., *The interface between psychiatry and anthropology.* New York: Brunner/Mazel, pp. 28-54.
1973. Anthropology and mental retardation. *In* L. Nader and T. Maretzki, eds., *Cultural illness and health.* Anthropological Studies, vol. 9. Washington, D.C.: American Anthropological Association, pp. 11-22.

1976. *Deviance: A cross-cultural perspective.* Menlo Park, Calif.: Cummings.

Edgerton, R. B., and L. L. Langness.
1974. *Methods and styles in the study of culture.* San Francisco: Chandler and Sharp.

Engelhardt, D. M., and N. Freedman.
1965. Maintenance drug therapy: The schizophrenic patient in the community. *International Psychiatry Clinics* 2(4):933-960.

Erickson, K. T.
1957. Patient role and social uncertainty: A dilemma of the mentally ill. *Psychiatry* 20:263-272.

Estroff, S. E.
1978. The anthropology-psychiatry fantasy: Can we make it a reality? *Transcultural Psychiatric Research Review* 15(10):209-213.

Etzioni, A.
1977. Opting out: The waning of the work ethic. *Psychology Today* 11(2):18.

Fabrega. H.
1972*a*. The study of disease in relation to culture. *Behavioral Science* 17:183-203.
1972*b*. Medical anthropology. *In* B. J. Siegel, ed., *Biennial review of anthropology.* Stanford: Stanford University Press, pp. 167-229.
1974*a*. Problems implicit in the cultural and social study of depression. *Psychosomatic Medicine* 36(5):377-398.
1974*b*. *Disease and social behavior: An interdisciplinary perspective.* Cambridge, Mass.: M.I.T. Press.
1975. The position of psychiatry in the understanding of human disease. *Archives of General Psychiatry* 32(12):1500-1512.
1978. Culture, behavior, and the nervous system. *In* B. J. Siegel et al., eds., *Annual review of anthropology,* 1978.

Fairweather, G. W., et al.
1969. *Community life for the mentally ill.* Chicago: Aldine.

Favazza, A. R., and M. Oman.
1978. Overview: Foundations of cultural psychiatry. *American Journal of Psychiatry* 135(3):293-303.

Fink, M.
1971. Long-acting (depot) phenothiazines in emergency and maintenance therapy of psychosis. *In* C. Shagass, ed., *The role of drugs in community psychiatry: Modern problems of pharmacopsychiatry,* vol. 6. Basel: Karger, pp. 78-92.

Firth, R., ed.
1967. *Themes in economic anthropology.* Association of Social Anthropologists, Monograph 6. London: Tavistock.

Floru, L., K. Heinrich, and F. Wittek.
1975. The problem of post-psychotic schizophrenic depressions and their pharmacological induction. *International Pharmacopsychiatry* 10:230-239.

Fortes, M.
1976. Foreword. *In* J. B. Loudon, ed., *Social anthropology and medicine.* New York: Academic Press, pp. ix-xx.

Foster, G. M.
1974. Medical anthropology: Some contrasts with medical sociology. *Medical Anthropology Newsletter* 6(1):1-6.

1976. Disease etiologies in nonwestern medical systems. *American Anthropologist* 78(4):773-782.

Fracchia, J., et al.
1976. Community perception of severity of illness levels of former mental patients: A failure to discriminate. *Comprehensive Psychiatry* 17(6):775-778.

Frank, J.
1961. *Persuasion and healing.* Baltimore: Johns Hopkins Press.

Freedman, M. J., et al.
1977. On the safety of long-term treatment with lithium. *American Journal of Psychiatry* 134(10):1123-1126.

Freud, S.
1961. *Civilization and its discontents.* New York: W. W. Norton.

Galdston, I.
1965. Community psychiatry: Its social and historical derivations. *Journal of the Canadian Psychiatric Association* 10:461-473.

G.A.P. (Group for the Advancement of Psychiatry)
1975. *Pharmacotherapy and psychotherapy: Paradoxes, problems, and progess.* New York: G.A.P.

1978. *The chronic mental patient in the community,* 10(102). New York: G.A.P.

Gardos, G., and J. Cole.
1976. Maintenance antipsychotic therapy: Is the cure worse than the disease? *American Journal of Psychiatry* 133:32-36.
1978. Maintenance antipsychotic therapy: For whom and how long? *In*

M. A. Lipton et al., eds. *Psychopharmacology: A generation of progress*. New York: Raven Press, pp. 1169-1178.
1980. Overview—Public health issues in tardive dyskinesia. *American Journal of Psychiatry* 137(7):776-781.

Gardos, G., J. Cole, and R. La Brie.
1977. The assessment of tardive dyskenesia. *Archives of General Psychiatry* 34(10):1206-1212.

Gardos, G., J. Cole, and D. Tarsy.
1978. Withdrawal syndromes associated with antipsychotic drugs. *American Journal of Psychiatry* 135(11)1321-1325.

Garfinkel, H.
1967. *Studies in ethnomethodology*. Englewood-Cliffs, N.J.: Prentice-Hall.

Geertz, C.
1973. *The interpretation of cultures*. New York: Basic Books.

Gillin, J.
1948. Magical fright. *Psychiatry* 11:387-400.

Glasscote, R. M., et al.
1971*a*. *Half-way houses for the mentally ill: A study of programs and problems*. Washington, D.C.: Joint Information Service of the American Psychiatric Association and National Association for Mental Health.
1971*b*. *Rehabilitating the mentally ill in the community*. Washington, D.C.: Joint Information Service of the American Psychiatric Association and National Association for Mental Health.

Glenn, T.
1975. Community programs for chronic patients: Administrative financing. *Psychiatric Annals* 5:174-177.

Glick, L. B.
1967. Medicine as an ethnographic category: The Gimi of the New Guinea Highlands. *Ethnology* 6(1):31-56.

Goffman, E.
1961. *Asylums: Essays on the social situation of mental patients and other inmates*. See especially, The moral career of the mental patient, pp. 125-170. Garden City, N.Y.: Anchor Books.
1963. *Stigma: Notes on the management of spoiled identity*. Englewood Cliffs, N.J.: Prentice-Hall.
1971. *Relations in public: Microstudies of the public order*. See especially, The insanity of place, pp. 335-390. New York: Basic Books.

Goldstein, M., et al.
1975. Long-acting phenothiazine and social therapy in the community

treatment of acute schizophrenia. *In* M. Greenblatt, ed., *Drugs in combination with other therapies*. New York: Grune and Stratton, pp. 35-48.

Gouldner, A. W.
1970. *The coming crisis of western sociology*. New York: Avon Books.

Greenblatt, M.
1978. Drugs, schizophrenia and the third revolution. *In* M. A. Lipton et al., eds., *Psychopharmacology: A generation of progress*. New York: Avon Books, pp. 1179-1184.

Greenblatt, M., and R. Budson.
1976. A symposium: Follow-up studies of community care. *American Journal of Psychiatry* 133(8):916-921.

Greenley, J., and R. Schoenher.
1975. Encounters with help-delivery organizations: Patient and client experiences. Madison: Dane County Health and Social Agency Project.

Greist, J. H., et al.
1977. The lithium librarian. *Archives of General Psychiatry* 34(4):456-459.

Groves, J. E., and M. R. Mandel.
1975. The long-acting phenothiazines. *Archives of General Psychiatry* 32(7):893-899.

Gutheil, T. G.
1977. Psychodynamics in drug prescribing. *Drug Therapy* (July):82-95.

Haley, J.
1969. *The power tactics of Jesus Christ and other essays*. New York: Avon Books. See especially, The art of being schizophrenic, pp. 145-176.

Hall, E. T.
1963. Proxemics: The study of man's spatial relations. *In* I. Galdston, ed., *Man's image in medicine and anthropology*. New York: International Universities Press, pp. 422-445.
1966. *The hidden dimension*. Garden City: Anchor Books.
1973. Mental health research and out-of-awareness cultural systems. *In* L. Nader and T. Maretzki, eds., *Cultural illness and health*. Anthropological Studies, vol. 9. Washington, D.C.: American Anthropological Association, pp. 97-103.

Hammer, M., et al.
1978. Social networks and schizophrenia. *Schizophrenia Bulletin* 4(4):522-545.

Hansell, N., and G. Willis.
1977. Outpatient treatment of schizophrenia. *American Journal of Psychiatry* 134(10):1082-1086.

Hatfield, A.
1979. The family and the chronically mentally ill. *In* R. T. Williams and H. M. Shetler, eds., *Proceeding of a conference: Advocacy for persons with chronic mental illness.* Madison: University of Wisconsin Extension, pp. 10-15.

Haynes, R. B., et al.
1978. Absenteeism from work after the detection and labeling of hypertensives. *New England Journal of Medicine* 299(14):741-744.

Heller, J.
1963. *Catch-22.* New York: Dell Publishing Co.

Henn, F. A.
1978. Dopamine and schizophrenia. *Lancet* 2(8084):293.

Henry, F., and S. Saberwal, eds.
1969. *Stress and response in fieldwork.* New York: Holt, Rinehart, and Winston.

Henry, J.
1964. Space and power on a psychiatric unit. *In* A. F. Wessen, ed., *The psychiatric hospital as a social system.* Springfield, Ill.: Charles C. Thomas, pp. 20-34.

Heston, L. L.
1970. The genetics of schizophrenic and schizoid disease. *Science* 16 January 1970:249-256.

Hirsch, S., et al.
1973. Outpatient maintenance of chronic schizophrenics with fluphenazine decanoate injections: A double-blind placebo trial. *British Medical Journal* 1:633 ff.

Hogarty, G. E.
1971. The plight of schizophrenics in modern treatment programs. *Hospital and Community Psychiatry* 22(7):197-203.

Hogarty, G. E., et al.
1973. Drug and sociotherapy in the aftercare of schizophrenic patients. *Archives of General Psychiatry* 28(1):54-64.
1975. Drug and sociotherapy in the aftercare of schizophrenia: A review. *In* M. Greenblatt, ed., *Drugs in combination with other therapies.* New York: Grune and Stratton, pp. 1-13.
1979. Fluphenazine and social therapy in the aftercare of schizophrenic patients. *Archives of General Psychiatry* 36:1283-1294.

Hokin, M.
1978. "Genetics, biochemistry, and psychopharmacology of psychiatric disorders." Unpublished manuscript.

Hospital and Community Psychiatry.
1974. Gold award: A community treatment program. 25:669-672.

Huessy, H. R.
n.d. "Caring: the stepchild of our medical care system." Unpublished manuscript.

Jarvie. I. C.
1967. *The revolution in anthropology.* Chicago: Henry Regnery Co.

Jefferson, J. W., and J. H. Greist.
1979. Lithium and the kidney. *In* J. Davis and D. Greenblat, eds., *Psychopharmacology update: New and neglected areas.* New York: Grune and Stratton, pp. 81-104.

Jeste, D. V., et al.
1979. Tardive dyskinesia—reversible and persistent. *Archives of General Psychiatry* 36(May):585-590.

Jones, M.
1968. *Social psychiatry in practise.* London: Penguin Books.

Jules-Rosette, B.
1978. The veil of objectivity: Prophecy, divination, and social inquiry. *American Anthropologist* 80(3):549-570.

Kane, J., F. Quitkin, and A. Rifkin.
1978. Comparison of incidence and severity of extrapyramidal symptoms with fluphenazine ethanate and fluphenazine decanoate. *American Journal of Psychiatry* 135(12):1539-1543.

Kaplan, B., ed.
1964. *The inner world of mental illness: A series of first-person accounts of what it was like.* New York: Harper and Row.

Kaplan, H. B.
1975. *Self attitudes and deviant behavior.* Pacific Palisades, Calif.: Goodyear Publishing Co.

Kennedy, J. G.
1967. Nubian Zar ceremonies as psychotherapy. *Human Organization* 26(4):185-194.
1973. Cultural psychiatry. *In* J. J. Honigman, ed., *Handbook of social and cultural anthropology.* Chicago: Rand McNally, pp. 1119-1198.

Kesey, K.
1962. *One flew over the cuckoo's nest.* New York: Viking Press.

Kiev. A., ed.
1964. *Magic, faith and healing*. New York: Free Press.
1968. *Curanderismo: Mexican American folk psychiatry*. New York: Free Press.

Kirk, S. A.
1974. The impact of labeling on rejection of the mentally ill: an experimental study. *Journal of Health and Social Behavior* 15:108-117.

Kirk, S. A., and M. E. Therrien.
1975. Community mental health myths and the fate of former hospitalized patients. *Psychiatry* 38:208-217.

Klein, D. M., and J. M. Davis.
1969. Psychotropic drug management. *In* D. Klein and J. Davis, eds. *Diagnosis and drug treatment of psychiatric disorders*. Baltimore: Williams and Wilkins, pp. 17-32.

Klerman, G. L.
1977. Better but not well: Social and ethical issues in the de-institutionalization of the mentally ill. *Schizophrenia Bulletin* 3(4):617-631.

Kluckhohn, C.
1944. The influence of psychiatry on anthropology in America in the past one hundred years. *In* J. K. Hall et al., eds., *One hundred years of American psychiatry*. New York: Columbia University Press, pp. 589-617.
1976. Cited in D. Kraft and B. Pepper, eds. *The social setting of mental health*. New York: Basic Books. pp. 40-47.

Knoedler, W. H.
1978. How the training in community living program helps patients work. *In* L. I. Stein, ed., *Support systems for the long-term patient*. New Directions for Mental Health Services, no. 2. San Francisco: Jossey-Bass, pp. 57-66.

Kochhar, S.
1979. Blind and disabled persons awarded federally administered SSI payments, 1975. *Social Secuity Bulletin* 42(6):13-23.

Kohn, M. L.
1973. Social class and schizophrenia: a critical review and reformulation. *Schizophrenia Bulletin* Winter:60-79.

Kreps, J. M.
1973. Modern man and his instinct of workmanship. *American Journal of Psychiatry* 130(2):179-183.

Kubie, L. S.
1968. Pitfalls of community psychiatry. *Archives of General Psychiatry* 18:257-266.

Lamb, H. R.
1979*a*. The new asylums in the community. *Archives of General Psychiatry* 36(2):129-138.
1979*b*. Roots of neglect in the long-term mentally ill. *Psychiatry* 42(3):201-207.

Lamb, H. R., et al.
1978. *Community survival for long-term patients*. San Francisco: Jossey-Bass.

Lamb, H. R., and V. Goertzl.
1971. Discharged mental patients: Are they really in the community? *Archives of General Psychiatry* 24:29-34.
1972. The demise of the state hospital: A premature obituary? *Archives of General Psychiatry* 26:489-495.
1977. The long-term patient in the era of community treatment. *Archives of General Psychiatry* 34:679-682.

Lamb, H. R., and A. S. Ragowski.
1978. Supplemental security income and the sick role. *American Journal of Psychiatry* 135(10):1221-1224.

Landy, D.
1958. The anthropologist and the mental hospital. *Human Organization* 17(3):30-35.

Langsley, D. D., and J. T. Barter.
1975. Treatment in the community or state hospital: An evaluation. *Psychiatric Annals* 5:163-170.

Largey, G. P., and D. R. Watson.
1974. The sociology of odors. *In* M. Truzzi, ed., *Sociology for pleasure*. Englewood-Cliffs, N.J.: Prentice-Hall. pp. 153-167.

Lehman, H. E.
1975. Psychopharmacological treatment of schizophrenia. *Schizophrenia Bulletin* 13, Summer: 27-45.

Leighton, A., et al., eds.
1957. *Explorations in social psychiatry*. New York: Basic Books.

Leininger, M.
1971. Some anthropological issues related to community mental health programs in the United States. *Community Mental Health Journal* 7(1):50-61.

Levine, D. S., and D. R. Levine.
1975. *The cost of mental illness*. Washington, D.C.: U.S. Government Printing Office, DHEW Publication (A.D.A.M.H.A.), pp. 76-265.

Levine, D. S., and S. G. Willner.
1976. The cost of mental illness, 1974. *Mental Health Statistical Note* no. 125. Washington, D.C.: Survey and Reports Branch.

Levinson, D. J., and E. B. Gallagher.
1964. *Patienthood in the mental hospital.* Boston: Houghton, Mifflin Co.

Levitan, T. E.
1975. Deviants as active participants in the labeling process: The visibly handicapped. *Social Problems* 22(4):548-557.

Levitz, L. S. and L. P. Ullman.
1969. The manipulation of indications of disturbed thinking in normal subjects. *Journal of Consulting Psychology* 33:633-641.

Lidz, T.
1958. Schizophrenia and the family. *Psychiatry* 21:21-27.

Lieban, R. W.
1973. Medical anthropology. *In* J. J. Honigman, ed., *Handbook of social and cultural anthropology.* Chicago: Rand McNally, pp. 1031-1072.

Linn, M. W., et al.
1979. Day treatment and psychotropic drugs in the aftercare of schizophrenic patients. *Archives of General Psychiatry* 36:1055-1066.

Lofland, J.
1979. *Deviance and identity.* Englewood-Cliffs, N.J.: Prentice-Hall.

Ludwig, A.
1971. *Treating the treatment failures: The challenge of chronic schizophrenia.* New York: Grune and Stratton.

Manis, J. G.
1968. The sociology of knowledge and community mental health research. *Social Problems* (Spring):488-501.

Manning, P. K., and H. Fabrega.
1973. The experience of self and body: Health and illness in the Chiapas Highlands. *In* G. Psathas, ed., *Phenomenological sociology.* New York: John Wiley and Sons, pp. 251-301.

Maretzki, T.
1973. Preface. *In* L. Nader and T. Maretzki, eds., *Cultural illness and health.* Washington, D.C.: American Anthropological Association Publication 9.

Maruyama, M.
1963. The second cybernetics: Deviation-amplifying mutual causation processes. *Society for general systems research yearbook* 8:233-241.

Marx, A. J., M. A. Test, and L. I. Stein.
1973. Extro-hospital management of severe mental illness. *Archives of General Psychiatry* 29:505-511.

Mauss, M.
1967. *The gift: Forms and functions of exchange in archaic societies.* New York: W. W. Norton.

May, P. R. A.
1976. When, what, and why? Psychopharmacology and other treatments in schizophrenia. *Comprehensive Psychiatry* 17(6):683-693.

May, P. R. A., and S. C. Goldberg.
1978. Prediction of schizophrenic patients' response to pharmacotherapy. *In* M. A. Lipton et al., eds., *Psychopharmacology: A generation of progress.* New York: Raven Press, pp. 1139-1153.

McClelland, H. A., et al.
1976. Very high dose fluphenazine decanoate. *Archives of General Psychiatry* 33(12)1435-1442.

Mechanic, D.
1972. Response factors in the study of illness: The study of illness behavior. *In* E. G. Jaco, ed., *Patients, physicians, and illness.* 2d ed. New York: Free Press, pp. 128-140.
1975. Social factors affecting psychotic behavior. Research and Analytic Report Series nos. 9-75. Madison: University of Wisconsin Center for Medical Sociology and Health Services Research.
1977*a*. Illness behavior, social adaptation, and the management of illness. Research and Analytic Report Series nos. 9-76. Madison: University of Wisconsin Center for Medical Sociology and Health Services Research.
1977*b*. Explanations of mental illness. Center for Medical Sociology and Health Services Research Paper 6-77. Madison: University of Wisconsin.
1978. Alternatives to mental hospital treatment: A sociological perspective. *In* L. I. Stein and M. A. Test, eds., *Alternatives to mental hospital treatment.* New York: Plenum Press.

Meehl, P. E.
1973. Schizotaxia, schizotypy, schizophrenia. *In* P. E. Meehl, *Psychodiagnosis: selected papers.* Minneapolis: University of Minnesota Press, pp. 135-155.

Mehan, H., and H. Wood.
1975. *The reality of ethnomethodology.* New York: John Wiley and Sons.

Mendel, W. M.
1978. Staff burn-out: Diagnosis, treatment, and prevention. *In* L. I. Stein, ed., *Community support systems for the long-term patient.* New Di-

rections for Mental Health Services no. 2. San Francisco: Jossey-Bass, pp. 75-84.

Mendel, W. M., and R. E. Allen.
1978. Rescue and rehabilitation. *In* L. I. Stein and M. A. Test, eds., *Alternatives to mental hospital treatment.* New York: Plenum Press.

Mendels, J.
1973. Lithium and depression. *In* G. S. Shopsin, ed., *Lithium: Its role in psychiatric research and treatment.* New York: Plenum Press, pp. 253-276.
1975. Lithium in the treatment of depressive states. *In* F. N. Johnson, ed., *Lithium research and therapy.* New York: Academic Press, pp. 43-62.
1976. Lithium in the treatment of depression. *American Journal of Psychiatry* 133(4):373-378.

Mendota Mental Health Institute
1976. Policies and procedures manual. Mineographed manuscript.

Menninger, W. W.
1978. Economic issues involved in providing effective care for the chronic mental patient. *In* J. A. Talbott, ed. *The chronic mental patient.* Washington, D.C.: American Psychiatric Association, pp. 151-155.

Meyerson, A. T.
1978. What are the barriers or obstacles to treatment and care of the chronically mentally disabled? *In* J. A. Talbott, ed., *The chronic mental patient.* Washington, D.C.: American Psychiatric Association, pp. 129-136.

Mikkelson, E. J.
1977. The psychology of disability. *Psychiatric Annals* 7(2):90-100.

Minkoff, K.
1978. A map of the chronic mental patient. *In* J. A. Talbott, ed., *The chronic mental patient.* Washington, D.C.: American Psychiatric Association, pp. 11-38.

Minuchin, S.
1974. *Families and family therapy.* Cambridge, Mass: Harvard University Press.

Moore, W. E.
1963. *Man, time, and society.* New York: John Wiley and Sons.

Morgan, R., and A. J. Cheadle.
1975. Unemployment impedes resettlement. *Social Psychiatry* 10:63-67.

Mosher, L., and S. Keith.
1979. Research on the psychosocial treatment of schizophrenia: A summary report. *American Journal of Psychiatry* 136(5):623-631.

Mosher, L., and A. Z. Menn.
1978. Lowered barriers in the community: The Soteria model. *In* L. I. Stein and M. A. Test, eds., *Alternatives to mental hospital treatment*. New York: Plenum Press.

Murdock. G. P.
1972. Anthropology's mythology. The Huxley Lecture, 1971. *Proceedings of the Royal Anthropological Institute of Great Britain and Ireland.* London, pp. 17-24.

Murphy, H. B. M., and A. C. Raman.
1971. The chronicity of schizophrenia in indigenous tropical peoples: 12 year follow-up in Mauritius. *British Journal of Psychiatry* 118:489-497.

Nader, L.
1970. From anguish to exultation. *In* P. Golde, ed., *Women in the field: Anthropological experiences*. Chicago: Aldine, pp. 57-118.

Neil, J. F., et al.
1976. Emergence of myasthenia gravis during treatment with lithium carbonate. *Archives of General Psychiatry* 33(9):1090-1092.

Olesen, V. L.
1974. Convergences and divergences: Anthropology and sociology in health care. *Medical Anthropology Newsletter* 6(1):6-10.

Opler, M. K.
1969. Anthropological contributions to psychiatry and social psychiatry. *In* S. Plog and R. Edgerton, eds., *Changing perspectives in mental illness*. New York: Holt, Rinehart, and Winston, pp. 88-105.

Ossowski, M., and G. Martony.
n.d. Program for special living arrangements. Final report to the 51.42 Board. Unpublished manuscript.

Ozawa, M. N., and D. Lindsey.
1977. Is SSI too supportive of the mentally ill? *Public Welfare* 35(4)48-52.

PACT Staff.
1977. Letter to the Veterans' Administration. Unpublished document.

Parsons, T.
1972. Definitions of health and illness in light of American values and

social structure. *In* E. G. Jaco, ed., *Patients, physicians, and illness.* 2d ed. New York: The Free Press, pp. 107-127.

Pasamanick, B., et al.
1967. *Schizophrenics in the community: An experimental study in the prevention of hospitalization.* New York: Appleton, Century, Crofts.

Paul, G. L.
1969. Chronic mental patient: Current status—future directions. *Psychological Bulletin* 71:81-94.

Paul, G. L., and R. J. Lentz.
1977. *Psychosocial treatment of chronic mental patients: Milieu versus social-learning programs.* Cambridge, Mass.: Harvard University Press.

Pearsall, M.
1963. *Medical behavioral science: A selected bibliography of cultural anthropology, social psychology and sociology in medicine.* Lexington: University of Kentucky Press.

Pelto, P. J.
1970. *Anthropological research: The structure of inquiry.* New York: Harper and Row.

Perrucci, R.
1974. *Circle of madness: On being insane and institutionalized in America.* Englewood Cliffs, New Jersey: Prentice-Hall.

Petroni, F.
1974. Correlates of the psychiatric sick role. *Journal of Health and Social Behavior* 13:47-54.

Plotkin, R.
1977. Limiting the therapeutic orgy: Mental patients' right to refuse treatment. *Northwestern University Law Review* 72(4):461-525.

Polack, P. R.
1978. A comprehensive system of alternatives to psychiatric hospitalization. *In* L. I. Stein and M. A. Test, eds., *Alternatives to mental hospital treatment.* New York: Plenum Publishers.

Prince, E. O.
1978. Welfare status, illness, and subjective health definition. *American Journal of Public Health* 68(9):865-871.

Psathas, G., ed.
1973. *Phenomenological sociology.* New York: John Wiley and Sons.

Quitkin, F., et al.
1978. Long acting oral vs. injectable antipsychotic drugs in schizophrenia. *Archives of General Psychiatry* 35(7):889-892.

Rabkin, J. G.
1979. Criminal behavior of discharged mental patients: A critical reappraisal of the research. *Psychological Bulletin* 86(1):1-28.

Rapoport, R. N.
1960. *The community as doctor*. Springfield, Ill.: C. C. Thomas Co.

Redlich, F.
1973. The anthropologist as observer: Ethical aspects of clinical observations of behavior. *Journal of Nervous and Mental Disease* 157(5):313-320.

Reich, R.
1973. Care of the chronically mentally ill: A national disgrace. *American Journal of Psychiatry* 130:911-912.

Reich, R., and L. Siegel.
1973. Chronically mentally ill shuffle to oblivion. *Psychiatric Annals* 3:35-48.

Reynolds, D. K., and N. L. Farberow.
1973. Experiential research: An inside perspective on suicide and social systems. *Life Threatening Behavior* 3(4):261-269.
1976. *Suicide: Inside and out*. Berkeley and Los Angeles: University of California Press.
1977. *Endangered hope: Experiences in psychiatric aftercare facilities*. Berkeley and Los Angeles: University of California Press.

Rifkin, A., et al.
1971. Very high dose fluphenazine for nonchronic treatment-refractory patients. *Archives of General Psychiatry* 25:398-403.
1977*a*. Fluphenazine decanoate, fluphenazine hydrochloride given orally, and placebo in remitted schizophrenics: I. Relapse rates after one year. *Archives of General Psychiatry* 34(1):43-47.
1977*b*. Fluphenazine decanoate, oral fluphenazine and placebo in treatment of remitted schizophrenics: II. Rating scale data. *Archives of General Psychiatry* 34:1215-1219.

Rivinus, T. M.
1977. The abuse of social security income. *Psychiatric Annals* 7(2):85-89.

Roberts, L. M.
1966. Introduction. *In* L. M. Roberts et al., eds., *Community psychiatry*. Madison: University of Wisconsin Press.

Roen, S. R., et al.
1966. Community adaptation as an evaluative concept in community mental health. *Archives of General Psychiatry* 15:36-44.

Roman, P. M.
1971. Labeling theory and community psychiatry. *Psychiatry* 34:378-390.

Rosenblatt, A., and J. E. Meyer.

1974. The recidivism of mental patients: A review of past studies. *American Journal of Orthopsychiatry* 44(5):697-706.

Rossi, A.

1969. Some pre-World War II antecedents of community mental health theory and practices. *In* A. J. Bindman and A. Spiegel, eds., *Perspectives in community mental health*. Chicago: Aldine, pp. 9-28.

Rutman, I. D., and R. C. Baron.

1975. *Community careers: An assessment of the life adjustment of former mental patients*. Horizon House Institute for Research and Development.

Sabshin, M.

1966. Theoretical models in community psychiatry. *In* L. M. Roberts et al., eds., *Community psychiatry*. Madison: University of Wisconsin Press.

Sanders, R., R. Smith, and B. S. Weinman.

1967. *Chronic psychoses and recovery*. San Francisco: Jossey-Bass.

Sapir, E.

1932. Cultural anthropology and psychiatry. *Journal of Abnormal Social Psychology* 27:229-242.

1938. Why cultural anthropology needs the psychiatrist. *Psychiatry*, 1:7-12.

Sartorius, N. A., A. Jablenski, and R. Shapiro.

1977. Two-year follow-up of the patients included in the WHO International Pilot Study of Schizophrenia. *Psychological Medicine* 7:529-541.

1978. Cross-cultural differences in the short term prognosis of schizophrenic psychoses. *Schizophrenia Bulletin* 4:102-113.

Schechter, E. S.

1979. Work experience of the disabled, 1972-1974. *1974 Follow-up of disabled and nondisabled adults*, no. 2. Washington, D.C.: Social Security Administration, SSA Publication 13-11725.

Scheff, T.

1966. *Being mentally ill*. Chicago: Aldine.

Scheper-Hughes, N.

1979. *Saints, scholars, and schizophrenics: Mental illness in rural Ireland.* Berkeley, Los Angeles, and London: University of California Press.

Schooler, N. R., et al.

1980. Prevention of relapse in schizophrenia: An evaluation of fluphenazine decanoate. *Archives of General Psychiatry* 37:16-24.

Schulberg, H. C.
1979. Community support programs—Program evaluation and public policy. *American Journal of Psychiatry* 136(11):1433-1437.

Schur, E.
1971. *Labeling deviant behavior: Its sociological implications.* New York: Harper and Row.

Schwartz, C. C., et al.
1974. Psychiatric labeling and the rehabilitation of the mental patient. *Archives of General Psychiatry* 31(Sept.):329-334.

Segal, S. P., and U. Aviram.
1978. *The mentally ill in community-based sheltered care: A study of community care and social integration.* New York: John Wiley and Sons.

Selby, H.
1974. *Zapotec deviance: The convergence of folk and modern sociology.* Austin: University of Texas Press.

Shader, R., ed.
1975. *Manual of psychiatric therapeutics.* New York: Little, Brown, and Company.

Shagass, C. L., ed.
1971. *The role of drugs in community psychiatry. Modern Problems of Pharmacopsychiatry* 6. New York: S. Karger.

Sharfstein, S. S., J. E. C. Turner, and H. W. Clark.
1978. Financing issues in providing services for the chronically mentally ill and disabled. *In* J. A. Talbott, ed. *The chronic mental patient.* Washington, D.C.: American Psychiatric Association, pp. 137-150.

Sheard, M. H., et al.
1976. The effect of lithium on impulsive aggressive behavior in man. *American Journal of Psychiatry* 133(12):1409-1413.

Shopshin, B. and S. Gershon.
1975. Cogwheel rigidity related to lithium maintenance. *American Journal of Psychiatry* 132(5):536-538.

Siegler, M. and H. Osmond.
1966. Models of madness. *British Journal of Psychiatry* 112:193-203.

Simon, P., et al.
1978. Standard and long-acting depot neuroleptics in chronic schizophrenia. *Archives of General Psychiatry* 35(7):893-897.

Simpson, G. M., and J. H. Lee.
1978. A ten-year review of antipsychotics. *In* M. A. Lipton et al., eds., *Psychopharmacology: A generation of progress.* New York: Raven Press, pp. 1131-1137.

Slovenko, R., and E. D. Luby.
1974. From moral treatment to railroading out of the mental hospital. *Bulletin of the American Academy of Psychiatry and the Law* 2:223-236.

Snyder, S., et al.
1974. Drugs, neurotransmitters, and schizophrenia. *Science* 184(21 June): 1243-1253.

Sokolovsky, J., et al.
1978. Personal networks of ex-mental patients in a Manhattan SRO hotel. *Human Organization* (Spring).

Spradley, J. P.
1970. *You owe yourself a drunk: An ethnography of urban nomads.* Boston: Little, Brown.
1973. The ethnography of crime in American society. *In* L. Nader and T. Maretzski, eds., *Cultural illness and health.* Washington, D.C.: American Anthropological Association Publication 9:23-34.

Staff of Committee on Finance of U.S. Senate.
1977. *The supplemental security income program.* Washington, D.C.: Government Printing Office 67:896-900.

Stein, L. I., M. A. Test, and A. J. Marx.
1975 Alternative to the hospital: A controlled study. *American Journal of Psychiatry* 132(5):517-522.

Stein, L. I., and M. A. Test.
1976. The revolving door syndrome: An empirical view. Paper presented at the 129th annual meetingof the American Pyschiatric Association (May), Miami, Florida.
1978. An alternative to mental hospital treatment. *In* L. I. Stein and M. A. Test, eds., *Aternatives to mental hospital treatment.* New York: Plenum Press.
n.d. The evolution of a treatment program: Training in community living. An alternative to the mental hospital. Unpublished manuscript.
1980. Alternative to mental hospital treatment. I. Conceptual model, treatment program, clinical evaluation. *Archives of General Psychiatry* 37(4):392-397.

Stein, L., and C. D. Wise.
1971. Possible etiology of schizophrenia: Damage to the norandrenergic reward system by 6-hydroxydopamine. *Science* 171:1032-1036.

Stephens, R. D., and D. C. McBride.
1976. Becoming a street addict. *Human Organization* 35(1):87-93.

Stevens, B.
1973. Role of fluphenazine decanoate in lessening the burden of chronic schizophrenics on the community. *Psychological Medicine* 3:41-50.

Sullivan, H. S.
1964. *The fusion of psychiatry and social science.* New York: W. W. Norton.

Susser, M.
1968. *Community psychiatry: Epidemiologic and social themes.* New York: Random House.

Swanson, R. M., and S. P. Spitzer.
1970. Stigma and the psychiatric patient career. *Journal of Health and Social Behavior* 11:44-51.

Szasz, T.
1960. The myth of mental illness. *American Psychologist* 5:113-118.
1974. *Ceremonial chemistry.* New York: Anchor Books.
1976. *Schizophrenia: The sacred symbol of psychiatry.* New York: Basic Books.

Takahashi, R., et al.
1975. Comparison of efficacy of lithium carbonate and chlorpromazine in mania. *Archives of General Psychiatry* 32(10):1310-1318.

Talbott, J. A., ed.
1978. *The chronic mental patient: Problems, solutions, and recommendations for public policy.* Washington, D.C.: American Psychiatric Association.

Talbott, J. A.
1979. Care of the chronically mentally ill—Still a national disgrace. *American Journal of Psychiatry* 136(5):688-689.

Tead, O.
1958. Toward the knowledge of man. *General Systems Yearbook* III:248-259.

Tepper, S. J., and J. F. Haas.
1979. Prevalance of tardive dyskinesia. *Journal of Clinical Psychiatry* 40:508-516.

Test, M. A., and L. I. Stein.
1977*a*. Use of special living arrangements: A model for decision-making. *Hospital and Community Psychiatry* 28:608-610.
1977*b*. A community approach to the chronically disabled patient. *Social*

Policy: Special Mental Health Issue (May-June):8-16.
1978*a*. The clinical rationale for community treatment: A review of the literature. *In* L. I. Stein and M. A. Test, eds., *Alternatives to mental hospital treatment*. New York: Plenum Press.
1978*b*. Training in community living: Research design and results. *In* L. I. Stein and M. A. Test, eds., *Alternatives to mental hospital treatment*. New York: Plemum Press.
1978*c*. Community treatment of the chronic patient: Research overview. *Schizophrenia Bulletin* 4:350-364.
1980. Alternative to Mental hospital treatment: III. Social Cost. *Archives of General Psychiatry* 37(4):409-412.

Thoits, P., and M. Hannan.
1979. Income and psychological distress: The impact of an income maintenance experiment. *Journal of Health and Social Behavior* 20 (June):120-138.

Tissot, R.
1977. Long-term drug therapy in psychoses. *In* C. Chiland, ed., *Long-term treatment of psychotic states*. New York: Human Sciences Press, pp. 89-111.

Torrey, E. Fuller.
1972. *The mind game: Witchdoctors and psychiatrists*. New York: Bantam Books.

Townsend, J. M.
1976. Self-concept and the institutionalization of mental patients: An overview and critique. *Journal of Health and Social Behavior* 17(3):263-271.

Turner, J. E. C.
1978. Philosophical issues in meeting the needs of people disabled by mental health problems: The psychosocial rehabilitation approach. *In* J. A. Talbott, ed., *The chronic mental patient*. Washington, D.C.: American Psychiatric Association, pp. 65-74.

Turner, R. J.
1977. Jobs and schizophrenia. *Social Policy* (May-June):32-40.

Turner, R. J., and J. W. Gartell.
1978. Social factors in psychiatric outcome: Toward the resolution of interpretive controversies. *American Sociological Review* 43(June): 368-382.

U.S. News and World Report.
1977. The growing controversy over putting mental patients on the street. (October 24):90-91.

Vacaflor, L.
1975. Lithium side effects and toxicity: The clinical picture. *In* F. N.

Johnson, ed., *Lithium Research and Therapy*. London: Academic Press, pp. 212-214.

Van Putten, T.
1974. Why do schizophrenic patients refuse to take their drugs? *Archives of General Psychiatry* 31(1):67-72.

Van Putten, T., and P. May.
1978. Akinetic depression in schizophrenia. *Archives of General Psychiatry* 35(9):1101-1111.

Van Putten, T., et al.
1976. Drug refusal in schizophrenia and the wish to be crazy. *Archives of General Psychiatry* 33(December):1443-1446.

Vaughn, C. E., and J. P. Leff.
1976. The influence of family and social factors in the course of psychiatric illness: A comparison of schizophrenic and depressed neurotic patients. *British Journal of Psychiatry* 129:125-137.

Von Mering, O.
1970. Medicine and psychiatry. *In* O. Von Mering and L. Kasdan, eds., *Anthropology and the Behavioral and Health Sciences*. Pittsburgh: University of Pittsburgh Press, pp. 272-306.

Vonnegut, Mark.
1976. *The eden express*. New York: Basic Books.

Wadeson, H., and W. T. Carpenter.
1976. Subjective experience of schizophrenia. *Schizophrenia Bulletin* 2(2):302-316.

Wallace, A. F. C.
1970. *Culture and personality*. 2d ed. New York: Random House.

Warren, C., and J. M. Johnson.
1972. A critique of labeling theory from the phenomenological perspective. *In* R. Scott and J. Douglas, eds., *Theoretical Perspectives on Deviance*. New York: Basic Books, pp. 69-92.

Watson, L. C.
1978. The study of personality and the study of individuals: Two approaches, two types of explanation. *Ethos* 6(1):3-21.

Wax, R.
1971. *Doing fieldwork: Warnings and advice*. Chicago: University of Chicago Press.

Waxler, N. E.
1977. Is mental illness cured in traditional societies? A theoretical analysis. *Culture, medicine, and psychiatry* 1(3):233-254.

Weidman, H. H.
1970. On ambivalence and the field. *In* P. Golde, ed., *Women in the field: Anthropological experiences*. Chicago: Aldine, pp. 239-266.

Weinman, B., et al.
1970. Community based treatment of the chronic psychotic. *Community Mental Health Journal* 6(1):13-21.

Weinstein, R. M.
1979. Patient attitudes toward mental hospitalization: A review of quantitative research. *Journal of Health and Social Behavior* 20:237-258.

Weisbrod, B., et al.
1980. Alternative to mental hospital treatment. II. Economic benefit-cost analysis. *Archives of General Psychiatry* 37(4):400-405.

Weissman, M.
1975. The assessment of social adjustment: A review of techniques. *Archives of General Psychiatry* 32(3):357-365.

Weissman, M., and S. Bothwell.
1976. Assessment of social adjustment by patient self-report. *Archives of General Psychiatry* 33:1111-1115.

Weppner, R. S.
1973. An anthropological view of the street addict's world. *Human Organization* 32(2):111-121.

Westermeyer, J., and R. Wintrob.
1979*a*. 'Folk' explanations of mental illness in rural Laos. *American Journal of Psychiatry* 136(7):901-905.
1979*b*. 'Folk' criteria for the diagnosis of mental illness in rural Laos: On being insane in sane places. *American Journal of Psychiatry* 136(6):755-761.

Wilkins, T. L.
1965. *Social deviance*. Englewood-Cliffs, N.J.: Prentice-Hall.

Williams, D. H., et al.
1980. De-institutionalization and social policy—historical perspectives and present dilemmas. *American Journal of Orthopsychiatry* 50(1):54-64.

Wing, J. K.
1978. The social context of schizophrenia. *American Journal of Psychiatry* 135(11):1333-1339.

Winslow, R., and V. Winslow.
1974. *Deviant reality: Alternative world views*. Boston: Allyn and Bacon, Inc.

Wise, C. D., and L. I. Stein.
1973. Dopamine-b-hydroxylase deficits in the brains of schizophrenic patients. *Science* 181:344-347.

Wittkower, E. D., and G. Dubreuil.
1971. Reflections on the interface between psychiatry and anthropology. *In* I. Galdston, ed., *The interface between psychiatry and anthropology.* New York: Brunner/Mazel, pp. 1-27.
1973. Psychocultural stress in relation to mental illness. *Social Science and Medicine* 7:691-704.

World Health Organization.
1973. *Report of the international pilot study of schizophrenia.* I. Geneva: World Health Organization.
1975. *Schizophrenia: A multinational study.* (Public Health Papers no. 63). Geneva: World Health Organization.
1979. *Schizophrenia: An international follow-up study.* New York: John Wiley and Sons.

Wyatt, R. J., and D. L. Murphy.
1976. Low platelet monoamine oxydase activity and schizophrenia. *Schizophrenia Bulletin* 2:77-89.

Yolles, S. F.
1968. The comprehensive national mental health program: An evaluation. *In* L. M. Roberts et al., eds., *Comprehensive mental health.* Madison: University of Wisconsin Press, pp. 279-290.
1969. Introduction. *In* A. Bindman and A. Spiegel, eds., *Perspectives in community mental health.* Chicago: Aldine.

Zander, T.
1977. Prolixin decanoate: A review of the research. *Mental Disability Law Reporter* 2(1):37-42.

Zitrin, A., et al.
1976. Crime and violence among mental patients. *American Journal of Psychiatry* 133:142-149.

Zusman, J.
1976. Can program evaluation be saved from its enthusiasts? *American Journal of Psychiatry* 133(11):1300-1305.

Zusman, J., and H. R. Lamb.
1977. In defense of community mental health. *American Journal of Psychiatry* 134(8):887-890.

INDEXES

INDEX OF CLIENTS

INDEX OF NAMES

SUBJECT INDEX